𝔖𝔱𝔞𝔫𝔡𝔞𝔯𝔡 𝔏𝔦𝔟𝔯𝔞𝔯𝔶 𝔈𝔡𝔦𝔱𝔦𝔬𝔫

THE HISTORICAL WRITINGS

OF

JOHN FISKE

ILLUSTRATED WITH MANY PHOTOGRAVURES,
MAPS, CHARTS, FACSIMILES, ETC.

IN TWELVE VOLUMES

VOLUME III

HERNAN CORTES.

Hernando Cortes

THE DISCOVERY OF AMERICA

WITH SOME ACCOUNT OF ANCIENT AMERICA AND THE SPANISH CONQUEST

BY

JOHN FISKE

IN THREE VOLUMES. VOLUME III

Then I unbar the doors; my paths lead out
The exodus of nations; I disperse
Men to all shores that front the hoary main.
I too have arts and sorceries;
Illusion dwells forever with the wave.
I make some coast alluring, some lone isle
To distant men, who must go there or die

EMERSON

BOSTON AND NEW YORK
HOUGHTON, MIFFLIN AND COMPANY
The Riverside Press, Cambridge

4436

CONTENTS

VIII

THE CONQUEST OF MEXICO

CONTENTS

CONTENTS

CONTENTS

IX

ANCIENT PERU

CONTENTS

CONTENTS

X

THE CONQUEST OF PERU

CONTENTS

CONTENTS

XI

LAS CASAS

CONTENTS

CONTENTS

XII

THE WORK OF TWO CENTURIES

CONTENTS

CONTENTS

xvi

CONTENTS

APPENDIX

LIST OF ILLUSTRATIONS

LIST OF ILLUSTRATIONS

THE
DISCOVERY OF AMERICA

VIII

THE CONQUEST OF MEXICO

IF we were engaged upon a philosophical history of the human mind, the career of maritime discovery in the fifteenth and six-teenth centuries would have great in-terest for us, with regard to its influ-ence upon men's habits of thought. In the long run, the effect of increased knowledge of the earth is to dispel mythological mystery and the kind of romance that goes with it, and to strengthen men's be-lief in the constancy of nature. As long as nothing was known of the lands beyond the equator, it was easy enough to people them with gnomes and griffins. There was no in-trinsic improbability in the existence of a " land east of the sun and west of the moon," or any of the other regions subject to the Queen of the Fairies, — any more than in the existence of Cipango or Cathay, or any other real coun-try which was indefinitely remote and had but rarely been visited. As long as men's fancy had free sweep, beyond the narrow limits of " the world as known to the ancients," there was plenty of room for fairyland. But in these prosaic days our knowledge of the earth's surface has become so nearly complete as to crowd out all thought of enchanted ground. Beyond the dark and perilous sea we no longer look for El Dorado, since maps and gazetteers have taught us to expect nothing better than the beautiful but cruel, the romantic but humdrum, world with which daily experience has already made us so well acquainted. In this respect the present age, compared with the sixteenth century, is like mature manhood compared with youth. The bright visions have fled, but the sober realities of life remain. The most ardent adventurer of our time has probably never indulged in such wild fancies as must have flitted through the mind of young Louis de Hennepin when he used to hide behind tavern doors while the sailors were telling of their voyages. " The tobacco smoke," he says, " used to make me very sick; but, notwithstanding, I listened attentively to all that was said about their adventures at sea and their travels in distant countries. I could have passed whole days and nights in this way without eating." [1]

[1] Hennepin, *Voyage Curieux* (1704), 12, cited in Parkman's *La Salle*, p. 120.

The first effect of the voyages of Columbus and his successors was to arouse this spirit of romantic curiosity to fever heat. Before the newly-found lands had been explored, there was no telling what they might not contain. Upon one point, however, most of the early adventurers were thoroughly agreed. The newly-found coasts must be near Cipango and Cathay, or at any rate somewhere within the territories of the " Grand Khan ; " and the reports of Marco Polo, doubtless bravely embellished in passing from mouth to mouth, whetted the greed for gold and inflamed the crusading zeal of the sturdy men who had just driven the Moor from Granada and were impatiently longing for " fresh woods and pastures new." It was taken for granted that the countries beyond the Sea of Darkness abounded in rich treasure which might be won without labour more prosaic than fighting ; for as heathen treasure it was of course the legitimate prey of these soldiers of the Cross. Their minds were in a state like that of the heroes of the Arabian Nights, who, if they only wander far enough through the dark forest or across the burning desert, are sure at length to come upon some enchanted palace whereof they may fairly hope, with the aid of some gracious Jinni, to become masters. But with all their unchecked freedom of fancy, it is not likely that the Span-

Romantic dreams of the Spanish explorers

3

iards who first set foot upon the soil of Mexico had ever imagined anything stranger than the sights they saw there ; nor did ever a slave of the lamp prepare for man a triumph so astounding as that of which the elements were in readiness awaiting the masterful touch of Hernando Cortes in the year 1519.

I have already described, in its most general outlines, the structure of society in ancient Mexico.[1] A glance at its history is now necessary, if we would understand the circumstances of its sudden overthrow. A very brief sketch is all that is here practicable, and it is all that my purpose requires.

The earliest date which we can regard as clearly established in the history of Mexico Prehistoric Mexico is 1325 A. D., the year in which the great Aztec pueblo was founded. For whatever happened before that time we have to grope our way in the uncertain light of vague or conflicting traditions and tempting but treacherous philological speculations. It is somewhat as in the history of Greece before the first Olympiad. Sundry movements of peoples and a few striking incidents loom up through the fog of oblivion, and there is room for surmises that things may have happened in this way or in that way, but whether we succeed in putting

[1] See above, vol. i. pp. 114–150.

4

events into their true order, or get them within a century or so of their real dates, remains very doubtful. According to Mr. Hubert Bancroft, the cool Mexican tableland, since often known as Anáhuac,[1] or "lake country," was occupied during the sixth and seventh centuries of the Christian era by tribes of various degrees of barbarism belonging to the group ever since known as Nahuas. In the fertile valleys horticulture became developed, population increased, arts of construction throve, and in course of time a kind of supremacy over the whole region east and south of the lakes is said to have been secured by certain confederated tribes The "Toltecs" called Toltecs, a name which has been explained as meaning "artificers" or "builders." It has been supposed that the name may have been loosely applied to pueblo-builders by other people who did not erect such structures. Among the principal seats of Toltec supremacy we hear much of the city or pueblo of Tollan, on the site of the modern village of Tula, some forty miles to the northwest of the city of Mexico. It is well to beware, however, about meddling much with these Toltecs. In

[1] There was no such thing as an "empire of Anáhuac," nor was the name peculiar to the Mexican tableland ; it was given to any country near a large body of water, whether lake or sea. See Brasseur de Bourbourg, *Ruines de Palenqué*, p. 32.

5

some respects they remind one of the Pelasgi.
Whatever seemed strange or inexplicable in the
early history of Greece, the old historians used
to dispose of by calling in that mysterious people, the Pelasgi. Greek history had its Pelas-
gic dark cupboard into which it used to throw
its nondescript rubbish of speculation; and I
suspect that the Toltecs have furnished a similar dark cupboard to the historians of Mexico.
There was doubtless, as we shall presently see,
a tribe of Toltecs which dwelt for a time at
Tollan, and it was the misfortune of this people to have its name become the vehicle of
divers solar myths associated with the fair god
Quetzalcoatl. The name Tollan, which means
"place of the sun," occurs in other parts of
Mexico; it was quite commonly applied to
Cholula, the pueblo especially sacred to Quetzalcoatl.[1] Wherever legends came to be located
in which the Fair God figured, his followers the
Toltecs naturally figured likewise. "All arts
and sciences, all knowledge and culture, were
ascribed to this wonderful mythical people; and
wherever the natives were asked concerning the
origin of ancient and unknown structures, they
would reply : 'The Toltecs built them.'"[2] In

[1] Bandelier, *Archæological Tour in Mexico*, p. 194.
[2] See Brinton, "The Toltecs and their Fabulous Empire,"
in his *Essays of an Americanist*, pp. 83–100, an admirable
treatment of the subject. The notion of the Toltec empire

6

this way seems to have been generated that notion of a " Toltec empire" which has bewildered and misled so many writers.

In opposition to the Toltecs we find frequent mention of the Chichimecs, whose name is said to mean " barbarians." Such an The "Chichimecs" epithet would indicate that their enemies held them in scorn, but does not otherwise give us much information. At the time of the Discovery it was applied in two very different senses ; 1. in general, to the roaming savage tribes far to the north of Anáhuac, and 2. in particular, to the " line of kings " (*i. e.* clan out of which the head war-chiefs were chosen) at Tezcuco.[1] This may indicate that at some time the great pueblo-town of Tezcuco was seized and appropriated by a people somewhat inferior in culture; or that neighbouring pueblos applied to the Tezcucans an oppro-

pervades M. de Charnay's *Ancient Cities of the New World*, and detracts from the value of that able book. M. de Charnay's archæological work is very good, but his historical speculations will bear considerable revision and excision.

[1] Their history has been written by their descendant Fernando de Ixtlilxochitl (born in 1570), *Histoire des Chichimèques, et des anciens rois de Tezcuco*, Paris, 1840, 2 vols. This work contains many valuable facts, but its authority is gravely impaired by the fact that Ixtlilxochitl " wrote for an interested object, and with the view of sustaining tribal claims in the eyes of the Spanish government." See Bandelier, *Archæological Tour*, p. 192.

brious epithet which stuck; or, perhaps, that at some time the Tezcucans may have repelled an invasion of lower peoples, so that their chiefs were called Chichimecs by way of compliment, as Roman warriors were called Germanicus or Africanus. Ingenuity may amuse itself with surmises, but the true explanation is often something that nobody would have thought of. It is not even certain that the name means barbarian, or anything of the sort.[1] The Chichimecs are no more than the Toltecs a safe subject for speculation.[2]

It may have been anywhere from the ninth to the eleventh century that a number of
The Nahua tribes, coming from some undetermined northerly region which they called Aztlan,[3] invaded the territory of

[1] Mr. Bandelier, improving upon a hint of the learned Veytia (*Historia antigua del Méjico*, cap. xii. p. 143), suggests that the word Chichimecs may mean "kin of red men." *Peabody Museum Reports*, ii. 393.

[2] The learned Rèmi Siméon, in his introduction to the *Annales de Chimalpahin Quauhtlehuanitzin*, Paris, 1889, has not quite succeeded in avoiding the pitfalls which surround this subject; *e. g.* "Ces trois grands peuples, les Toltèques, les Mexicains, et les Chichimèques, avaient donc chacun leur caractère particulier. Les Toltèques étaient artisans, les Mexicains guerriers et commerçants, les Chichimèques agriculteurs," etc., p. xxxvi. This sort of generalization does not help us much.

[3] The situation of Aztlan, and the meaning of the name, have furnished themes for much speculation. Mr. Morgan,

Anáhuac, and planted themselves at various commanding points. It is probable that there was a series of waves of invasion by peoples essentially the same in blood and speech. As Dr. Brinton has ably pointed out, the story of Tollan and its people as we find it in three of the most unimpeachable authorities — Father Duran, Tezozomoc, and the Codex Ramirez — virtually identifies Toltecs with Aztecs. The situation of that Tollan which is now called Tula was on one of the prin- cipal ancient trails from the north into the elevated Valley of Mexico. It was a natural pass or gateway, and had the importance which belongs to such places. The ruins of the

Tollan and the Serpent Hill

following Acosta and Clavigero, interpreted Aztlan as " place of cranes," and inferred that it must have been in New Mexico, where cranes abound (*Houses and House-Life*, p. 195). Duran translated it " place of whiteness " (*Historia de Nueva España*, i. 19); but, as Dr. Brinton observes, it may mean " place by salt water " (*Essays of an Americanist*, p. 88). Father Duran thought that Aztlan was situated within the region of our Gulf States; cf. Brasseur, *Hist. des nations civilisées de l' Amerique centrale*, ii. 292. Some writers have supposed it was the home of the " mound-builders " in the Mississippi, and in recent times a group of earthworks in Wisconsin has been named Aztlan or Aztalan. Much more probable are the views of Mendieta (*Historia Ecclesiastica*, p. 144), who places it in the province of Xalisco; or of Orozco y Berra (*Historia antigua de Mexico*, tom. iii. cap. 4), who places it in Michoacan. Albert Gallatin expressed a similar view in *Trans. Amer. Ethnolog. Soc.*, ii. 202.

ancient town are upon a small hill, known as Coatepetl, or Serpent Hill, which figures largely in the legends about the Toltecs. The town consisted of large edifices built of rubble-stone mingled with adobe-brick, with flat and terraced roofs, somewhat after the fashion, perhaps, of the pueblos in New Mexico. Mural painting and figure carving were practised by its inhabitants. According to the authorities just cited, there was a division among the Nahua tribes migrating from Aztlan. Some passed on into the Valley of Mexico, while others fortified themselves on the Serpent Hill and built a temple to the war-god Huitzilopochtli. The city of Tollan thus founded lasted for some generations, until its people, hard pressed by hostile neighbours, retreated into the Valley of Mexico, and afterward built the city which has become famous under that name.[1]

In this story the founders of Mexico are virtually identified with those of Tollan. Following this hint, we may suppose the "Toltec period" in Mexican tradition to have been simply the period when the pueblo-town of Tollan was flourishing, and domineered most likely over neighbouring pueblos. One might thus speak of it as one

The fabulous "Toltec empire"

[1] Duran, *Historia de las Indias de Nueva España*, cap. iii. ; Tezozomoc, *Crónica Mexicana*, cap. ii. ; *Codex Ramirez*, p. 24.

would speak of the " Theban period " in Greek history. After the " Toltec period," with perhaps an intervening " Chichimec period " of confusion, came the " Aztec period ; " or in other words, some time after Tollan lost its importance, the city of Mexico came to the front. Such, I suspect, is the slender historical residuum underlying the legend of a " Toltec empire." [1]

The Codex Ramirez assigns the year 1168 as the date of the abandonment of the Serpent Hill by the people of Tollan. We begin to leave this twilight of legend when we meet the Aztecs already encamped in the Valley of Mexico. Finding the most obviously eligible sites preoccupied, they were sagacious enough to detect the advantages of a certain marshy spot through which the outlets of lakes Chalco and Xochimilco, besides sundry rivulets, flowed northward and eastward into Lake Tezcuco. Here in the year 1325 they began to build their pueblo, which they called Tenochtitlan, — a name whereby hangs a tale. When the Aztecs, hard pressed by foes, took refuge among these marshes, they came upon a sacrificial stone which they recognized as one upon which some years before one of their priests had immolated a captive chief. From a crevice in this stone, where a little earth was imbedded, there grew a

The Aztecs, and the founding of the city of Mexico

[1] See Brinton, *op. cit.* p. 89.

cactus, upon which sat an eagle holding in its beak a serpent. A priest ingeniously interpreted this symbolism as a prophecy of signal and long-continued victory, and forthwith diving into the lake he had an interview with Tlaloc, the god of waters, who told him that upon that very spot the people were to build their town. The place was therefore called Tenochtitlan, or " place of the cactus-rock," but the name under which it afterward came to be best known was taken from Mexitl, one of the names of the war-god Huitzilopochtli. The device of the rock and cactus, with the eagle and serpent, formed a tribal totem for the Aztecs, and has been adopted as the coat-of-arms of the present Republic of Mexico. The pueblo of Tenochtitlan was surrounded by salt marshes, which by dint of dikes and causeways the Aztecs gradually converted into a large artificial lake, and thus made their pueblo by far the most defensible stronghold in Anáhuac, — impregnable, indeed, so far as Indian modes of attack were concerned.[1]

The advantages of this commanding position were slowly but surely realized. A dangerous neighbour upon the western shore of the lake

[1] According to Mr. Bandelier the only Indian position comparable with it for strength was that of Atitlan, in Guatemala. *Peabody Museum Reports,* vol. ii. p. 97.

was the tribe of Tecpanecas, whose principal
pueblo was Azcaputzalco. The Aztecs succeeded
in making an alliance with these Tecpanecas, but
it was upon unfavourable terms and involved the
payment of tribute to Azcaputzalco. It gave the
Aztecs, however, some time to develop their
strength. Their military organization was gradually perfected, and in 1375 they elected their first
tlacatecuhtli, or "chief-of-men," whom European
writers, in the loose phraseology formerly current, called "founder of the Mexican empire."
The name of this official was Acamapichtli, or
"Handful-of-Reeds." During the eight and
twenty years of his chieftaincy the The first
pueblo houses in Tenochtitlan began four Aztec
to be built very solidly of stone, and men"
the irregular water-courses flowing between
them were improved into canals. Some months
after his death in 1403 his son Huitzilihuitl,
or "Humming-bird," was chosen to succeed
him. This Huitzilihuitl was succeeded in 1414
by his brother Chimalpopoca, or "Smoking
Shield," under whom temporary calamity visited
the Aztec town. The alliance with Azcaputzalco was broken, and that pueblo joined its
forces to those of Tezcuco on the eastern shore
of the lake. United they attacked the Aztecs,
defeated them, and captured their chief-of-men,
who died a prisoner in 1427. He was succeeded

by Izcoatzin, or " Obsidian Snake," an aged chieftain who died in 1436.

During these nine years a complete change came over the scene. Quarrels arose between Azcaputzalco and Tezcuco; the latter pueblo entered into alliance with Tenochtitlan, and together they overwhelmed and de-

Destruction of Azcaputzalco stroyed Azcaputzalco, and butchered most of its people. What was left of the conquered pueblo was made a slave mart for the Aztecs, and the remnant of the people were removed to the neighbouring pueblo of Tlacopan, which was made tributary to Mexico. By this great victory the Aztecs also acquired secure control of the springs upon Chepultepec, or " Grasshopper Hill," which furnished a steady supply of fresh water to their island pueblo.

The next step was the formation of a partnership between the three pueblo-towns, Tenochtitlan, Tezcuco, and Tlacopan, for the organized and systematic plunder of other pueblos. All the tribute or spoils extorted was to be divided into five parts, of which two parts each were for Tezcuco and Tenochtitlan, and one part for Tlacopan. The Aztec chief-of-men became mil-

The Mexican Confederacy itary commander of the confederacy, which now began to extend operations to a distance. The next four chiefs-of-men were Montezuma, or " Angry Chief," the First, from 1436 to 1464; Axayacatl, or " Face-in-

14

TABLE OF THE SUCCESSION (ELECTIVE) AND OF THE RELATIONSHIPS OF THE ELEVEN MEXI-
CAN *TLACATECUHTLI*, OR "CHIEFS-OF-MEN."

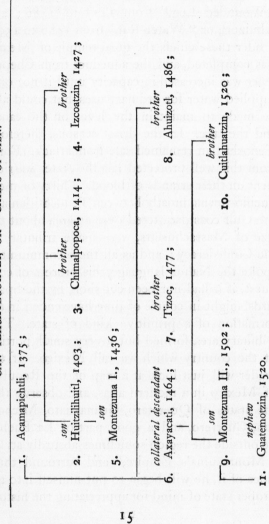

1. Acamapichtli, 1375 ;

2. Huitzilihuitl, 1403 ; *son*

3. Chimalpopoca, 1414 ; *brother*

4. Izcoatzin, 1427 ; *brother*

5. Montezuma I., 1436 ; *son*

6. Axayacatl, 1464 ; *collateral descendant*

7. Tizoc, 1477 ; *brother*

8. Ahuizotl, 1486 ; *brother*

9. Montezuma II., 1502 ; *son*

10. Cuitlahuatzin, 1520 ; *brother*

11. Guatemotzin, 1520. *nephew*

15

the-Water," from 1464 to 1477; Tizoc, or "Wounded Leg," from 1477 to 1486; and Ahuizotl, or "Water-Rat," from 1486 to 1502. Under these chiefs the great temple of Mexico was completed, and the aqueduct from Chepultepec was increased in capacity until it not only supplied water for ordinary uses, but could also be made to maintain the level of the canals and the lake. In the driest seasons, therefore, Tenochtitlan remained safe from attack. Forth from this well-protected lair the Aztec warriors went on their errands of blood. Thirty or more pueblo-towns, mostly between Tenochtitlan and the Gulf coast, scattered over an area about the size of Massachusetts, were made tributary to the Confederacy; and as all these communities spoke the Nahua language, this process of conquest, if it had not been cut short by the Spaniards, might in course of time have ended in the formation of a primitive kind of state. This tributary area formed but a very small portion of the country which we call Mexico. If the reader will just look at a map of the Republic of Mexico in a modern atlas, and observe that the states of Queretaro, Guanaxuato, Michoacan, Guerrero, and a good part of La Puebla, lie outside the region sometimes absurdly styled "Montezuma's Empire," and surround three sides of it, he will begin to put himself into the proper state of mind for appreciating the history

of Cortes and his companions. Into the outlying region just mentioned, occupied by tribes
for the most part akin to the Nahuas in blood
and speech, the warriors of the Confederacy
sometimes ventured, with varying fortunes.
They levied occasional tribute among the pueblos in these regions, but hardly made any of
them regularly tributary. The longest range of
their arms seems to have been to the eastward,
where they sent their tax-gatherers along the
coast into the isthmus of Tehuantepec, and
came into conflict with the warlike Mayas and
Quiches. On the other hand, as already observed, the Confederacy did not effect any true
military occupation of the country near at hand,
and within twenty or thirty leagues of Tenochtitlan such pueblo-towns as Cholula and Tlascala, with populations of about 30,000 persons,
retained their independence. The   The hostile
Tlascalans, indeed, were a perpetual Tlascalans
thorn in the side of the Confederacy. Occupying a strong defensive position, they beat back
repeatedly the forces of the chief-of-men and
aided and abetted recalcitrant pueblos in refusing tribute. The state of feeling between Tlascalans and Aztecs was like that between Romans
and Carthaginians, or Turks and Montenegrins.

Such was, in general outline, what we may
call the political situation in the time of the son

of Axayacatl, the second Montezuma, who was elected chief-of-men in 1502, being then thirty-four years of age. One of the first expeditions led by this Montezuma, in 1503, was directed against the Tlascalans for the purpose of obtaining captives for sacrifice ; it met with disastrous defeat, and furnished victims for the Tlascalan altars. A raid of Montezuma's into Michoacan was also repulsed, but upon the eastern coast he was more successful in wringing tribute from the pueblo-towns, and in arousing in their inhabitants a desperate rage, ready to welcome any chance of delivery from the oppressor. Many towns refused tribute and were savagely punished ; and as always happens upon the eve of a crisis in history, we hear wild rumours of supernatural portents. There was the usual tale of comet and eclipse, and the volcanic craters in the Cordillera were thought to be unwontedly active.[1] At length, in the course of the year 1518, came the handwriting on the wall. A certain Indian named Pinotl was Montezuma's tax-gatherer (*calpixca*) and spy at the pueblo of Cuetlachtlan, some thirty miles inland from the Gulf coast and about as far to the southward from San Juan de Ulloa. To this officer there came one day an Indian from the neighbouring pueblo of Mictlan-Quauhtla on the coast, with a story

The second Montezuma

An amazing story

[1] Bancroft, *History of Mexico,* i. 113.

the like of which no man in all that country had
ever heard. He had seen a great tower, with
wings, moving hither and thither upon the sea.
Other Indians, sent to verify the rumour, saw
two such towers, and from one of them a canoe
was let down and darted about on the water,
and in it were a kind of men with white faces
and heavy beards, and they were clad in a strange
and shining raiment.[1] At this news the tax-
gatherer Pinotl, with a body of attendants, hastened down to the shore and met the Spanish
squadron of Juan de Grijalva. Pinotl went on
board one of these marvellous winged
towers, and exchanged gifts with its
commander, who was pleased to hear
about the wealth and power of Pinotl's master,
and promised some day before long to come and
pay him a visit in his great city among the mountains. When the dread strangers had gone on
their way, the tax-gatherer's party took the short-
est trail to Tenochtitlan, and hurrying to the
tecpan, or council-house, informed Montezuma
that they had seen and talked with gods. On
strips of maguey paper they had made sketches
of the Spaniards and their ships and arms, along
with abundant hieroglyphic comments; and

*Pinotl visits
the mysteri-
ous strangers*

[1] Tezozomoc, ii. 232; Duran, ii. 359–377; Bancroft,
loc. cit. Tezozomoc says that this Indian's ears, thumbs, and
big toes were mutilated; concerning the purport of which a
query will presently be made.

when all this was presently laid before the tribal council for consideration, we may dimly imagine the wild and agitated argument that must have ensued.

No doubt the drift of the argument would be quite undecipherable for us were it not for the clue that is furnished by the ancient Mexican beliefs concerning the sky-god and culture-hero, Quetzalcoatl. This personage was an object of reverence and a theme of mythical tales among all the Nahua and Maya peoples.[1] Like Zeus and Woden he has been supposed to have been at some time a terrestrial hero who became deified after his death, but it is not likely that he ever had a real existence, any more than Zeus or Woden. In his attributes Quetzalcoatl resembled both the Greek and the Scandinavian deity. He was cloud gatherer, wielder of the thunderbolt, and ruler of the winds. As lord of the clouds he was represented as a bird; as lord of the lightning he was represented as a serpent;[2] and his name *Quetzal-Coatl* means " Bird-Serpent."[3] In this char-

Quetzalcoatl

---

[1] The Mayas called him Cukulcan.

[2] I have fully explained this symbolism in *Myths and Myth-Makers*, chap. ii., " The Descent of Fire."

[3] Or " Feathered Serpent." Mr. Bandelier (*Archæol. Tour*, p. 170) suggests that the word *quetzalli* " only applies to feathers in the sense of indicating their bright hues," and that the name therefore means " Shining Serpent." But in

BAS-RELIE

NQUE

acter of elemental deity he was commonly associated with Tlaloc, the god of rain, of waters, and
of spring verdure.[1] This association is depicted
upon the two famous slabs discovered by Mr.
Stephens in 1840 in the course of his researches
at Palenque. The slabs were formerly inlaid in
the pillars that supported the altar in the building known as the "Temple of the Cross, No.
1." They are about six feet in length by three
in width. On the left-hand slab Tlaloc appears
as a "young man magnificently arrayed; he
wears a richly embroidered cape, a collar and
medallion around his neck, a beautiful girdle to

the Mexican picture-writing the rebus for Quetzalcoatl is
commonly a feather or some other part of a bird in connection with a snake ; and the so-called " tablet of the cross "
at Palenque represents the cross, or symbol of the four winds,
" surmounted by a bird and supported by the head of a serpent " (Brinton, *Myths of the New World*, p. 118). Here
the symbolism is complete and unmistakable. The cross is
the symbol of Tlaloc, the rain-god, who is usually associated
with Quetzalcoatl.

Two very learned and brilliant accounts of Quetzalcoatl are
those of Bandelier (*Archæol. Tour*, pp. 168–216), and
Brinton (*American Hero-Myths*, pp. 63–142). It seems to
me that the former suffers somewhat from its Euhemerism,
and that Dr. Brinton, treating the subject from the stand-
point of comparative mythology, gives a truer picture. Mr.
Bandelier's account, however, contains much that is invaluable.

[1] Sahagun, *Hist. de las cosas de la Nueva España*, lib. ii.
cap. 1.

21

his waist; the ends of the maxtli [1] are hanging down front and back, cothurni cover his feet and legs up to the knee. On the upper end of Quetzalcoatl and Tlaloc his headdress is the head of a stork, having a fish in his bill, whilst other fishes are ranged below it." [2] The right-hand slab represents Quetzalcoatl as an old man, clad in the skin of an ocelot, or Mexican "tiger," and blowing puffs of air through a tube. The bird's brilliant feathers and sharp beak are seen in his headdress, and about his waist is the serpent twisting and curling before and behind.

The building at Palenque in which these sculptured slabs once adorned the altar appears to Specialization of Tlaloc as elemental deity have been a temple consecrated to Quetzalcoatl and Tlaloc. The connection between the two deities was so close that their festivals " were celebrated together on the same day, which was the first of the first month of the Aztec calendar, in February." [3] There was nothing like equality between the two, however. Tlaloc remained specialized as the god of rains and giver of harvests; he was attached as a subordinate appendage to the mighty Blower of Winds and Wielder of Lightning, and his symbolism served to com-

[1] " Maxtlatl, bragas, o cosa semejante," Molina, *Vocabulario*, s. v.

[2] Charnay, *Ancient Cities of the New World*, p. 216.

[3] Brinton, *American Hero-Myths*, p. 125.

22

memorate the elemental character of the latter. On the other hand Quetzalcoatl, without losing his attributes as an elemental deity, acquired many other attributes. As has frequently happened to sky-gods and solar heroes, Generalization of Quet-he became generalized until almost zalcoatl as all kinds of activities and interests culture-hero were ascribed to him. As god of the seasons, he was said to have invented the Aztec calendar. He taught men how to cut and polish stones; he was patron of traders, and to him in many a pueblo ingenious thieves prayed for success, as Greek thieves prayed to Hermes. It was he that promoted fertility among men, as well as in the vegetable world; sterile wives addressed to him their vows. Yet at the same time Quetzalcoatl held celibacy in honour, and in many pueblos houses of nuns were consecrated to him. Other features of asceticism occurred in his service; his priests were accustomed to mutilate their tongues, ears, and other parts of the body by piercing them with cactus thorns.

As Zeus had his local habitation upon Mount Olympus and was closely associated with the island of Crete, so Quetzalcoatl had his favourite spots. Cholula was one of them; another was Tollan, but, as already observed, this place was something more than the town which commanded the trail from Mexico into the north country. Like Cadmus and Apollo, this New World culture-deity had his home in the far east; there was his Tollan, or "place of the sun." And here we come to the most interesting part of the story, the conflict between Light and Darkness, which in all aboriginal American folk-lore appears in such transparent and unmistakable garb.[1] One of the most important figures in the Mexican pantheon was Tezcatlipoca, the dread lord of night and darkness, the jealous power that visited mankind with famine and pestilence, the ravenous demon whose food was human hearts. No deity was more sedulously worshipped than Tezcatlipoca, doubtless on the theory, common among barbarous people, that it is by all means desirable to keep on good terms with the evil powers. Between Quetzalcoatl and Tezcatlipoca there was everlasting hostility. The latter deity had once been the sun, but Quetzalcoatl had knocked him out of the sky with a big club, and jumping into his place had become the sun instead of him. Tezcatlipoca, after tumbling into the sea, rose again in the night sky as the Great Bear; and

The dark Tezcatlipoca

---

[1] In this aspect of the power of light contending against the power of darkness, Quetzalcoatl is the counterpart of the Algonquin Michabo, the Iroquois Ioskeha, and the Peruvian Viracocha, to whom we shall by and by have occasion to refer. See Brinton, *Myths of the New World*, chap. vi.

so things went on for a while, until suddenly the Evil One transformed himself into a tiger, and with a blow of his paw struck Quetzalcoatl from the sky. Amid endless droll and uncouth incidents the struggle continued, and the combatants changed their shapes as often as in the Norse tale of Farmer Weathersky.[1] The contest formed the theme of a whole cycle of Mexican legends, some grave, some humorous, many of them quite pretty.[2] In some of these legends the adversaries figured, not as elementary giants, but as astute and potent men. The general burden of the tale, the conclusion most firmly riveted in the Mexican mind, was that Quetzalcoatl had been at last outwitted by his dark enemy and obliged to for- Exile of sake the land.[3] Accompanied by a Quetzalcoatl few youthful worshippers he fared forth from

[1] See, also, the delicious story of the Gruagach of Tricks, in Curtin's *Myths and Folk-Lore of Ireland*, pp. 139–156.

[2] Quite a number were taken down by Father Sahagun (about 1540) from the lips of the natives, in the original Nahuatl, and are given in his *Hist. de las cosas de Nueva España*, lib. iii., and in Brinton's *American Hero-Myths*, pp. 106–116.

[3] What a pathos there is in these quaint stories ! These poor Indians dimly saw what we see, that the Evil One is hard to kill and often seems triumphant. When things seem to have arrived at such a pass, the untutored human mind comforts itself with Messianic hopes, often destined to be rudely shocked, but based no doubt upon a sound and whole-

25

Cholula, and when he had reached the eastern shore, somewhere in the Coatzacualco country, between Cuetlachtlan and Tabasco, he bade farewell to his young companions, saying that he must go farther, but at some future time he should return from the east with men as fair-skinned as himself and take possession of the country. As to whither he had gone, there was a difference of opinion. Some held that he had floated out to sea on a raft of serpent skins; others believed that his body had been consumed with fire on the beach, and that his soul had been taken up into the morning star. But in whatever way he had gone, all were agreed that in the fulness of time Quetzalcoatl would return from the eastern ocean, with white-faced companions, and renew his beneficent rule over the Mexican people.[1]

His return, it would seem, must needs involve the dethronement of the black Tezcatlipoca. According to one group of legends the fair culture-hero condemned the sacrifice of Expectation human beings, and held that the perof his return fume of flowers and incense was sufficient without the shedding of blood; in similar wise he was said to look with disapproval

some instinct, and one that the future career of mankind will justify. It is interesting to watch the rudimental glimmerings of such a hope in such a people as the ancient Mexicans.

[1] Brinton, *op. cit.* pp. 117, 133.

26

upon wars and violence of whatever sort. If the theory which found expression in these legends should prove correct, the advent of Quetzalcoatl would overturn the worship of Tezcatlipoca, who demanded human victims, and likewise that of his gruesome ally Huitzi-lopochtli, the war-god who presided over the direful contests in which such victims were obtained. In short, it would revolutionize the whole system upon which the political and social life of the Nahua peoples had from time immemorial been conducted. One is naturally curious to know how far such a theory could have expressed a popular wish and not merely a vague speculative notion, but upon this point our information is lamentably meagre. It does not appear that there was any general longing for the reign of Quetzalcoatl, like that of the Jews for their Messianic Kingdom. But the notion that such a kingdom was to come was certainly a common one in ancient Mexico, and even in that fierce society there may well have been persons to whom the prevalence of wholesale slaughter did not commend itself, and who were ready to welcome the hope of a change.

When the Spanish ships arrived upon the Mexican coast in 1518, the existence of this general belief was certainly a capital fact, and probably the supreme fact, in the political and military situation. It effectually paralyzed the opposition to their entrance into the country. Fulfilment of prophecy; extraordinary coincidences Surely such a grouping of fortunate coincidences was never known save in fairy tales. As the Spanish ships came sailing past Tabasco, they were just reversing the route by which Quetzalcoatl had gone out into the ocean; as he had gone, so they were coming in strict fulfilment of prophecy! Mictlan-Quauhtla was evidently a point from which the returning deity was likely to be seen; and when we read that the Indian who ran with the news to Cuetlachtlan had his ears, thumbs, and toes mutilated, how can we help remembering that this particular kind of self-torture was deemed a fit method of ingratiating oneself into the favour of Quetzalcoatl? When Pinotl went on board ship he found the mysterious visitors answering in outward aspect to the requirements of the legend. In most mythologies the solar heroes are depicted with abundant hair. Quetzalcoatl was sometimes, though not always, represented with a beard longer and thicker than one would have been likely to see in ancient America. The bearded Spaniards were, therefore, at once recognized as his companions. There were sure to be some blonde Visigoth complexions among them,[1] and their

[1] Indeed, we know of at least one such blonde on this fleet, Pedro de Alvarado, whom the Mexicans called *Tonatiuh*,

28

general hue was somewhat fairer than that of the red men. Nothing more was needed to convince the startled Aztecs that the fulfilment of the prophecy was at hand. Montezuma could hardly fail thus to understand the case, and it filled him with misgivings. We may be sure that to the anxious council in the tecpan every shooting-star, every puff from the crater of Popocatepetl, and whatever omen of good or evil could be gathered from any quarter, came up for fresh interpretation in the light of this strange intelligence. Let us leave them pondering the situation, while we turn our attention to the Spaniards, and observe by what stages they had approached the Mexican coast.

From the island of Hispaniola as a centre, the work of discovery spread in all directions, and not slowly, when one considers the difficulties involved in it. With the arrival of Diego Columbus, as admiral and governor of the Indies, in 1509, there was increased activity. In 1511 he sent Velasquez to conquer Cuba, and two years later Juan Ponce de Leon, governor of Porto Rico, landed upon the coast of Florida. In the autumn of 1509 the ill-fated expeditions of Ojeda and Nicuesa began their work upon the coast of Da-

Diffusion of the work of discovery from Hispaniola

" sun-faced," on account of his shaggy yellow hair and ruddy complexion.

rien; and in 1513 Balboa crossed that isthmus and discovered the Pacific Ocean. Rumours of the distant kingdom of the Incas reached his ears, and in 1517 he was about starting on a voyage to the south, when he was arrested on a charge of premeditating treason and desertion, and was put to death by Pedrarias, governor of Darien. This melancholy story will claim our attention in a future chapter. It is merely mentioned here, in its chronological order, as having a kind of suggestiveness in connection with the conduct of Cortes.

After the fall of Balboa the Spaniards for some time made little or no progress to the southward, but their attention was mainly directed to the westward. In 1516 food was scarce in Darien, and to relieve the situation about a hundred of the colonists were sent over to Cuba; among them was the soldier of fortune, Bernal Diaz de Castillo, afterward one of the most famous of chroniclers. These men had plenty of Indian gold, with which they fitted up a couple of ships to go slave-catching in the bay of Honduras. The governor, Velasquez, added a ship of his own to the expedition, and the chief command was given to Francisco Hernandez de Córdova, a man "very prudent and courageous, and strongly disposed to kill and kidnap Indians."[1]

Córdova's expedition, 1517

[1] Las Casas, *Historia de las Indias*, tom. iv. p. 369. This

The chief pilot was Antonio de Alaminos, who had been with Columbus on his fourth voyage, and there were in all more than a hundred soldiers. From Santiago they sailed, in February, 1517, through the Windward Passage around to Puerto Principe to take in sundry supplies. While they were waiting there the pilot, recalling to mind some things that Columbus had told him, was seized with the idea that a rich country might be discovered within a short distance by sailing to the west. Córdova was persuaded by his arguments, and loyally sent word to Velasquez, asking if he might be allowed to act as governor's lieutenant in any new lands he might discover.[1] Assent having been given, the

sort of expedition was illegal, and so it was publicly announced that the expedition was fitted out for purposes of discovery. See Bancroft's *Mexico*, vol. i. p. 6.

[1] This is graphically told by Las Casas : " Y estando allé, dijo el piloto Alaminos al capitan Francisco Hernandez que le parecia que por aquella mar del Poniente, abajo de la dicha isla de Cuba, le daba el corazon que habia de haber tierra muy rica, porque cuando andaba con el Almirante viejo, siendo él muchacho, via que el Almirante se inclinaba mucho à navegar hacia aquella parte, con esperanza grande que tenia que habia de hallar tierra muy poblada y muy más rica que hasta allí, é que así lo afirmaba, y porque le faltaron los navíos no prosiguió aquel camino, y tornó, desde el cabo que puso nombre de Gracias á Dios, atras á la provincia de Veragua. Dicho ésto, el Francisco Hernandez, que era de buena esperanza y buen ánimo, asentándosele aquestas palabras, determinó de enviar por licencia á Diego Velasquez,"

little fleet finally sailed from the lately founded town of Havana, and presently reached the northeastern corner of the peninsula of Yucatan. Here the Spaniards for the first time saw signs of that Oriental civilization for which they had so long been looking in vain. Strange-looking towers or pyramids, ascended by stone steps, greeted their eyes, and the people, who came out in canoes to watch the ships, were clad in quilted cotton doublets, and wore cloaks and brilliant plumes. These Mayas were bitterly hostile. Apparently they had heard of the Spaniards. It would have been strange indeed if, in the·six years since Velasquez had invaded Cuba, not a whisper of all the slaughter and enslavement in that island had found its way across the one hundred miles of salt water between Cape San Antonio and Cape Catoche. At several places along the shore the natives are said to have shouted "Castilians! Castilians!" At Catoche their demeanour was at first friendly, but after the Spaniards had come ashore they drew them into an ambush and attacked them, killing two and wounding several. The Spaniards then reëmbarked, tak-

Hostile demeanour of the Mayas

etc. *Op. cit.* p. 350. Alaminos had evidently confused in his memory the fourth voyage of Columbus with the second. It was in the second that Columbus felt obliged to turn back, and it is clear that in the fourth he had no intention of going west of Cape Honduras.

ing with them a couple of young captives whom they trained as interpreters. After a fortnight's sail along the coast they arrived at Campeche. Here the Maya natives invited them into the town, and showed them their huge pueblo fortresses and their stone temples, on the walls of which were sculptured enormous serpents, while the altars dripped fresh blood. "We were amazed," says Bernal Diaz, "at the sight of things so strange, as we watched numbers of natives, men and women, come in to get a sight of us with smiling and careless countenances."[1] Presently, however, priests approaching with fragrant censers requested the visitors to quit the country; and they deemed it prudent to comply, and retired to their ships. Proceeding as far as Champoton, the Spaniards were obliged to go ashore for water to drink. Then the Indians set upon them in overwhelming numbers and woefully defeated them, slaying more than half their number, and wounding nearly all the rest. The wretched survivors lost no time in getting back to Cuba, where Córdova soon died of his wounds. Worse luck they could hardly have had, but they brought back a little gold and some carved images stolen from a temple, and their story incited Velasquez to prepare a new expedition.

Defeat of the Spaniards at Champoton

[1] Diaz, *Historia verdadera*, cap. iii.

Four caravels were accordingly made ready and manned with 250 stout soldiers. The chief command was given to the governor's nephew, Juan de Grijalva, and the captains of two of the ships were Pedro de Alvarado and Francisco de Montejo. Sailing from Santiago early in April, 1518, they landed first at the island of Cozumel, and then followed the Yucatan coast till they reached Champoton, where they came to blows with the natives, and being fully prepared for such an emergency defeated them. In June they came to a country which they called Tabasco, after the name of a chief[1] with whom they had some friendly interviews and exchanged gifts. It was a few days later, at the little bay near the shore of which stood the pueblo of Mictlan-Quauhtla, that they were boarded by the tax-gatherer Pinotl, who carried such startling intelligence of them to Montezuma. The demeanour of the Nahua people in this neighbourhood was quite friendly; but the Spaniards were more and more struck with horror at the ghastly sights they saw of human heads raised aloft on poles, human bodies disembowelled, and grinning idols dripping blood from their jaws. On St. John's day they stopped at an island, the name of

Grijalva's
expedition
1518

---

[1] The Spaniards often mistook the name of some chief for a territorial name, as for example Quarequa, Pocorosa, Birú, etc., of which more anon.

34

which they understood to be Ulua,[1] and so they gave it the name now commonly written San Juan de Ulloa. Here Alvarado was sent back to Cuba with fifty or more sick men, to report what had been done and get reinforcements with which to found a colony. Grijalva kept on with the other three ships, as far, perhaps, as the river Pánuco, beyond the region of pueblos tributary to the Aztecs. By this time their ships were getting the worse for wear, and they began once more to encounter fierce and hostile Indians. Accordingly they turned back, and retracing their course arrived in Cuba early in November.

The effect of this expedition was very stimulating. A quarter of a century had elapsed since Columbus's first voyage, and the Spaniards had been active enough in many directions, but until lately they had seen no indications of that Oriental civilization and magnificence which they had expected to find. They had been tossed on weather-beaten coasts, and had wandered mile after mile half starved through tropical forests, for the most part without finding anything but rude and squalid villages inhabited by half-naked barbarians. Still hope had not deserted them ; they were as confident as ever that, in-

Excitement of the Spaniards

[1] An imperfect hearing of Culhua, a name common in Mexico.

asmuch as they were in Asia, it could not be so very far to the dominions of the Great Khan. Now Grijalva's tidings seemed to justify their lingering hope. Pinotl and other Indians had told him that far up in that country dwelt their mighty king who ruled over many cities and had no end of gold. Of course this must be the Great Khan, and the goal which Columbus had hoped to attain must now be within reach! The youthful Grijalva was flushed with anticipations of coming glory.

No sooner had he arrived in Cuba, however, than he was taught the lesson that there is many a slip betwixt the cup and the lip. He had found occasion to censure Alvarado, and that captain, nursing his spite and getting home some time before his young commander, had contrived to poison the mind of his uncle the governor. So Grijalva was set aside, all his fine hopes turned sick with chagrin. The prize was not for him, but for another young man, a native of Estremadura, who in 1504 had come over to the Indies. The name of this knight-errant, now in his thirty-fourth year, bold and devout, fertile in devices and unscrupulous, yet perhaps no more so than many a soldier whose name is respected, an Achilles for bravery, an Hernando Odysseus for craft and endurance, was Cortes Hernando Cortes. In 1511 he had served with distinction under Velasquez in the

36

expedition which conquered Cuba, and he was at this time *alcalde* (chief judge) of the newly founded town of Santiago on that island. He now persuaded Velasquez to appoint him to command the important expedition fitted out in the autumn of 1518 for operations on the Mexican mainland.

Before Cortes started, Velasquez began to worry lest he might prove too independent a spirit, and he twice sent messengers after him to recall him and put another in his place. Cortes politely disregarded the messages, thus verifying the governor's fears. Early in March, 1519, he landed at Tabasco, found the natives unfriendly, defeated them in a sharp skirmish, seized a fresh stock of pro- visions, and proceeded to San Juan de Ulloa, whence he sent messengers to Montezuma with gifts and messages as from his sovereign Charles V. Presently he ascertained that the yoke of the Aztec confederacy was borne unwillingly by many tributary towns and districts, and this was one of the main facts that enabled him to conquer the country. At first Cortes contrived to play a double game, encouraging the tributary towns to arrest Montezuma's tax-gatherers, and then currying favour with these officials by quietly releasing them and sending them with soft words to Montezuma.

It was now desirable to make a quick, bold

Expedition of Cortes, 1519

37

stroke and enlist all his followers irrevocably in the enterprise. Cortes laid the foundations of the town of Vera Cruz (a little to the north of its present site), and a municipal government was then and there framed.

Cortes then resigned his commission from Velasquez, and was at once reëlected captain-general by his municipality. He was doing pretty much the same thing that Balboa had been wrongly accused of doing, and he knew well that the alternative before him was victory or the headsman's block. He sent his flagship to Spain, with Montejo and a few other influential and devoted friends, to gain the ear of the grave young king who, while these things were going on, had been elected to the imperial throne of Charlemagne and the Othos. Then, with a strange mixture of persuasion and stealth, he had his ships one after another scuttled and sunk.[1] Nothing was left but to march on Mexico-Tenochtitlan.

---

[1] It is often carelessly said that Cortes burned his ships. Three or four were at first secretly scuttled, and there was more or less discussion as to whether the sinking was done by worms. Then the mariners who were in the secret reported other ships unseaworthy. Cortes's first argument was that it would not be worth while to waste time in trying to repair such extensive damages ; then he advanced to the position that perhaps it would be wise to sink all that were left, so as to be able to take the sailors along on the march into the country. All were then scuttled but one. Presently some of the mal-

Cortes sinking his Ships

A wonderful march! At one point (Iztac-mixtitlan) they came upon a valley where " for

contents in the camp discovered how the scuttling had been done, and loudly upbraided Cortes. He then boldly faced them, and asked for whom but cowards were means of retreat necessary! There was one ship left ; if there were any craven-hearted enough to wish to abandon the enterprise, in God's name let them go at once and in that ship. Cortes well knew what chord to touch in a soldier's heart. As the complaints were drowned in cheers, he went on and suggested that inasmuch as that last ship was of no use it might as well be sunk likewise ; which was forthwith done. See Bernal Diaz, *Historia verdadera,* cap. xxx.–xl.

It was the Sicilian general Agathokles who *burned* his ships when he invaded the territory of Carthage in 310 B. C., and it is interesting to compare the graphic description of Diodorus Siculus (lib. xx. cap. 7) with that of Bernal Diaz. The characteristics of the two commanders and the two different ages are worth noting. After crossing the Mediterranean, despite some real danger from Carthaginian cruisers of superior strength and much fancied danger from a total eclipse of the sun, Agathokles determined to destroy his ships, since guarding them would detain a part of his force, while in the event of his defeat they would not avail to save him from the Carthaginian fleet. So he gathered his army together and performed the customary sacrifices to the patron goddesses, Demeter and Persephone. The auspices turned out to be favourable. Then he told the soldiers that in an anxious moment upon the water he had vowed, if these goddesses should conduct him safely to the African shore, to make a burnt-offering of his fleet in honour of them. The peremptory obligation was at once recognized by the army. Agathokles with a torch set fire to his flagship, and at the same moment all the other ships were set blazing by their own captains, amid the murmured prayers of

39

four successive leagues there was a continuous line of houses, and the Lord of the valley," we are told, " lived in a fortress such as was not to be found in the half of Spain, surrounded by walls and barbicans and moats." What was The Spanish the force with which our knight-errant force ventured into such a country ? It consisted of 450 Spaniards, many of them clad in mail, half a dozen small cannon, and fifteen horses. It was not enough that the Spanish soldier of that day was a bulldog for strength and courage, or that his armour was proof against stone arrows and lances, or that he wielded a Toledo blade that could cut through silken cushions, or that his arquebus and cannon were not only death-dealing weapons but objects of superstitious awe. More potent than all else together were those frightful monsters, the horses. Before these animals men, women, and children fled like sheep, or skulked and peeped from behind their walls in an ecstasy of terror. It was that paralyzing, blood-curdling fear of the supernatural, against which no amount of physical bravery, nothing in the world but modern knowledge, is of the slightest avail. Perhaps Sir Arthur Helps is right in saying that it was the horse that overthrew the

the soldiers and the solemn notes of the trumpet. The event, on the whole, justified the daring policy of Agathokles.

kingdoms of the Aztecs and the Incas.[1] But
besides all this, there was the legend of the
bright Quetzalcoatl coming to win back his
ancient kingdom from the dark Tezcatlipoca.
And strongly coöperating with all other circumstances was the readiness of the hounded and
crestfallen tributary pueblos to welcome any
chance that might humble the Triple Tyrant
of the Lake! Surely, if ever the stars in their
courses fought for mortal man, that man was
Hernando Cortes. This luck, however, should
not lessen our estimate of his genius, for never
was man more swift and sure in seizing opportunities. To offer chances to a dull-witted man
is like casting pearls before swine.

As the little army advanced, its progress was
heralded by awe-struck couriers who made pictures of the bearded strangers and their hoofed
monsters, and sent them, with queer hieroglyphic notes and comments, to the Great
Pueblo on the lake. Cortes soon divined the
situation, albeit imperfectly, and displayed an audacity the like of which
was perhaps never seen before in the
world. At the town of Cempoala he had already
set free the victims held for sacrifice, and hurled
the misshapen idols from the temple. But his

Audacity of
Cortes at
Cempoala

[1] See the striking passage in his *Spanish Conquest*, vol. iii.
p. 547.

in their tribal council which reveals to us the opposing views that were probably entertained in every pueblo in the land. One chieftain, Maxixcatzin, argued that the Spaniards were probably gods whom it was idle to think of resisting. Another chieftain, Xicotencatl,[1] thought that this view was at least doubtful enough to be worth testing; the strangers assumed odious airs of authority, but they were a mere handful in number, and the men of Tlascala were invincible; by way of experiment, at all events, it was worth while to fight. After much debate this counsel prevailed, and the tawny warriors went forth against the Spaniards. Bernal Diaz says there were 50,000 of them in the field, and later writers have swelled the number to 150,000. In studying the conquest of Mexico one soon gets used to this sort of thing. Too many of its historians belong to a school of which Falstaff, with his men in buckram, was the founder. Bernal Diaz was an eyewitness; he took part in the battle, and, if we strike off about one cipher from his figure and make it 5000, we shall get somewhere within the bounds of credibility, and the odds will remain sufficiently great to attest the

Battle between Spaniards and Tlascalans

[1] Mr. Bandelier regards Maxixcatzin and Xicotencatl as sharing the office of head war-chief, an instance of dual executive quite common in ancient America. *Peabody Museum Reports*, ii. 660.

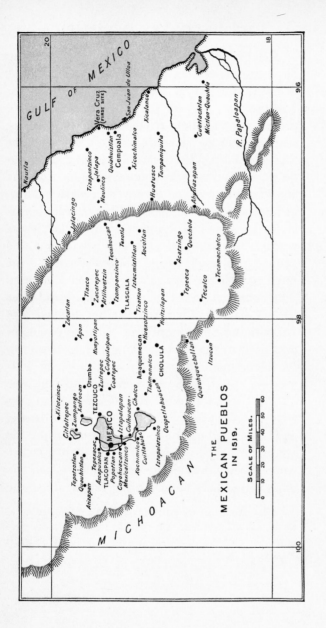

THE
MEXICAN PUEBLOS
IN 1519.

SCALE OF MILES.

0   10   20   30   40   50   60

GULF OF MEXICO

Tlaula

Vera Cruz (FIRST SITE)
San Juan de Ulloa

Quiahuiztlan
Cempoala

Tizapantinco
Jalapa
Naulinco

Xicochimalco
Xicalanco

Cuetlachtlan
Michtlan-Quauhtla

R. Papaloapan

Huatusco
Tampaniquita

Atlatlauzapan

Quechola
Acatzingo

Tecamachalco

Tepeaca
Tecalco

Huitzilapan

Ixtacmixtitlan
Tizatlan
TLASCALA
Tizompantzinco
Atlihuetzin
Zocatepec
Tlaxco

Zacatlan

Ixcotlan
Tzotla
Teuxihuacan

Apan
Hueyotlipan

Otumba
Xaltocan

Tzitrepec
Calpulalpan
Coatepec

Amaquemecan
Tlalmanalco
CHOLULA

Quauhquechollan

Itzucan

Xiltotzinco
Zumpango

TEZCUCO
Ixtapalapan
MEXICO
Culhuacan
Chalco

Izcapuzalco
Tepozotlan
Quauhtitlan
Tepeacac
TLACOPAN
Popotlan
Coyohuacan
Mexicaltzinco
Xochimilco
Cuitlahuac
Izcapalatzinco
Ocpetlahuacan

Anzapan

M I C H O A C A N

valour of the Spaniards. The Tlascalan army was apparently marshalled in phratries, one of them from the allied pueblo of Huexotzinco. They were distinguished by the colours of their war-paint. They wore quilted cotton doublets, and carried leather shields stretched upon a framework of bamboo and decorated with feathers. Upon their heads they wore helmets of stout leather fashioned and trimmed with featherwork so as to look like heads of snakes or jaguars, and the chiefs were distinguished by gorgeous plumes. Their weapons were long bows, arrows tipped with obsidian, copper-pointed lances, slings, javelins, and heavy wooden swords with sharp blades of obsidian inserted in both edges.[1] With this barbaric host the Spaniards had two days of desultory fighting. By the end of that time a great many Tlascalans had been killed; a few Spaniards had been wounded, and one or two had been killed,[2] but they were so carefully buried by their comrades that the enemy did not learn the fact, and it was sagely

[1] Bancroft, *Native Races of the Pacific States*, vol. ii. pp. 406–410.

[2] The ingrained Mexican custom of trying to capture their enemies for sacrifice, instead of slaying them on the field, is cited by Bandelier as a reason why more Spaniards did not get killed in these straggling fights. "Thus, for the sake of capturing a single horseman, they recklessly sacrificed numbers of their own, when they thought to be able to surround him, and cut him off from his corps or detachment. The custom

45

concluded that the white men must be more than mortal.

The sturdy Xicotencatl, however, was not willing to give up the case without one more trial. He took counsel with soothsayers, and the opinion was suggested that the strangers, as solar deities, were very probably dependent for their strength, and perhaps for their invulnerability, upon direct contact with the solar radiance. Possibly in the night-time they might turn out to be mortal. At all events it was worth trying, and Xicotencatl made up his mind to act on his own account that very night. In making his preparations for an attack he sent a small party of spies to the Spanish camp with presents and soft words. They were to watch things keenly, and bring back such information as might prove useful. Some were to stay in the camp and at an appointed signal set fire to it. Cortes received these Indians graciously, but presently their behaviour excited suspicion, and to their utter terror and confusion they suddenly found themselves arrested and charged with treachery! There was no use in lying to superhuman beings who clearly possessed the godlike power of reading the secret thoughts of men; so the spies, or some of them, made

Scheme of the Tlascalan soothsayers

was general among the Nahuatlac tribes." *Peabody Museum Reports*, ii. 128.

confession. Thus informed of the situation, Cortes waited till nightfall, and then cut off the thumbs of the spies and sent them to tell Xicotencatl that he would find the white man as invincible by night as by day.[1] Cortes followed the messengers at no great distance with a party of horsemen; and while the Tlascalan warriors were limp with amazement at this penetration of their design, the party charged in among them at full gallop, scattering them in wildest panic and cutting them down by the score.[2]

It was clear that nothing was to be gained by opposing these children of the sun. The unfortunate soothsayers who had advised the night attack were disembowelled, stewed with chile pepper, and served in a ragout; and the Tlascalan tribal council, taught wisdom by adversity, decided to improve the situation by making an alliance with the wielders of thunder and lightning, and enlisting, if possible, their resistless strength in the work of humbling Tlascala's ancient enemy. Upon the people of the Aztec

[1] "Y los embió para que dixessen a Xicotĕcatl su capitan-general, que lo mismo haria de quantas espias pudiesse auer, y que fuesse cõ su exercito, porque siempre conoceria que los Castellanos eran inuencibles de dia y de noche." Herrera, decad. ii. lib. vi. cap. 8.

[2] Diaz, *Historia verdadera*, cap. xlvii.–l.

Confederacy these events made a most profound impression. They freely acknowledged that beings who could so easily defeat the Tlascalans must be more than human. But when it was learned that these dreaded strangers had entered into friendly alliance with the " republic " of Tlascala,[1] and were now leading an army of its warriors toward Tenochtitlan, we can well imagine the consternation that must have pervaded the streets of that great pueblo.

From this time the community of interests kept the Tlascalans faithful to the white men even after the illusion as to their supernatural qualities had died away. If we would form a true conception of the conquest of Mexico by a handful of Spaniards, we must remember that Tlascala, with its few allied pueblos, had shown itself nearly a match for the Aztec Confederacy; and the advantage of this alliance was now added to the peculiar combination of circumstances that made the Spaniards so formidable.

Affairs having duly been arranged at Tlascala, the little army, now followed by a formidable

[1] It is curious to see Tlascala commonly mentioned as a " republic " and the Aztec Confederacy as an " empire," ruled by an absolute monarch, when in reality the supreme power in both was vested in the tribal councils. This indicates that the Aztec *tlacatecuhtli* had acquired higher dignity than that merely of head war-chief. He had joined to this the dignity of chief priest, as we shall see.

48

body of dusky allies, approached Cholula, a strong pueblo allied with the Confederacy and especially identified with the worship of Quetzalcoatl.[1] The town was not only one of the principal markets in Mexico, but it was held in much reverence for its religious associations. With the aid and approval of emissaries from Tenochtitlan, the chiefs of Cholula prepared an ambuscade for the Spaniards, who were politely and cordially admitted into the town with the intention of entrapping them. But with Cortes there was a handsome young Indian woman from Tabasco, who had fallen in love with him there and remained his faithful companion through all the trials of the conquest. Her aid was invaluable, since to a thorough familiarity with the Nahuatl and Maya languages she soon added a knowledge of Spanish, and for quick wit and fertility of resource she was like Morgiana in the story of the Forty Thieves. The name given to this young woman on the occasion of her conversion and baptism was Marina, which in Nahuatl mouths became Malina, and oddly enough the most common epithet applied to Cortes, by Montezuma and others, was Malintzin or Malinche, "lord of Marina." It was through her keenness that the plot of the Cholultec chiefs

Treachery at Cholula, discovered by Doña Marina

---

[1] There is an excellent account of Cholula in Bandelier's *Archæological Tour*, pp. 79–262.

was discovered and frustrated. Having ascertained the full extent of their plans, Cortes summoned the principal chiefs of Cholula to a conference, announced his intention of starting on the morrow for Tenochtitlan, and with an air of innocent trust in them, he asked them to furnish him with an additional supply of food and with an auxiliary force of Cholulans. In childish glee at this presumed simplicity, and confident that for once the white stranger was not omniscient, the chiefs readily promised the men and provisions. Several three-year-old babes had been sacrificed that day, and the auspices were favourable. So the chiefs spent the night in arranging their *coup de main* for the next morning, while Cortes saw that his cannon were placed in suitable positions for raking the streets. In the morning a throng of Cholultec warriors crowded into the square where the Spaniards were quartered, and the chiefs felt so sure of their game that to the number of thirty or more they accepted an invitation to meet " Malinche " in private and receive his parting blessing. When they were assembled, and with them the Aztec emissaries, whom Cortes took care to have at hand, they heard such words as froze them with terror. It seems that, here as well as at Tlascala, there were two parties, one counselling submission, the other resistance, only here the

The gods too confident

50

resistance had assumed the form of treachery. Having been primed by Marina with full and accurate information, Cortes conveyed to the astounded chiefs the secret history of their little scheme, and informed them that they were his prisoners, but he knew how to separate sheep from goats and only the guilty should be punished. As for Montezuma, though it was said that he was privy to the Cholulan plot, Cortes declared himself unwilling to believe such a slander against one whom he had always understood to be a worthy prince. It was his policy for the moment to soothe the emissaries from Tenochtitlan while he exhibited his fiend-like power. We can dimly imagine the paralyzing amazement and terror as the chiefs who had counselled submission were picked out and taken aside. At this moment the thunder of artillery, never heard before in Cholula, burst upon the ear. Bloody lanes were ploughed through the mass of dusky warriors in the square, hippocentaurs clad in shining brass charged in among them, and the Tlascaltec warriors, who had been encamped outside, now rushed into the town and began a general massacre. Several hundred, perhaps some thousands, were slain, including the head war-chief. Of the captured chiefs a few were burned at the stake, doubtless as a warning example for Montezuma. Cortes then released

Massacre at Cholula

all the caged victims fattening for sacrifice, and resumed his march.

From Cholula the little army proceeded to Huexotzinco and thence to Amaquemecan, where they were met by chiefs from Tlalman-alco, inveighing against the tyranny of the Aztecs and begging for deliverance. Passing Tlalmanalco and Iztapalatzinco, the Spaniards went on to Cuitlahuac, situated upon the cause-way leading across the lake of Chalco. This was one of the many towns in the lately found Indies which reminded the Spaniards of Venice ; *i. e.* it was built over the water, with canals for streets. Its floating gardens and its houses glistening in their stucco of white gypsum delighted the eyes of the Spaniards. Crossing the cause-way they marched on to Iztapalapan, where First sight of they arrived on the 7th of November, Tenochtitlan 1519, and saw before them the Queen of Pueblos. " And when we beheld," says Bernal Diaz, " so many cities and towns rising up from the water, and other populous places situated on the terra firma, and that causeway, straight as a level, which went into Mexico, we remained astonished, and said to one another that it appeared like the enchanted castles which they tell of in the book of Amadis, by reason of the great towers, temples, and edifices which there were in the water, and all of them work of

Citlaltepec

Zumpango

Tepotzotlan

Quauhtitlan

Xaltocan

Otumba

Zultepec

Tepexacac

TEZCUCO

Calpulalpan

Azcapuzalco

Lake of Tezcuco

TLACOPAN

Popotlan

TENOCHTITLAN
MEXICO

Chimalhuacan

Coatepec

Coyohuacan

Iztapalapan

Mexicaltzinco

Culhuacan

Xochimilco

Cuitlahuac
Lake of
Chalco

Chalco

Amaquemecan

Iztapalatzinco

Tlalmanalco

Ocoperlahuacan

Spanish Leagues.

1 2 3 4   6

THE VALLEY OF MEXICO IN 1519

masonry. Some of our soldiers asked if this that they saw was not a thing in a dream."[1]

It may well be called the most romantic moment in all history, this moment when European eyes first rested upon that city of wonders, the chief ornament of a stage of social evolution two full ethnical periods behind their own. To say that it was *A most romantic moment* like stepping back across the centuries to visit the Nineveh of Sennacherib or hundred-gated Thebes is but inadequately to depict the situation, for it was a longer step than that. Such chances do not come twice to mankind, for when two grades of culture so widely severed are brought into contact, the stronger is apt to blight and crush the weaker where it does not amend and transform it. In spite of its foul abominations, one sometimes feels that one would like to recall that extinct state of society in order to study it. The devoted lover of history, who ransacks all sciences for aid toward understanding the course of human events, who knows in what unexpected ways one stage of progress often illustrates other stages, will sometimes wish it were possible to resuscitate, even for one brief year, the vanished City of the Cactus Rock. Could such a work of enchantment be performed, however, our first feeling would

[1] Diaz, *Historia verdadera*, cap. lxxxvii.

doubtless be one of ineffable horror and disgust, like that of the knight in the old English ballad, who folding in his arms a damsel of radiant beauty finds himself in the embrace of a loathsome fiend.

But inasmuch as the days of magic are long since past, and the ointment of the wise dervise, that enabled one to see so many rich and buried secrets, has forever lost its virtues, the task for the modern student is simply the prosaic one of setting down such few details as can be gathered from the Spanish narratives [1] and sifted in view of what little we know about such points as the Spaniards were liable to misinterpret. A few such details will help us to understand the way

[1] My authorities for the description of Tenochtitlan are Cortes, *Cartas y relaciones al emperador Carlos V.*, Paris, 1866; Bernal Diaz, *Historia verdadera*, Madrid, 1632; Icazbalceta, *Coleccion de documentos*, etc., Mexico, 1858–66; *Relatione fatta per un gentil' huomo del Signor Fernando Cortese*, apud Ramusio, *Navigationi et Viaggi*, Venice, 1556; Tezozomoc, *Histoire de Mexique*, Paris, 1853; Ixtlilxochitl, *Relaciones*, apud Kingsborough's *Mexican Antiquities*, London, 1831–48, vol. ix.; Sahagun, *Historia general de las cosas de Nueva España*, Mexico, 1829; Torquemada, *Monarquía indiana*, Madrid, 1723; Clavigero, *Storia antica del Messico*, Cesena, 1780; Oviedo, *Historia general y natural de las Indias*, Madrid, 1851–55; Gomara, *Historia de Mexico*, Antwerp, 1554; Herrera, *Historia general de los hechos de los Castellanos*, etc., Madrid, 1601; Veytia, *Historia antigua de Mejico*, Mexico, 1836; Vetancurt, *Teatro mexicano*, Mexico, 1870.

in which this archaic phase of human development was so abruptly cut short.

The city of Mexico stood in a salt lake, and was approached by three causeways of solid masonry, each, as the Spanish soldiers said, two lances in breadth, which might mean from twenty to thirty feet. Being from four to five miles in length, and assailable on both sides by the canoes of the city's defenders, they were very dangerous avenues for an enemy, whether advancing or retreating. Near the city *The cause-* these causeways were interrupted by *ways* wooden drawbridges. Then they were continued into the city as main thoroughfares, and met in the great square where the temple stood. The city was also connected with the mainland by an aqueduct in solid masonry leading down from Chepultepec. The streets might have reminded one of Venice, in so far as some were canals alive with canoes, while others were dry footpaths paved with hard cement, and the footways often crossed the canals on bridges. These paths and canals ran between immense houses of red stone, many of them coated with a hard white stucco. The houses in- *The houses* closed great courtyards, and vast as were the spaces covered by them there was seldom a third story. The low flat roofs, often covered with flower gardens, were protected by

stone parapets with small towers at intervals, so
that every house was a fortress. The effect must
have been extremely picturesque. Military pre-
cautions were everywhere visible. The bridges
across the canals could be drawn up at a moment's notice. The windows were mere loop-
holes, and they as well as the doorways were
open. The entrance to the house could be bar-
ricaded, but doors had not been invented. Sometimes a kind of bamboo screen was hung in the
doorway and secured by a crossbar; sometimes,
especially in interior doorways, there were hang-
ings of cotton or feather-work.[1]

---

[1] The portière is much more ancient than the door, and
goes back at least as far as the lower period of barbarism; as
e. g. the Mandan buffalo robe above mentioned, vol. i. p. 95.
The Greeks in the upper period of barbarism had true doors
with hinges and latches. One of the cosiest pictures in the
delicious Odyssey is that of the old nurse Eurykleia showing
Telemachus to his chamber, when leaving him tucked under the
woollen rug she goes out, and closes the door with its silver
ring and fastens the latch with a thong : —

> ὤϊξεν δὲ θύρας θαλάμου πύκα ποιητοῖο,
> ἕζετο δ' ἐν λέκτρῳ, μαλακὸν δ' ἔκδυνε χιτῶνα·
> καὶ τὸν μὲν γραίης πυκιμηδέος ἔμβαλε χερσίν.
> ἡ μὲν τὸν πτύξασα καὶ ἀσκήσασα χιτῶνα,
> πασσάλῳ ἀγκρεμάσασα παρὰ τρητοῖς λεχέεσσιν,
> βῆ ῥ' ἴμεν ἐκ θαλάμοιο, θύρην δ' ἐπέρυσσε κορώνη
> ἀργυρέη, ἐπὶ δὲ κληῖδ' ἐτάνυσσεν ἱμάντι.
> ἔνθ' ὅγε παννύχιος, κεκαλυμμένος οἰὸς ἀώτῳ,
> βούλευε φρεσὶν ᾗσιν ὁδὸν τὴν πέφραδ' Ἀθήνη.
>
> *Odyssey*, i. 436.

M. Charnay, in his investigations at Uxmal, found " four
rings or stone hooks inside the doorways near the top, from

56

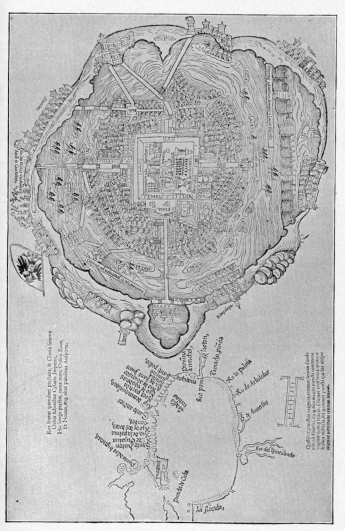

CORTES'S MAP OF THE LAKE AND CITY OF MEXICO, 1524

The number of the houses and of their occupants has been the subject of curious misapprehensions. The Licentiate Zuazo, a scholarly and careful man whom Cortes left in charge of the city in 1524, and who ought to be good authority, said that there were 60,000 *vecinos*.[1] As I have before observed,[2] this Spanish word may mean either " inhabitants " or " householders." The latter interpretation was given to it by Gomara and Peter Martyr,[3] and has been generally adopted ; but as nobody has given the circumference of the city as more than four leagues, and as it was in all probability less than that,[4] there would not have begun to be room enough for 60,000 of these huge houses, The population along with the space occupied by canals and open squares, temples with their pyramids, and gardens between the houses.[5] The

which it is easy to conjecture that a wooden board was placed inside against the opening, and kept in place by two transversal bars entering the stone hooks.'' *Ancient Cities of the New World*, p. 398.

[1] *Carta de Licenciado Zuazo*, MS., apud Prescott, *Conquest of Mexico*, bk. iv. chap. i.

[2] See above, vol. i. p. 108.

[3] Gomara, *Crónica de la Nueva España*, Saragossa, 1554, cap. lxxviii.; Martyr, *De Orbe Novo*, dec. v. cap. iii.

[4] Bandelier, *Archæological Tour*, p. 50.

[5] '' Nearly all the old authors describe the public buildings as surrounded by pleasure-grounds or ornamental gardens. It is very striking that, the pueblo having been founded in 1325,

book of one of Cortes's companions, known as
the Anonymous Conqueror, survives only in an

and nearly a century having been spent in adding sufficient
artificial sod to the originally small solid expanse settled, the
Mexicans could have been ready so soon to establish purely
decorative parks within an area, every inch of which was valuable to them for subsistence alone !'' Bandelier, in *Peabody
Museum Reports*, vol. ii. p. 422. That the corn-growers of
Tenochtitlan were cramped for room is plain from the fact
that they constructed '' floating gardens,'' or rafts covered
with black loam which were moored at various points in the
shallow lake. These artificial gardens (*chinampas*) were usually rectangular in shape and from thirty to fifty yards in
length ; maize, beans, tomatoes, and other vegetables were
raised in them. See Torquemada, *Monarquía indiana*, tom.
ii. p. 483 ; Acosta, *Historia de las Indias*, p. 472 ; Clavigero, *Storia di Messico*, tom. ii. p. 152. This practice indicates that there was no superfluous space in the city. Nevertheless the testimony of '' nearly all the old authors,'' that
extensive flower gardens were to be seen, is not to be lightly
rejected. Flowers were used in many of the religious festivals, and there is abundant evidence, moreover, that the
Mexicans were very fond of them. This is illustrated in
the perpetual reference to flowers in old Mexican poems :
'' They led me within a valley to a fertile spot, a flowery
spot, where the dew spread out in glittering splendour, where
I saw various lovely fragrant flowers, lovely odorous flowers,
clothed with the dew, scattered around in rainbow glory ;
there they said to me, ' Pluck the flowers, whichever thou
wishest, mayest thou the singer be glad, and give them to thy
friends, to the chiefs, that they may rejoice on the earth.' So
I gathered in the folds of my garment the various fragrant
flowers, delicate scented, delicious,'' etc. Brinton, *Ancient
Nahuatl Poetry*, p. 57. Of the twenty-seven ancient Mexi-

Italian translation, and this has 60,000 *habita-tori*, which can mean nothing but inhabitants.[1] Taking 60,000 as the population, which seems a reasonable figure, the number of communal houses can hardly have exceeded 300, as the number of persons in a house can hardly have averaged less than 200. We have already, in the first chapter of this work, seen how the organization of the Aztec tribe in four phratries divided the city into four quarters, each with its curial temple and peculiar ceremonies. It reminds one of the three-fold division of Rome by tribes at the time when the Ramnes occupied the Palatine hill, while the Tities lived on the Quirinal, and the Luceres on the Esquiline.[2] The communal

The four wards

can songs in this interesting collection, there is scarcely one that does not abound with ecstatic allusions to flowers : " The delicious breath of the dewy flowers is in our homes in Chiapas ; " " my soul was drunken with the flowers ; " " let me gather the intoxicating flowers, many coloured, varied in hue," etc.

[1] *Relatione fatta per un gentil' huomo del Signor Fernando Cortese*, apud Ramusio, *Navigationi et Viaggi*, Venice, 1556, tom. iii. fol. 309. Mr. Morgan (*Ancient Society*, p. 195) thinks the number of inhabitants could not have exceeded 30,000, but I see no reason for doubting the statements of Zuazo and the Anonymous Conqueror.

[2] Tlatelulco constituted a fifth quarter, for the Tlatelulcans, who had been conquered in 1473, deprived of tribal rights, and partially re-adopted ; an interesting case, for which see Bandelier, *Peabody Museum Reports*, ii. 593.

houses, as Richard Eden has it, were "palaices of maruelous bygnes, and curiously buylded with many pleasaunt diuises." Upon the front of each was sculptured the totem or beast-symbol of the clan to which it belonged, that upon the one in which Montezuma received the strangers being an eagle with a wildcat (*ocelotl*) grasped in its beak. It was customary to carve upon the jambs, on either side of the doorway, enormous serpents with gaping mouths.

The dress of the people was of cotton, the men wearing loose cloaks and ample fringed sashes, and the women long robes reaching to the ground. These cotton garments were often elaborately embroidered and dyed with the rich scarlet of the cochineal. Capes of fur or doublets of feather-work were worn in cold weather. The feet were protected by a kind of sandal, and the head by a white cotton hood. The hair was ordinarily worn long, and a deep violet hair-dye was used by the women. Faces were sometimes smeared with red or yellow ointment, and the teeth stained with cochineal. Gold and silver bracelets and anklets and rings for fingers, ears, and nose were worn by men and women.

Dress

In the interior of the houses cedar and other fine woods were used for partitions and ceilings. The chief decorations were the mural tapestries woven of the gorgeous

Interiors

60

plumage of parrots, pheasants, cardinals, and humming-birds, and one purpose of the many aviaries was to furnish such feathers. Except a few small tables and stools, there was not much furniture. Palm-leaf mats piled on the hard cemented floor served as beds, and sometimes there were coverlets of cotton or feather-work. Resinous torches were used for lights. The principal meal of the day was served on low tables, the people sitting on mats or cushions in long rows around the sides of the room, with their backs against the wall. A lighted brazier stood in the middle, and before tast- _Dinner_ ing the food each person threw a morsel into the brazier as an offering to the fire-god. The commonest meat was the turkey, a bird as characteristic of Mexico as its cactuses. The name of this fowl preserves a curious illustration of the mixture of truth and error which had led to the discovery of America. When it was first introduced into European barnyards in 1530, people named it on the theory that it was an Asiatic fowl. The Germans for a while called it _Calecutische hahn_ or Calicut cock; the French still call it _dinde_, which at first was _poulet d'Inde_ or India fowl; and the English called it the Turkey fowl; but the Oriental country which it came from was really Mexico, many thousand miles east of Asia.

Cookery had made some progress among the Aztecs. Indian meal beaten up with eggs was baked in loaves, and there were cakes resembling the modern *tortilla*. Then there was the *tamale*, a kind of pie of meat and vegetables with a covering of Indian meal. Fresh fish were abundant. There were various ragouts intensely hot with tabasco and chile sauce. Bernal Diaz counted thirty such dishes upon Montezuma's table. One favourite mess was frog spawn and stewed ants peppered with chile; another was human flesh cooked in like manner. To the cannibalism almost universal among American aborigines the people of Mexico and Central America added this epicure's touch.[1]

Dishes

---

[1] The first dish mentioned by Bernal Diaz seemed to Mr. Prescott both startling and apocryphal, and even the old soldier himself, in spite of the cannibalism he had witnessed, was slow to admit the truth of what he was told. It was a fricassee of very young children : " E como por passatiempo oi dezir, que le solian guisar carnes de muchachos de poca edad," etc. (*Historia verdadera*, cap. xci.) When we bear in mind, however, that in times of public excitement and peril it was customary to obtain the auspices by sacrificing young children, and that the flesh of the human victim seems invariably to have been eaten, there is nothing at all improbable in what was told to Diaz.

Sir Henry Yule, in one of his learned notes to Marco Polo, mentions instances which show the connection between cannibalism and sundry folk-lore notions, *e. g.* " after an execution at Peking certain large pith balls are steeped in the

These viands were kept hot by means of chafing dishes and were served on earthenware

blood, and under the name of *blood-bread* are sold as a medicine for consumption. It is only to the blood of decapitated criminals that any such healing power is attributed." There is evidence that this remnant of cannibalism is not yet extinct in China. Among civilized peoples in modern times instances of cannibalism have been for the most part confined to shipwrecked crews in the last stages of famine. Among savages and barbarians of low type, famine and folk-lore probably combine to support the custom. When the life of the Jesuit priest Brébeuf had gone out amid diabolical torments, during which he had uttered neither cry nor groan, an Iroquois chief tore out his heart and devoured it for the very practical purpose of acquiring all that courage ; on the other hand, when one of Mr. Darwin's party asked some Fuegians why they did not eat their dogs instead of their grandmothers, they replied, probably in some amusement at his ignorance of sound economical principles, "Doggies catch otters ; old women no !" In mediæval Europe instances of cannibalism can be traced to scarcity of food, and among the Turks there seem to have been cases quite sufficient to explain the fabulous picture of King Richard, in the presence of Saladin's ambassadors, dining on a curried Saracen's head

> " soden full hastily
> With powder and with spysory,
> And with saffron of good colour."

In the interior of northern Sumatra dwell a people called Battas, civilized enough to use a phonetic alphabet. Their ancient cannibalism is now restricted by law. Three classes of persons are condemned to be eaten : 1. a commoner guilty of adultery with a Rajah's wife ; 2. enemies taken in battle outside their own village ; 3. traitors and spies, in default of a ransom equivalent to 60 dollars a head. See Yule's *Marco Polo*, vol. i. pp. 275–277 ; vol. ii. p. 231 ; Parkman,

bowls or plates, for the making of which Cho-lula was especially noted. Chocolate, flavoured

Drinks

with vanilla, was the ordinary bever-age. Food was handled with the fin-gers, but bowls of water and towels were brought in at the end of the meal, and the next thing in order was to smoke tobacco and get drunk with *pulque*, the fermented juice of the century plant.[1]

The trade implied by this sort of life was not done in shops. There were no shops in this Aztec pueblo, but two spacious market-places,

Markets

with fairs every fifth day. There were displayed foods, cloths, and orna-ments ; tools, weapons, and building materials ; mats and stools, dye-stuffs and pottery. Traffic was chiefly barter, but there were such rudi-mentary attempts at currency as quills packed with gold-dust, bags of cocoa seed, and queer little bits of copper and tin shaped like the let-

Jesuits in North America, p. 389 ; Darwin, *Voyage of the Beagle*, London, 1870, p. 214.

[1] The maguey, or *Agave americana*, sometimes called American aloe. One of these plants in a green tub stood on either side of the steps leading up to the front door of George Nupkins, Esq., magistrate, in Ipswich (*Pickwick Papers*, chap. xxv.). For a good account of the many and great uses of the century-plant, see Bandelier, *Archæological Tour*, p. 217 ; Garcilasso, *Comentarios reales*, pt. i. lib. viii. cap. 13. From the pulque, a kind of strong brandy, called *mescal*, is distilled.

ter T. There were no coins or scales, and sell-
ing by weight was unknown. In most of the
pueblos traders came in from the country, or
from other towns, with their wares borne on
litters, the only kind of wagon or carriage in
use ; but in Mexico such conveyance was done
chiefly by canoes. In the market-place there
were booths where criminals were tried and
sentenced. Crime was frequent, and punishment swift and cruel.[1] Another feature of the
market-place would seem in itself to epitomize
all the incongruousness of this strange Aztec
world. A barber's shop seems to suggest civilization as vividly as a stone knife suggests barbarism. In the Mexican market there were
booths where the scanty beards of the dusky
warriors were shaved with razors of obsidian ![2]

Close by the principal market and in the centre of the pueblo was the great enclosure of
the temple, surrounded by stone walls
                                              The temple
eight feet in height, and entered by
four gateways, one from each of the wards or
quarters above described. Within were not less
than twenty *teocallis*, or truncated pyramids, the

[1] The subject of crimes and punishments in ancient Mexico is well summarized by Bandelier, *Peabody Museum Reports*, vol. ii. pp. 623–633.

[2] Prescott, *Conquest of Mexico*, bk. iv. chap. ii. ; on
American beards, cf. Brinton, *The American Race*, p. 40.

tallest of which was the one dedicated to the war-god. It was ascended by stone stairs on the outside, and as the Spaniards counted 114 stairs it was probably not far from 100 feet in height. This height was divided into five stages, in such wise that a man, after ascending the first flight of stairs, would walk on a flat terrace or ledge around to the opposite side of the pyramid, and there mount the second flight. Thus the religious processions on their way to the summit would wind four times about the pyramid, greatly enhancing the spectacular effect. This may or may not have been the purpose of the arrangement ; it was at any rate one of its results. On the summit was a dreadful block of jasper, convex at the top, so that when the human victim was laid upon his back and held down, the breast was pushed upward, ready for the priest to make one deep slashing cut and snatch out the heart. Near the sacrificial block were the altars and sanctuaries of the gods Tezcatlipoca, Huitzilopochtli, and others, with idols as hideous as their names.[1] On these altars smoked fresh human hearts, of which the gods were fond, while other parts of the bodies were made ready for the kitchens

Human sacrifices

[1] See the photograph of an idol, probably of Huitzilopoch-tli, dug up in 1790 near the cathedral, which stands on the site of the heathen temple, in Bandelier, *Archæological Tour*, p. 59.

of the communal houses below. The gods were voracious as wolves, and the victims were numerous.[1] In some cases the heart was thrust into the mouth of the idol with a golden spoon, in others its lips were simply daubed with blood. In the temple a great quantity of rattlesnakes, kept as sacred objects, were fed with the entrails of the victims. Other parts of the body were given to the menagerie beasts, which were probably also kept for purposes of religious

[1] A native Mexican author, born in 1579, says that at the dedication of the new temple to Huitzilopochtli, in 1487, the number of victims was 80,600 (Chimalpahin Quauhtlehuanitzin, *Sixième et Septième Relations*, ed. Siméon, Paris, 1889, p. 158). I rather think that, even for such a grand occasion, we must at least cut off a cipher. There can be little doubt, however, that within this whole snake-worshipping world of Mexico and Central America there were many thousand victims yearly, — men, women, and children. A very complete view, with many of the hideous details, is given in Bancroft's *Native Races of the Pacific States*, vol. ii. pp. 302–341, 687–714 ; see also Fergusson, *Tree and Serpent Worship*, p. 40 ; Stephens, *Central America*, vol. ii. p. 185. For a human sacrifice among the Pawnees, somewhat similar to the Mexican custom, see Brinton, *The American Race*, p. 97. For some references to human sacrifices among the ancient Germans and Huns, see Gibbon, chap. xxx., xxxiv.; Leo, *Vorlesungen über die Geschichte des Deutschen Volkes*, Halle, 1854, bd. i. p. 96; Mone, *Geschichte des Heidenthums*, Leipsic, 1822, ii. 20, 136; Milman, *Latin Christianity*, vol. i. p. 244; among the Saxons, Sidonius Apollinaris, lib. viii. epist. 6 ; among the Carthaginians, Grote, *History of Greece*, vol. xii. p. 565.

symbolism.   Blood was also rubbed in the mouths of the carved serpents upon the jambs and lintels of the houses.   The walls and floor of the great temple were clotted with blood and shreds of human flesh, and the smell was like that of a slaughter-house.   Just outside the temple, in front of the broad street that led across the causeway to Tlacopan, stood the *tzompantli*, which was " an oblong sloping parallelogram of earth and masonry, one hundred and fifty-four feet [long] at the base, ascended by thirty steps, on each of which were skulls.   Round the summit were upwards of seventy raised poles about four feet apart, connected by numerous rows of cross-poles passed through holes in the masts, on each of which five skulls were filed, the sticks being passed through the temples.   In the centre stood two towers, or columns, made of skulls and lime, the face of each skull being turned outwards, and giving a horrible appearance to the whole.   This effect was heightened by leaving the heads of distinguished captives in their natural state, with hair and skin on.   As the skulls decayed, or fell from the towers or poles, they were replaced by others, so that no vacant place was left." [1]   If Lucretius could have visited such a *tzompantli* he would have found a fit text for his sermon on the evils of religion.

The place of skulls

[1] Bancroft, *Native Races*, etc., vol. ii. p. 586.

It was into this strange city that on the 8th of November, 1519, Montezuma, making the best of bitter necessity, welcomed his long-bearded visitors with timorous polite- *Entry of* ness, and assigned them a great house *the Spaniards* near the temple for their lodgings. *titlan* This house is supposed to have been a *tecpan* or tribal council-house built in the time of Axayacatl, but for some reason superseded in general use by another tecpan since built in the same neighbourhood. It was large enough to afford ample accommodation for the 450 Spaniards with their 1000 or more Tlascalan allies, and Cortes forthwith proceeded quietly to station his sentinels along the parapet and to place his cannon where they could do the most good. After a few days spent in accepting the hospitalities proffered by Montezuma and in studying the city and its people, the Spanish commander went to work with that keen and deadly sagacity which never failed him. Safety required that some step should be taken. From what had occurred at Tlascala and Cholula, it is fair to suppose that in Tenochtitlan also there were two parties, the one inclined to submit to the strangers as representatives of Quetzalcoatl, the other disposed to resist them as interlopers. With time the latter counsels were almost certain to prevail. Familiarity with the sight of the strangers about the streets would deaden

the vague terror which their presence at first
inspired. Ceasing to be dreaded as gods they
would not cease to be regarded as foreigners, and
to the warrior of Tenochtitlan a foreigner was
interesting chiefly as meat, — for his idols, his
rattlesnakes, and himself. Whether as strangers or as emissaries of Quetzalcoatl, the Spaniards had already incurred the deadly hatred of
those obscene carrion-birds, the priests of the
black Tezcatlipoca and his ally Huitzilopochtli.
And then had they not brought into the city a
host of its eternal enemies the Tlascalans ? How
would the Romans of Hannibal's time have felt
and acted toward anybody who should insolently
have brought into Rome a force of Carthagin-
A dangerous   ians ? It was clear enough to Cortes
situation   and his men that their situation was
excessively dangerous. Sooner or later an outbreak was to be expected, and when it should
come the danger was immeasurably greater than
before Tlascala or in Cholula ; for if the people
should simply decide to blockade and starve the
Spaniards, there would be no escape save by a
desperate fight through the streets and along
those interminable causeways. Truly no hero
of fairyland astray in an ogre's castle was ever
in worse predicament than Cortes and his little
army cooped in this stronghold of cannibals !
There was no ground for surprise if they should
one and all get dragged to the top of the great

pyramid on their way to the kettles of the communal kitchens.

It was therefore necessary to act decisively and at once, while all the glamour of strangeness still enveloped them. Cortes acted upon the principle that the boldest course was the safest. A blow must be struck so promptly and decisively as to forestall and fatally cripple resistance, and here Cortes was aided by his experience at Cempoala. *Effect of seizing the head war-chief* One can hardly fail to see that on that occasion, as at present, his own extraordinary sagacity must have derived no little aid from such facts about the ideas and habits of the people as his keenly observant and devoted Marina could tell him. We have seen that at Cempoala the capture of a few chiefs quite paralyzed the people, so that even if the party opposed to the Spaniards had prevailed in the council it would probably have been for a time incapacitated for action. It seems to me that this incapacity arose from the paramount necessity of performing sacrifices and taking the auspices before fighting, and that nobody but the head war-chief — or, in the case of a dual executive, perhaps one of the two head war-chiefs — was properly qualified to perform these ceremonies. Early Greek and Roman history afford abundant illustrations of a stage of culture in which people did not dare to precipitate hostilities without the needful preliminary rites; since to do so would simply enrage the tutelar deities and invite destruction. If we would understand the conduct of ancient men we must not forget how completely their minds were steeped in folk-lore.

Now we have already had occasion to observe that the people of the Aztec Confederacy had joined the priestly to the military function in their *tlacatecuhtli*, or "chief-of-men," thus taking a step toward developing the office to the point attained by the Greek *basileus*, or king, of the Homeric period.[1] We learn from Sahagun that in ancient Mexico there were two high-priests, and the first of these was called Quetzalcoatl and surnamed *Totec*, "our Lord."[2] Now one of Montezuma's titles, as shown by his picture in the Codex Vaticanus, was *Quetzalcoatl Totec-tlamazqui* (*i. e.* Quetzalcoatl our Lord Priest) of Huitzilopochtli. As supreme military commander, Montezuma'a title was *Tlacochtecuhtli* or *Tlacochcalcatl*. For the generalissimo to become chief priest of the war-god is a development so natural and so practical that we find it repeated in every society where we have data for tracing back the kingship to its origins. In Mexican mythology the primitive Totec was a comrade of the fair god Quetzalcoatl; this cheer-

Montezuma was a priest-commander

---

[1] See above, vol. i. p. 130.

[2] Sahagun, *Historia*, lib. iii. cap. ix.

72

the pueblo of Nautla — had picked a quarrel with these Spaniards, and there had been a fight in which the white men were victorious, but not without losing half a dozen of their number. The fact was thus revealed that the strangers were mortal. Cortes decided to make this affair the occasion for taking possession of Montezuma's person. After a night spent with his captains and priests in earnest prayer,[1] he visited the " chief-of-men," in company with the big blonde " sun-faced " Alvarado and other mail-clad warriors, and taking, as usual, his trusty Marina as interpreter. Cortes told Montezuma that charges had been brought against him of having instigated the conduct of Quauhpopoca; not that Cortes believed these charges, O dear, no! he had too much respect for the noble *tlacatecuhtli* to believe them, but still it was his duty to investigate the facts of the case. Montezuma promptly despatched a messenger to bring home the unlucky Quauhpopoca. Very good, pursued Cortes with much suavity, but until the inquiry should be brought to some satisfactory termination, of course his august friend could not entertain the slightest objection

---

[1] " E como teniemos acordado el dia antes de prender al Monteçuma, toda la noche estuuimos en oracion con el Padre de la Merced, rogando á Dios, que fuesse de tal modo, que redundasse para su santo servicio." Diaz, *Historia verdadera*, cap. xcv. fol. 74 verso.

75

to coming and making his quarters in the tecpan occupied by the white men. It appeared, however, that Montezuma did entertain most decided objections to any such surrender of himself.

Seizure of Montezuma But his arguments and entreaties were of no avail against the mixture of soft persuasion with ominous threats in which Cortes knew so well how to deal. So when the Spanish captains returned to their fortress they took Montezuma with them, paying him every outward mark of respect. It was a very subtle scheme. The *tlacatecuhtli* was simply transferred from one tecpan to another; the tribal council could meet and public business be transacted in the one place as well as in the other. That the fact of Montezuma's virtual imprisonment might not become too glaring, Cortes sometimes let him go to the temple, but on such occasions not less than a hundred Spaniards, armed to the teeth, served as an escort. Cortes was now acting governor of Tenochtitlan and of the Confederacy, with Montezuma as his mouthpiece and the *tlatocan*, or tribal council, holding its meetings under his own roof!

When Quauhpopoca arrived, a couple of weeks after the seizure of Montezuma, Cortes had him tried for treason, and condemned him, with several of his friends, to be burned alive in the square in front of his tecpan; and with a refinement of prudence and of audacity at which

76

one cannot sufficiently marvel, he sent his men around to the dart-houses and collected a vast quantity of arrows and javelins which he caused to be piled up about the stakes to which the victims were chained, so that weapons and warriors were consumed in the same blaze. A conspiracy for the release of Montezuma, in which his brother Cuitlahuatzin and the tribal chiefs of Tezcuco and Tlacopan were implicated, was duly discovered, and it was not long before Cortes had these three dignitaries safely confined in his tecpan and in irons, while he contrived, through Montezuma, to dictate to the tribal councils at Tezcuco and Tlacopan the summary deposition of the old chiefs and the election of such new ones as he deemed likely to be interested on their own account in his safety. He does not seem to have realized the full importance of his capture of Cuitlahuatzin, who stood next to Montezuma in the customary line of succession. In Tenochtitlan Cortes began an image-breaking crusade. The cruel custom of human sacrifices greatly shocked him, as men are wont to be shocked by any kind of wickedness with which they are unfamiliar; and devil-worship was something that his notions of Christian duty required him to suppress. His action in this direction might have been over rash but for the sagacious counsel of his spiritual adviser, Father Olmedo, who

Burning of Quauhpopoca

77

warned him not to go too fast. So at first he contented himself with taking possession of one of the pyramids, where he threw down the idols, cleansed the reeking altar and sprinkled it with holy water, set up the crucifix and an image of the Virgin, and had the mass performed there, while the heathen multitude in the square below looked on and saw it all. If we did not understand the possible interpretation of these acts as sanctioned by Quetzalcoatl, and also the superstitious incapacity of the people to act without their priest-commander, it would be utterly incomprehensible that the fires of Aztec wrath should have smouldered so long. The long winter passed in sullen quiet, and April flowers were blooming, when picture-writing, sent up from the coast, was fraught with sudden intelligence alarming to Cortes. Pánfilo de Narvaez, with 18 ships and not less than 1200 soldiers, had anchored at San Juan de Ulloa, sent from Cuba by Velasquez, with orders to pursue the disobedient knight-errant and arrest him.

Cleansing of one of the pyramids

Arrival of Narvaez

Cortes was not the man to waste precious moments in wondering what he had better do. He left Pedro de Alvarado, with about 150 men, to take charge of Montezuma and Mexico. With the remaining 300 he hastened to the coast, came down upon Narvaez unawares like a thief in the night, defeated and captured him, entranced his troops with tales of the great Mexican pueblo, whetted their greed *Defeat of* with hopes of plunder, kindled the *Narvaez* missionary zeal of the priests, and ended by enlisting every man of them under his own banner. Thus with more than quadrupled force he marched back to Mexico. There evil news awaited him. Alvarado's cast of mind was of far lower grade than that of Cortes. He had in him less of Reynard and more of Isegrim. Not fathoming the reasons of the Aztecs for forbearance, he made the grave mistake of despising them as spiritless cowards. There were some grounds for a suspicion that the chiefs of the clans were meditating an attack upon the Spaniards in the city, and Alvarado, in this imminent peril, with nerves intensely strained, made up his mind to be beforehand. There was in the Aztec city a great spring festival, the gladdest of the year, the May day of rejoicing over the return of verdure and flowers. Every year at this season a young man, especially chosen for manly beauty and prowess, was presented with four brides and feasted sumptuously during a honeymoon of twenty days. On *Festival of* the twenty-first day all military deeds *Tezcatlipoca* and plans were held in abeyance, and the city was given up to festivities, while a solemn procession of youths and maidens, clad in dainty

79

white cotton and crowned with garlands of roasted maize, escorted the chosen young man to the summit of the great pyramid. There they knelt and adored him as an incarnation of the god Tezcatlipoca. Then he was sacrificed in the usual manner, and morsels of his flesh were sent about to the clan chiefs to be stewed and eaten with devout hymns and dances.[1]

It was this day of barbaric festivity in the year 1520 that the imprudent Alvarado selected for delivering his blow. In the midst of the ceremonies the little band of Spaniards fell upon Alvarado's massacre the people and massacred about 600, including many chiefs of clans. Thus Alvarado brought on the sudden calamity which he had hoped to avert. The Aztecs were no cowards, and had not the Spaniards still possessed the priest-commander Montezuma it

[1] The sacrifice of a she-goat by some of the barbarians in the army of Alboin, King of the Lombards, afforded Gibbon an opportunity for one of his ingenious little thrusts at the current theology of his time. " Gregory the Roman (*Dialog.*, iii. 27) supposes that they likewise adored this she-goat. I know of but one religion in which the god and the victim are the same " (!) *Decline and Fall*, chap. xlv., note 14. Ancient Mexico would have furnished the learned historian with another example, and a more extensive study of barbarous races would have shown him that the case of Christianity is by no means exceptional. Indeed, the whole doctrine of vicarious sacrifice, by which Christianity was for a time helped, but has now long been encumbered, is a survival from the gross theories characteristic of the middle period of barbarism.

would have gone hard with them. As it was
they soon deemed it best to retreat to their
fortress, where they were surrounded and besieged by a host of Indians who began trying in
places to undermine the walls. By threats Alvarado compelled Montezuma to go out upon
the roof and quiet the outbreak. Things went
on for some weeks without active fighting, but
the Indians burned the brigantines on the lake
which Cortes had built during the winter as a
means of retreat in case of disaster. The Spaniards by good luck found a spring in their
courtyard and their store of corn was ample, so
that thirst and hunger did not yet assail them.

When Cortes entered the city on the 24th
of June, he found the streets deserted, the markets closed, and many of the drawbridges raised.
A few Indians from their doorways scowled at
the passing troops. When Cortes met Alvarado he told him that he had behaved like a
madman, but it was now the turn of Return of
Cortes himself to make a mistake. Cortes
He could not be expected to know that in that
community there was an ulterior power behind
the throne. That ulterior power was the *tlatocan*, or tribal council, which elected the priest-
commander from the members of a particular
family, in accordance with certain customary
rules of succession. In a great emergency the
council which thus elected the ruler could de-

pose him and elect another. Now Cortes had in his fortress Montezuma's brother Cuitlahuatzin, who stood next in the regular line of succession, and he evidently did not understand the danger in letting him out. The increase of numbers was fast telling upon the stock of food, and Cortes sent out Cuitlahuatzin with orders to have the markets opened. This at once brought matters to a terrible crisis. Cuitlahuatzin con-

Deposition of Montezuma vened the *tlatocan*, which instantly deposed Montezuma and elected him in his place. Early next morning came the outbreak. A hoarse sound arose, like the murmur of distant waters, and soon the imprisoned Spaniards from their parapet saw pyramids, streets, and housetops black with raging warriors. They attacked with arrows, slings, and javelins, and many Spaniards were killed or wounded. The Spanish cannon swept the streets with terrible effect and the canals near by ran red with blood, but the Indians pressed on, and shot burning arrows through the embrasures until the interior woodwork began to take fire.

At Cortes's direction Montezuma presented himself on the terraced roof and sought to assuage the wrath of the people, but now he found that his authority was ended. Another now wore the golden beak of the war-god. He was no longer general, no longer priest, and his

person had lost its sacred character. Stones
and darts were hurled at him ; he was struck
down by a heavy stone, and died a
few days afterward, whether from the   His death
wound, or from chagrin, or both. Before his
death the Spaniards made a sortie, and after
terrific hand to hand fighting stormed the great
temple which overlooked and commanded their
own quarters and had sadly annoyed them.
They flung down the idols among the people
and burned the accursed shrines. It was on the
last day of June that Montezuma died, and on
the evening of the next day, fearing lest his
army should be blockaded and starved, Cortes
evacuated the city. The troops marched through
quiet and deserted streets till they reached the
great causeway leading to Tlacopan. Its three
drawbridges had all been destroyed. The Spaniards carried a pontoon, but while they were
passing over the first bridgeway the Indians fell
upon them in vast numbers, their light canoes
swarming on both sides of the narrow road.
The terrible night that ensued has   The Melan-
ever since been known in history as choly Night
la noche triste. Cortes started in the evening
with 1250 Spaniards, 6000 Tlascalans, and 80
horses. Next morning, after reaching terra firma
he had 500 Spaniards, 2000 Tlascalans, and 20
horses. All his cannon were sunk in the lake ;
and 40 Spaniards were in Aztec clutches to be

offered up to the war-god. Then Cortes sat down upon a rock, and buried his face in his hands and wept.

Not for one moment, however, did he flinch in his purpose of taking Mexico. In a few days the Indians from that and other neighbouring pueblos attacked him in overwhelming force in the valley of Otumba, hoping to complete his destruction, but he won such a decisive and murderous victory as to reëstablish his shaken prestige. It was well, for Mexico had sent an embassy to Tlascala, and in that pueblo the council of clan chiefs were having an earnest debate much like those that one reads in Thucydides or Xenophon. There were speakers who feared that success for the Spaniards would ultimately mean servitude for Tlascala, and the Aztec envoys played upon this fear. Nothing could have happened at this time so likely to insure the destruction of Cortes as the defection of the Tlascalans. But his victory at Otumba determined them to keep up their alliance with him. During the autumn Cortes occupied himself with operations, military and diplomatic, among the smaller pueblos, defeating any that ventured to resist him and making alliances with such as were eager to wreak their vengeance upon the hated Tenochtitlan. It is enough to say that all this work was done with characteristic skill.

Victory at Otumba and its effects

Cortes now found ships useful. Taking some of those that had come with Narvaez, he sent them to Hispaniola for horses, cannon, and soldiers; and by Christmas Eve he found himself at the head of a thoroughly equipped army of 700 infantry armed with pikes and crossbows, 118 arquebusiers, 86 cavalry, a dozen cannon, and several thousand Indian allies. Though the belief that white men could not be killed had been quite overthrown, yet the prestige of Cortes as a resistless warrior was now restored, and the prospect of humbling the Aztecs kindled a fierce enthusiasm in the men of Quauquechollan, Huexotzinco, Chalco, and other pueblos now ranked among his allies.

Starting at Christmas on his final march against the mighty pueblo, Cortes first proceeded to Tezcuco. In that community there was disaffection toward its partner on the lake, resulting from recent quarrels between the chiefs, and now Ixtlilxochitl, the new war-chief of the Tezcucans, gave in his adherence to Cortes, ad- Gaining of mitted him into the town, and enter- Tezcuco tained him hospitably in the tecpan. This move broke up the Aztec Confederacy, placed all the warriors of Tezcuco at the disposal of Cortes, and enabled him without opposition to launch a new flotilla of brigantines on the lake and support them with swarms of agile Tezcucan canoes. Thus the toils were closing in upon doomed Tenochtitlan. Meanwhile smallpox had carried off Cuitlahuatzin, and his nephew Guatemotzin was now "chief-of-men," — a brave warrior whom Mexicans to this day regard with affectionate admiration for his gallant defence of their city. For ferocious courage the Aztecs were not surpassed by any other Indians on the continent, and when Cortes at length began the siege of Mexico, April 28, 1521,[1] the fighting that ensued was incessant and terrible. The fresh water supply was soon cut off, and then slowly but surely the besiegers upon the three causeways and in the brigantines closed in upon their prey. Points of advantage were sometimes lost by the Aztecs through their excessive anxiety to capture Spaniards alive. Occasionally they succeeded, and then from the top of the great pyramid would resound the awful tones of the sacrificial drum made of serpent skins, a sound that could be heard in every quarter of this horrible city; and the souls of the soldiers sickened as they saw their wretched comrades dragged up the long staircase, to be offered as sacrifices to Satan. Every inch of ground was contested by the Aztecs with a fury that reminds one of the resistance of Jerusalem to the soldiers of Titus. At last, on the 13th of August, the resistance came to an end.

Siege of Mexico

[1] The death of Magellan, at Matan, occurred the day before, April 27.

86

Carta de relació ẽbiada a su .S. majestad del ẽpa=
dor nro señor por el capitã general dela nueua spaña: llamado fernãdo cor
tes. Enla q̃l haze relació dlas tierras y prouicias sin cuẽto q̃ hã descubierto
nueuamẽte enel yucatã del año de .xix. a esta pte: y ha sometido ala corona
real de su .S. A. En especial haze relació de vna grãdissima prouicia muy
rica llamada Culua: ẽla q̃l ay muy grãdes ciudades y de marauillosos edi=
ficios: y de grãdes tratos y riq̃zas. Entre las q̃les ay vna mas marauillosa
y rica q̃ todas llamada Timirtitã: q̃ esta por marauillosa arte edificada so
bre vna grãde laguna. dela q̃l ciudad y prouicia es rey vn grãdissimo señor
llamado Muteeçuma : dõde le acaeciẽró al capitã y alos españoles espãto
sas cosas de oyr. Cuenta largamẽte del grãdissimo señorio del dicho Mu
teeçuma y de sus ritos y cerimonias. y de como se sirue.

TITLE–PAGE OF CORTES'S CARTA DE RELACION, 1522

Canals and footways were choked with corpses, and a great part of the city lay in ruins. The first work of the conquerors was to cleanse and rebuild. The ancient religion soon passed away, the ancient society was gradually metamorphosed, and Mexico assumed the aspect of a Spanish town. On the site of the heathen temple a Gothic church was erected, which in 1573 was replaced by the cathedral that still stands there.

The capture of Tenochtitlan was by no means equivalent to the conquest of the vast territory that now goes under the name of Mexico. Much work was yet to be done in all directions, but it is not necessary for the purposes of this book that I should give an account of it. I am concerned here with the Conquest of Mexico only in so far as it is an episode in the Discovery of America, only in so far as it illustrates a phase of the earliest contact between the two hemispheres, each hitherto ignorant of the other, each so curiously affected by its first experience of the other ; and for my purpose the story here given will suffice. Nor is it necessary to recount the vicissitudes of the later years of Cortes, who had to contend against the enmity of Bishop Fonseca, and a series of untoward circumstances connected therewith. His discovery of the peninsula of California will be mentioned in a future chapter. He returned finally to Spain in 1540, and served with great merit in the expedition against Algiers in the following year ; but he

Death of Cortes

was neglected by the emperor, and passed the rest of his life in seclusion at Seville. He died at a small village near that city on the 2d of December, 1547.

A great deal of sentimental ink has been shed over the wickedness of the Spaniards in crossing

How the Spanish conquest should be regarded

the ocean and attacking people who had never done them any harm, over-turning and obliterating a " splendid civilization," and more to the same effect. It is undeniable that unprovoked aggression is an extremely hateful thing, and many of the cir-cumstances attendant upon the Spanish conquest in America were not only heinous in their atro-city, but were emphatically condemned, as we shall presently see, by the best moral standards of the sixteenth century. Yet if we are to be guided by strict logic, it would be difficult to condemn the Spaniards for the mere act of con-quering Mexico without involving in the same condemnation our own forefathers who crossed the ocean and overran the territory of the United States with small regard for the proprietary rights of Algonquins, or Iroquois, or red men of any sort. Our forefathers, if called upon to justify themselves, would have replied that they were founding Christian states and diffusing the bless-

88

ings of a higher civilization ; and such, in spite of much alloy in the motives and imperfection in the performance, was certainly the case. Now if we would not lose or distort the historical perspective, we must bear in mind that the Spanish conquerors would have returned exactly the same answer. If Cortes were to return to this world and pick up some history book in which he is described as a mere picturesque adventurer, he would feel himself very unjustly treated. He would say that he had higher aims than those of a mere fighter and gold-hunter ; and so doubtless he had. In the complex tangle of motives that actuated the mediæval Spaniard — and in his peninsula we may apply the term mediæval to later dates than would be proper in France or Italy — the desire of extending the dominion of the Church was a very real and powerful incentive to action. The strength of the missionary and crusading spirit in Cortes is seen in the fact that where it was concerned, and there only, was he liable to let zeal overcome prudence.

There can be no doubt that, after making all allowances, the Spaniards did introduce a better state of society into Mexico than they found there. It was high time that an end should be put to those hecatombs of human victims, slashed, torn open, and devoured on all the little occasions of

It was a good thing for Mexico

life. It sounds quite pithy to say that the Inquisition, as conducted in Mexico, was as great an evil as the human sacrifices and the cannibalism; but it is not true.[1] Compared with the ferocious barbarism of ancient Mexico the contemporary Spanish modes of life were mild, and this, I think, helps further to explain the ease with which the country was conquered. In a certain sense the prophecy of Quetzalcoatl was fulfilled, and the coming of the Spaniards did mean the final dethronement of the ravening Tezcatlipoca. The work of the noble Franciscan and Dominican monks who followed closely upon Cortes, and devoted their lives to the spiritual welfare of the Mexicans, is a more attractive subject than any picture of military conquest. To this point I shall return hereafter, when we come to consider the sublime career of Las Casas. For the present we may conclude in the spirit of one of the noblest of Spanish historians, Pedro de Cieza de Leon, and praise God that the idols are cast down.[2]

The conquest of Mexico was followed at intervals by the reduction of Guatemala, Honduras, and Yucatan; and while this work was

[1] As Llorente, the historian of the Inquisition who has fully set forth its enormities, once wittily observed, "Il ne faut pas calomnier même l'Inquisition."

[2] *Crónica del Peru*, pt. i. cap. lviii.

going on, captains from Darien overran Nicaragua, so that what we may call the northern and southern streams of Spanish conquest — the stream which started from Hispaniola by way of Cuba, and that which started from Hispaniola by way of Darien — at length came together again. The southern stream of Spanish conquest, thus stopped in one direction at Nicaragua, kept on its course southward along the Pacific coast of South America until it encountered a kind of semi-civilization different from anything else that was to be seen in the western hemisphere. We are now prepared for the sketch, hitherto postponed, of Ancient Peru.

IX

ANCIENT PERU

FROM the elevated table-lands of New Mexico and Arizona to the southward as far as the mountain fastnesses of Bolivia, the region of the Cordilleras was the seat of culture in various degrees more advanced than that of any other parts of the New World. Starting from Central America, we find in the tombs of the little province of Chiriqui, between Costa Rica and Veragua, a wealth of artistic remains that serve in some respects to connect the culture of Central America with that of the semi-civilized peoples beyond the Isthmus of Darien.[1] Of these peoples the first were the Muyscas, or Chibchas, whose principal towns were near the site of Bogotá. There were many tribes of Chibchas, speaking as many distinct dialects of a common stock language. They had no writing except rude pictographs and no means of recording

Chiriqui

[1] See Holmes, " Ancient Art of the Province of Chiriqui," *Reports of the Bureau of Ethnology*, vol. vi. pp. 13–187 ; Bollaert, *Antiquarian Researches in New Granada*, London, 1860.

events. Their family was in a rudimentary state
of development, and kinship was traced only
through the female line. There was a
priesthood, and the head war-chief, ^{The Chibchas}
whose office was elective, had begun to exercise the highest priestly functions. They were
idolaters, with human sacrifices, but seem to
have abandoned cannibalism. Their funeral
customs deserve mention. We have observed
that the Mexicans practised cremation. In
some parts of Central America the dead were
buried, in others burnt. But in coming down to
the Isthmus of Darien we begin to find mummies. Among the people of the Andes in the
middle status of barbarism, it was customary
to embalm the bodies of chiefs and other important personages, and to wrap them closely
in fine mantles adorned with emeralds. The
mummy was then buried, and food, weapons,
and living concubines were buried with it.
Such was the practice among the Chibchas.

The houses of these people were very large,
and shaped either like the frustum of a cone or
like that of a pyramid. The walls were built
of stout timbers fastened with wedges and
cemented with adobe clay. Maize and cotton
were cultivated, and cotton cloth of various coloured designs was made. The rafts and rope
bridges resembled those of the Peruvians hereafter to be mentioned. Chiefs and priests were

carried on wooden litters. In every town there were fairs at stated intervals. Goods were sold by measure, but not by weight. Round tiles of gold, without stamp or marking of any sort, served as a currency, and when there was not enough of it salt was used as a medium of exchange. Trade, however, was chiefly barter. The Chibchas had some slight intercourse with the people of Quito and some knowledge of the Inca kingdom beyond.[1]

This Chibcha culture, in many respects lower, but in some respects higher, than that of the Mexicans, was probably typical of the whole Andes region for unknown centuries before its various peoples were brought under the comparatively civilizing sway of the Incas. On the eastern slopes of the giant mountains this semi-

[1] The principal sources of information about the Chibchas are Piedrahita, *Historia del Nuevo Reyno de Granada*, Antwerp, 1688; Simon, *Tercera (y cuarta) noticia de la segunda parte de las Noticias Historiales de las Conquistas de Tierra Firme en el Nuevo Reyno de Granada*, 1624 (in Kingsborough's *Mexican Antiquities*, vol. viii.) ; Herrera, *Historia General de los hechos de los Castellanos*, etc., Madrid, 1601 (especially the fifth book); Joaquin Acosta, *Compendio Historico del Descubrimiento y Colonizacion de la Nueva Granada*, Paris, 1848; Cassani, *Historia de la Compagnia de Jesus del Nuevo Reino de Granada*, Madrid, 1741; Uricoechea, *Memoria sobre las Antiguedades Neo-Granadinas*, Berlin, 1854. The subject is well tabulated in Spencer's *Descriptive Sociology*, No. ii.

civilization maintained itself precariously against the surging waves of lower barbarism and savagery. The ethnology of South America has been much less thoroughly studied than that of North America, and our subject does not require us to attempt to enumerate or characterize these lower peoples. They have been arranged provisionally in four groups, although it is pretty clear that instances of non-related tribes occur in some if not in all the groups. At the time of the Discovery the ferocious Caribs inhabited the forests of Venezuela and Guiana, and had established *The Caribs* themselves upon many of the West India islands. Their name, first written in Latin form " Caribales " by Columbus in 1498, was presently corrupted into " Canibales," and has thus furnished European languages with an epithet since applied to all eaters of human flesh. Adjacent to the Caribs, but distinct from them, were the Maypures, whose tribes ranged from the headwaters of the Orinoco southward into Bolivia. The Caribs and Maypures make up what is geographically rather than ethnologically known as the Orinoco group of Indians. A second group, called Amazonians, *Various savage groups* includes a great number of tribes, mostly in the upper status of savagery, ranging along the banks of the Amazon and its tributaries ; about their ethnology very

THE DISCOVERY OF AMERICA

little is known. Much better defined is the
third or Tupi-Guarani group, extending over
the vast country southward from the Amazon
to La Plata. This family of tribes, speaking
a common stock language, is more widely dif-
fused than any other in South America; and it
is certain that within the area which it occupies
there are other tribes not related to it and not
yet classified. The fourth group is merely geographical, and includes families so different as
the Pampas Indians of the Argentine Republic,
the inhabitants of Patagonia and Tierra del
Fuego, and the brave Araucanians of Chili.[1]

All the peoples here mentioned were, when
discovered, either in the upper status of savagery or the lower status of barbarism, and to
many of them the same description would still
be applicable. Lowest of all were the Fuegians
and some of the tribes on the Amazon; highest of all were the Araucanians, with their habitat on the western slope of the Andes.

The whole of this Pacific slope, from the
country of the Araucanians northward to that
of our friends the Chibchas, was occupied by
the family of Quichua-Aymara tribes, since commonly known as Peruvians. These tribes were

[1] See Keane's essay on the "Ethnography and Philology
of America," appended to Bates's *Central and South America*, 2d ed. London, 1882, pp. 443-561.

probably the first in all America to emerge from the lower status of barbarism, and at the time of the Discovery they had ap- Quichua- proached much nearer to the formation Aymara of a true nationality than any others. tribes In some important respects they were much more civilized than the people of Mexico and Central America, but they had not attained to the beginnings of true civilization, inasmuch as they had neither an alphabet nor any system of hieroglyphic writing. In preserving traditions the Peruvian *amautas*, or " wise men," were aided by a queer system of mnemonics worked out by tying complicated knots in cords of divers colours.[1] These knotted cords, or

[1] Mr. Tylor's description of the *quipus* is so good that I cannot do better than insert it here in full : — " When a farmer's daughter ties a knot in her handkerchief to remember a commission at market by, she makes a rudimentary *quipu*. Darius made one when he took a thong and tied sixty knots in it, and gave it to the chiefs of the Ionians, that they might untie a knot each day, till, if the knots were all undone and he had not returned, they might go back to their own land. (Herodotus, iv. 98.) . . . This is so simple a device that it may have been invented again and again. . . . It has been found in Asia (Erman's *Siberia*, i. 492), in Africa (Klemm's *Culturgeschichte*, i. 3), in Mexico, among the North American Indians (Charlevoix, vi. 151) ; but its greatest development was in South America." The Peruvian *quipu* consists " of a thick main cord, with thinner cords tied on to it at certain distances, in which the knots are tied. . . . The cords are often of various colours, each with its

quipus, were also used in keeping accounts, and in some ways they were curiously analogous on

own proper meaning ; red for soldiers, yellow for gold, white for silver, green for corn, and so on.   This knot-writing was especially suited for reckonings and statistical tables ; a single knot meant ten, a double one a hundred, a triple one a thousand, two singles side by side twenty, two doubles two hundred.   The distances of the knots from the main cord were of great importance, as was the sequence of the branches, for the principal objects were placed on the first branches and near the trunk, and so in decreasing order.   This art of reckoning is still in use among the herdsmen of the Puna (the high mountain plateau of Peru)," and they explained it to the Swiss naturalist Tschudi " so that with a little trouble he could read any of their *quipus*.   On the first branch they usually register the bulls, on the second the cows, these again they divide into milch cows and those that are dry ; the next branches contain the calves, according to age and sex, then the sheep in several subdivisions, the number of foxes killed, the quantity of salt used, and lastly the particulars of the cattle that have died.   On other *quipus* is set down the produce of the herd in milk, cheese, wool, etc.   Each heading is indicated by a special colour or a differently twined knot.   It was in the same way that in old times the army registers were kept ; on one cord the slingers were set down, on another the spearmen, on a third those with clubs, etc., with their officers ; and thus also the accounts of battles were drawn up. In each town were special functionaries whose duty was to tie and interpret the *quipus ;* they were called *quipucamayocuna,* or ' knot-officers.' . . . They were seldom able to read a *quipu* without the aid of an oral commentary ; when one came from a distant province, it was necessary to give notice with it whether it referred to census, tribute, war, etc. . . . They carefully kept the *quipus* in their proper depart-

the one hand to Indian wampum belts and on the other hand to the tally-sticks used in old times by officers of the exchequer in France and England. Learned Spaniards were astonished at seeing how many things the Peruvians could record with their *quipus*. Nevertheless, as

ments, so as not, for instance, to mistake a tribute-cord for one relating to the census. . . . In modern times all the attempts made to read the ancient *quipus* have been in vain. The difficulty in deciphering them is very great, since every knot indicates an idea, and a number of intermediate notions are left out. But the principal impediment is the want of the oral information as to their subject-matter, which was needful even to the most learned decipherers." As to the ancient use of the *quipu* in Mexico, "Boturini placed the fact beyond doubt by not only finding some specimens in Tlascala, but also recording their Mexican name, *nepohualtzitzin*, a word derived from the verb *tlapohua*, ' to count.' (Boturini, *Idea de una nueva Historia*, etc., Madrid, 1746, p. 85.) . . . *Quipus* are found in the Eastern Archipelago and in Polynesia proper, and they were in use in Hawaii forty years ago, in a form seemingly not inferior to the most elaborate Peruvian examples. . . . The fate of the *quipu* has been everywhere to be superseded, more or less entirely, by the art of writing. . . . When, therefore, the Chinese tell us (Goguet, *Origine des Lois*, etc., tom. iii. p. 322 ; Mailla, *Hist. générale de la Chine*, Paris, 1777, tom. i. p. 4) that they once upon a time used this contrivance, and that the art of writing superseded it, the analogy of what has taken place in other countries makes it extremely probable that the tradition is a true one." Tylor, *Researches into the Early History of Mankind*, London, 1865, pp. 154–158. See also Garcilasso, *Comentarios reales*, lib. ii. cap. 13 ; lib. vi. cap. 8, 9.

compared with hieroglyphics even as rude as those of Mexico, these knotted cords were very inefficient instruments for recording knowledge. For this reason the historic period of the Peruvian people goes but a short distance back of the Discovery. All lists of the Incas agree in beginning with Manco Capac ;[1] and there is practical unanimity as to the names and order of succession of the Incas. But when we come to dates for the earlier names, all is indefinite. Manco has been variously placed from the eleventh to the thirteenth century, the later date being far more probable than the earlier if we have regard for the ordinary rules of human longevity. The first Inca whose career may be considered strictly historical is Viracocha, whose reign probably began somewhere about A. D. 1380, or a century and a half before the arrival of the Spaniards in Peru.[2] Moreover throughout the fifteenth cen-

Lists of Incas

[1] The pronunciation of this name is more correctly indicated by writing it *Ccapac*. The first *c* is " a guttural far back in the throat ; the second on the roof of the mouth." Markham's *Quichua Grammar*, p. 17. The result must be a kind of guttural click.

[2] The following list of the Incas will be useful for reference : —

1. Manco Capac . . . cir. 1250?
2. Sinchi Rocca . . .
3. Lloque Yupanqui . . .
4. Mayta Capac . . .

account of the matter is given by Garcilasso de
la Vega, who must be regarded as an authority
scarcely less important than Cieza de Leon.
Garcilasso says that the fortress was fifty years
in building and was not finished until the reign
of Huayna Capac, if indeed it could
properly be said to have been finished
at all. " These works," says Garcilasso, " with many others thoughout the empire, were cut short by the civil wars which

Testimony of
Cieza and
Garcilasso

author most to admire, Sarmiento or Cieza ! but we now
know that his praise, bestowed upon both, belongs wholly to
the latter.   Part III. and the first two books of Part IV. are
not yet to be obtained.   We are assured by Don Ximenez de
Espada that he knows where the manuscript is, though he has
not seen it.   The manuscript of the third book of Part IV. is
in the Royal Library at Madrid; a copy of it found its way
in 1849 into the hands of the late Mr. James Lenox, of New
York, who paid $3000 for it.   It was at length edited by
Espada, and published at Madrid in 1877.   The fourth and
fifth books of Part IV. and the two commentaries were completed by Cieza de Leon before his death, but whether they
are in existence or not is not known.   Perhaps we may yet
be so fortunate as to recover the whole of this magnificent
work, which ranks indisputably foremost among the sources
of information concerning ancient Peru.   The first two parts
have been translated into English, and edited, with learned
notes and introductions, by Mr. Clements Markham, to whom
I am indebted for this sketch of the strange vicissitudes of the
book. See Markham, *The Travels of Cieza de Leon, contained in the First Part of his Chronicle of Peru*, London,
1864 ; *The Second Part of the Chronicle of Peru*, London,
1883 (both published by the Hakluyt Society).

broke out soon afterwards between the two
brothers Huascar Inca and Atahualpa, in whose
time the Spaniards arrived and destroyed everything; and so all the unfinished works remain
unfinished to this day." [1] It has become fash-

[1] Compare Garcilasso, *Royal Commentaries*, ed. Markham,
vol. ii. p. 318, with Markham's *Cieza de Leon*, vol. ii. p.
163. The father of the historian Garcilasso Inca de la Vega
belonged to one of the most distinguished families of Spain.
In 1531, being then twenty-five years old, he went to Guatemala and served under Pedro de Alvarado as a captain of infantry. When Alvarado invaded Peru in 1534, but consented
to retire and left a great part of his force behind him (see
below, p. 225), the captain Garcilasso was one of those that
were left. For eminent military services he received from
Pizarro a fine house in Cuzco and other spoils. In 1538
he was married to Chimpa Ocllo, baptized as Doña Isabel,
a granddaughter of the great Inca Tupac Yupanqui. Mr.
Markham informs us that "a contemporary picture of this
princess still exists at Cuzco — a delicate looking girl with
large gentle eyes and slightly aquiline nose, long black tresses
hanging over her shoulders, and a richly ornamented woollen
mantle secured in front by a large gold pin." The Inca
Garcilasso de la Vega, son of this marriage, was born in
Cuzco in 1540. He was carefully educated by an excellent
Spanish priest, and became a good scholar. His father, one
of the most honourable and high-minded of the Spanish cavaliers, was made governor of Cuzco, and his home was a place
where Spaniards and Incas were hospitably entertained. From
infancy the young Garcilasso spoke both Spanish and Quichua,
and while he was learning Latin and studying European history, his mother and her friends were steeping him in Peruvian
traditions. At about the age of twelve he lost this gentle
mother, and in 1560 his gallant father also died. Garcilasso

ionable in recent times to discredit this testimony of Garcilasso and Cieza, on the ground
of their want of extensive archæological knowledge; but it seems to me that in this case
scepticism is carried rather too far. Garcilasso
was great-great-grandson of the Inca Pacha-

then went to Spain and served for some years in the army.
After retiring from the service, somewhere from 1570 to 1575,
he settled in Cordova and devoted himself to literary pursuits
until his death in 1616. His tomb is in the cathedral at Cordova. Besides other books Garcilasso Inca wrote *The Royal
Commentaries of the Incas*, in two parts, the first of which,
treating of the history and antiquities of Peru before the arrival of the Spaniards, was published at Lisbon in 1609 ; the
second part, treating of the conquest of Peru and the civil wars
of the conquerors, was published at Cordova in 1616. There
have been several editions and translations in various languages.
An English translation of the first part, by Mr. Clements
Markham, has been published by the Hakluyt Society, London, 1869, 2 vols. Garcilasso's unrivalled opportunities for
gathering information, and his excellent use of them, give to
his book an authority superior to all others except that of
Cieza de Leon, and Garcilasso was better able than the latter
to understand the Peruvian view of the situation. He often
quotes from Cieza, and always with high respect. His book
is at once learned and charming ; its tone is kindly and courteous, like the talk of a thoroughbred gentleman. One cannot
read it without a strong feeling of affection for the writer.

Throughout this chapter — except in a few cases, where it
seems desirable to give the Spanish — I cite from Mr. Markham's version of Garcilasso and Cieza ; but, as I cite by book
and chapter, instead of volume and page, the references are
equally convenient for any edition or version.

cutec under whom the work at Sacsahuaman is said to have begun, and his statements as to the progress of that work which went on until it was stopped by the civil war between his mother's cousins Huascar and Atahualpa are too nearly contemporaneous to be lightly set aside, especially when independently confirmed by so careful an inquirer as Cieza. This testimony is positive that the cyclopean architecture at Sacsahuaman was the work of recent Incas. With Tiahuanacu the case may be quite different. Garcilasso, indeed, in giving the names of the four chief architects who were successively employed at Sacsahuaman, lets drop the remarkable statement, "The third was Acahuana Inca, to whom is also attributed a great part of the edifices at Tiahuanacu."[1] But in another place Garcilasso quotes without dissent the statement of Cieza that contemporary Peruvians believed the buildings at Tiahuanacu to be much older than the Sacsahuaman fortress, and indeed that the recent Incas built the latter work in emulation of the former.[2] So, perhaps, in his remark about the architect Acahuana having superintended the works at Tiahuanacu, Garcilasso's memory, usually so strong and precise,[3] may for

[1] Garcilasso, lib. vii. cap. xxix.

[2] Cieza, pt. i. cap. cv.; Garcilasso, lib. iii. cap. i.

[3] He often observes, with winning modesty, that it is so long since he left Peru that his memory may deceive him ; but

once have tripped. It might fail to serve him about works at distant Lake Titicaca, but such a slip, if it be one, should not discredit his testimony as to the great edifice near Cuzco, about the stones of which he had often played with his Spanish and Peruvian schoolfellows, regarding them as the work of his mother's immediate ancestors.

Assuming as correct the statement in which Garcilasso and Cieza agree, that the Incas of the fifteenth century built the Sacsahuaman fortress in emulation of the ancient structures at Tiahuanacu, in order to show that they could equal or surpass the mighty works of by-gone ages, it must be acknowledged that they were successful. Sacsahuaman is, according to Mr. Markham, "without comparison the grandest monument of an ancient civilization in the New World. Like the Pyramids and the Coliseum, it is imperishable." [1]

If this colossal building could have been

in such cases, whenever we can bring other evidence to bear, the dear old fellow turns out almost invariably to be correct.

[1] Winsor, *Narr. and Crit. Hist.*, vol. i. p. 221. Cf. Squier's remarks, in his *Peru: Incidents of Travel and Exploration in the Land of the Incas*, New York, 1877, p. 470: "The heaviest works of the fortress . . . remain substantially perfect, and will remain so . . . as long as the Pyramids shall last, or Stonehenge and the Colosseum shall endure, for it is only with those works that the fortress of the Sacsahuaman can be properly compared."

erected under the later Incas, it is clearly un-
necessary to suppose for the works at Tiahuanacu any intrusive agency from the Old World,
or any condition of society essentially different
from that into which the mother of the historian
Garcilasso Inca was born. This style of building will presently furnish us with an instructive
clue to the state of Peruvian society in the century preceding the arrival of the Spaniards.
Meanwhile there is no occasion for supposing
any serious break in the continuity of events in
prehistoric Peru. It is not necessary to suppose
that the semi-civilization of the Incas was preceded by some other semi-civilization distinct
from it in character. As for the Pirua dynasty
of sixty-five kings, covering a period of thirteen
centuries, it does not seem likely that the " wise
men " of Cieza's time, with their knotted strings,
could have preserved any trustworthy testimony
as to such a period.

Without assuming, however, any historical
knowledge of the times that preceded the rule
of the Incas, we have other grounds for believing that the Peruvian culture was much older
than that of the Mexicans and Mayas. In other
words, the Peruvians had probably attained to
the middle status of barbarism at a much earlier
date than the Mexicans and Mayas, and had
in many striking features approached nearer to
civilization than the latter. First, we may note

that the Peruvians were the only American aborigines that ever domesticated any other animal than the dog. The *llama*, de- Domesticated veloped from the same stock with the animals wild *huanacu*, is a very useful beast of burden, yielding also a coarse wool; and the *alpaca*, developed from the ancestral stock of the wild *vicuña*, is of great value for its fine soft fleece.[1] While the huanacu and vicuña are to-day as wild as chamois, the llama is as thoroughly domesticated as cows or sheep, while the alpaca has actually become unable to live without the care of man; and Mr. Markham argues, with much force, that such great variation in these animals implies the lapse of many centuries since men first began to tame them. A similar infer-ence is drawn from the facts that while the ancient Peruvians produced several highly cultivated varieties of maize, that cereal in a wild state is unknown in their country; "the Peruvian spe-cies of the cotton plant also is known only under cultivation. The potato is found wild The potato in Chili, and probably in Peru, as a very insignificant tuber. But the Peruvians, after cultivating it for centuries, increased its size and produced a great number of edible varieties."[2]

---

[1] Darwin, *Variation of Animals and Plants under Do-mestication*, London, 1868, vol. ii. p. 208. These four spe-cies belong to the genus *auchenia* of the family *camelidæ*.

[2] Markham, "The Inca Civilization in Peru," in Winsor,

Now the wild potato seems to be a refractory vegetable. There is a variety in Mexico, no bigger than a nut, and sedulous efforts, kept up during many years, to increase its size and improve its quality, have proved futile; from which Mr. Markham reasonably infers that the high state of perfection to which the Peruvians brought the potato indicates a very considerable lapse of time since they began to work upon its wild ancestral form.[1]

Narr. and Crit. Hist., i. 213. As for maize, Mr. Darwin found ears of it, along with sundry species of recent sea-shells, on the coast of Peru, "embedded in a beach which had been upraised at least eighty-five feet above the level of the sea." Darwin, *Geological Observations on South America*, London, 1846, p. 49.

[1] Cieza de Leon (pt. 1. cap. xl.) describes the potato as "a kind of earth nut, which, after it has been boiled, is as tender as a cooked chestnut, but it has no more skin than a truffle, and it grows under the earth in the same way. This root produces a plant like a poppy." Humboldt says, "La pomme de terre n'est pas indigène au Pérou" (*Essai sur la Nouvelle Espagne*, Paris, 1811, 8vo, tom. iii. p. 113); but Cuvier declares, "il est impossible de douter qu'elle ne soit originaire de Pérou" (*Histoire des sciences naturelles*, Paris, 1831, p. 185). Further research seems to sustain Cuvier's view. The legitimate conclusion from Humboldt's facts, however, does not carry the original home of the potato very far from Peru, but points to the Chilian or Bolivian Andes, whence its cultivation seems to have spread northward, until at the time of the Discovery it was found among the people of Quito and among the Chibchas. The potato was not cultivated anywhere north of the Isthmus of Darien.

In cultivating such vegetables the Peruvians
practised irrigation on an extensive scale, and

The ships of Raleigh's expedition, returning from Albemarle
Sound in 1586, carried the first potatoes to Ireland (Beckmann,
Grundsätze der teutschen Landwirthschaft, 1806, p. 289),
and in Gerarde's *Herball*, published in 1597, these vegetables
were called " Virginia potatoes ; " whence it is sometimes
said that Raleigh's people " found potatoes in Virginia." But
that is highly improbable. As Humboldt says, potatoes were
common all over the West Indies before 1580, and had even
found their way into the gardens of Spain and Italy. In 1586
Lane's party of Raleigh's people, a hundred or more in number, had been staying for a year upon Roanoke Island, where
they had hoped to found a colony. They were terribly short
of food, when all at once Sir Francis Drake arrived from the
West Indies and brought them a supply of provisions, with
which they prudently decided to go home to England. Evidently their potatoes, which were planted on an estate of Raleigh's in Ireland, did not come from " Virginia," but from
the West Indies. The potato was very slow in coming into
general use in Europe. It was not raised on an extensive scale
in Lancashire until about 1684; it was first introduced into
Saxony in 1717, into Scotland in 1728, into Prussia in 1738
(cf. Humboldt, *op. cit.* tom. iii. p. 120). It has been said
that potatoes were first made known in France about 1600 by
the celebrated botanist Charles de Lécluse (Legrand d'Aussy,
Hist. de la vie privée des Français, tom. i. p. 143); but they
certainly did not begin to come into general use among the
people till just before the Revolution. A very graphic account
of their introduction into Alsace from Hanover is given in that
charming story of Erckmann-Chatrian, *Histoire d'un paysan*,
tom. i. pp. 54–83. They were at first received with cries of
" à bas les racines du Hanovre! " and a report was spread
that persons had been seized with leprosy after eating them;

had from time immemorial been accustomed to use guano as manure.[1] By right of such careful and methodical agriculture, as well as by right of having domesticated animals for other purposes than hunting, the ancient Peruvians had entered upon the middle period of barbarism, and evidently at a much earlier date than any other known people of aboriginal America. At the time of the Discovery an unknown number of centuries had elapsed since the general condition of these people had begun to be that which characterized the middle period of barbarism in North America. The interval was no doubt long enough for very remarkable social

so for a while people kept aloof from them until it was learned that the king had them on his table ; " alors tout le monde voulut en avoir." This account of the matter is strictly correct. See the works of Parmentier, *Examen chimique des pommes de terre*, Paris, 1773; *Recherches sur les végétaux nourrissants*, Paris, 1781; *Traité sur la culture des pommes de terre*, Paris, 1789. Parmentier was largely instrumental in introducing the potato. Accurate statistics are given in Arthur Young's *Travels in France*, 2d ed., Bury St. Edmunds, 1794, 2 vols. 4to, vol. i. p. 77.

For further mention of the Peruvian potato, see Ulloa, *Voyage to South America*, London, 1772, vol. i. p. 287; Tschudi, *Travels in Peru*, London, 1847, pp. 178, 368, 386. The importance of the study of cultivated plants in connection with the early history of mankind receives some illustration in Humboldt's *Essai sur la géographie des plantes*, Paris, 1805.

[1] Cieza, pt. i. cap. lxxv.; Garcilasso, lib. v. cap. iii.

changes to have taken place, and in point of
fact such changes had taken place. Yet, as already observed, true civilization, in the sense in
which we have agreed with Mr. Morgan to
understand it, had not been attained by people
who could record events only by *quipus*. Nor
had Peruvian society acquired the characteristic
features which in the Old World marked the
upper period of barbarism, the stage reached by
the Hebrew patriarchs and the conquerors of
Troy. Though iron mines were at hand, the
Peruvians did not know how to work the ore.[1]
Their axes, gimlets, chisels, and knives were of
bronze ;[2] they had no tongs or bel- Tools
lows, and no nails, in lieu of which
they fastened pieces of wood together with
thongs.[3] Their ploughs were made of a hard
wood, and were commonly pulled through the
ground by men, though now and then llamas
may have been employed.[4]

In another respect the Peruvians lacked the
advantages which in the Old World gave to
the upper period of barbarism some of its most
profoundly important characteristics. We have
seen that in the eastern hemisphere the middle
period was the time when horses were tamed to

[1] Garcilasso, lib. ii. cap. xxviii.
[2] Markham's *Cieza*, p. xxviii.
[3] Garcilasso, lib. vi. cap. iv.
[4] Garcilasso, lib. v. cap. ii. ; see also above, vol. i. p. 73.

men's uses and great herds of kine were kept. This was not only a vast enlargement of men's means of subsistence, affording a steady diet of meat and milk ; it not only added greatly to men's control of mechanical forces by enlisting the giant muscular strength of horses and oxen in their service ; but its political and social consequences were far-reaching. In the absence of a pastoral life, the only possible advance out of a hunting stage, with incipient horticulture, into any higher stage, was along the line of village communities like those of Iroquois or Mandans into pueblo-houses and pueblo-towns like those of Zuñis and Aztecs. The clan must remain the permanent unit of organization, because the inchoate family could not acquire strength enough to maintain a partial independence. It could not release itself from the compact communal organization without perishing from lack of the means of subsistence and defence. But in a pastoral society the needs of pasturage extended the peaceful occupations of the clan over a considerable territory ; and the inchoate family, with its male chief, his underling warrior herdsmen and his horses and cattle, could maintain itself in a partial isolation which would have been impossible in a society of mere hunters, or of hunters and primitive corn-growers, with no helping animal but the dog. Life came to

Influence of cattle upon the evolution of society

be more successfully conducted in scattered
tents than in the communal household. Thus
there grew up a tendency to relax or break
down the compact communal organization ; the
primeval clan, based upon the tie of a common
maternal descent, declined in authority, and the
family of patriarchal type became the most important unit of society. In course of time a
metamorphosis was wrought in the structure
of the clan ; it came to be a group of closely
related patriarchal families, and such is the sort
of clan we find in Old World history, for the
most part, from the days of Esau to those of
Rob Roy.

One phase of the growing independence of
cow-keeping patriarchal families, and of the
loosening of the primitive communal clan or-
ganizations,[1] was the rapid and masterful development of the notion of private property.
The earliest instance of property on a large
scale, which was not the common possession of
a clan, but the private possession of a Private pro-
family represented by its patriarchal perty (*pecu-
head, was property in cattle. Of very *lium*)
little save his blanket and feathers, his tomahawk

---

[1] As a general rule social progress has been achieved
through successive tightenings and loosenings of sundry forms
of social or political organization, the proper condition of development being neither anarchy nor despotic rigidity, but
plastic mobility. See my *Cosmic Philosophy*, part ii. chap. xx.

and his string of scalps, could the proudest Indian sachem say " it is mine ; " of nothing that was part of the permanent stock of food could he say as much, for it all belonged to the clan ; and his own official importance was simply that of a member of the clan council. But the Arab sheikh, as head of a patriarchal group, could say " this family is mine, and these are my cattle." This early preëminence of the cow as private property has been commemorated in the numerous Aryan words for money and wealth derived from the name of that animal.[1]

[1] For example, in Latin, *pecus* is " herd," *pecunia* is " money," *peculium* is " private property," whence we have *peculiarity*, or " that which especially pertains to an individual." Sir Henry Maine sees no reason for doubting the story " that the earliest coined money known at Rome was stamped with the figure of an ox " (*Early History of Institutions*, London, 1875, p. 49). Gothic *faihu* = Old English *feoh* = modern German *Vieh* is " cow ; " in modern English the same word *fee* is " pecuniary reward." In Gaelic, *bosluag* is " herd of cows," and *bosluaiged* is " riches." When you go to a tavern to dine you pay your *shot* or *scot* before leaving ; or perhaps you get into a ticklish situation, but escape *scot-free*. In King Alfred's English *sceat* was " money," and the Icelandic *skattr* and Gothic *skatts* had the same meaning ; while the same word in Gaelic, *skath*, means " herd," and in Old Bulgarian, as *skotu*, it means " cow." So in Sanskrit, *rupa* is " cow," and *rupya* is " money," whence we have the modern *rupee* of Bengal. The great importance of the cow in early Aryan thought is shown not only by the multitude of synonyms for the creature, but still more strikingly by the frequency of similes,

Now in ancient Peru the llama and alpaca played an important part,[1] but in nowise comparable to that taken by cattle in the eastern hemisphere. Camels and sheep, the nearest Old World equivalents to the llama and alpaca, would be far from adequate to the functions that have been performed by horses and cows. The contrast, moreover, was not merely in the animals, but in the geo-

No true pastoral life in ancient Peru

metaphors, and myths in the Vedas in which the cow plays a leading part.

[1] According to Garcilasso the llamas gave no more milk than was required for their own young, and were therefore not available for dairy purposes (lib. viii. cap. xvi.). Garcilasso has many amusing reminiscences connected with the introduction of European animals and plants into Peru, — how he came upon a litter of pigs in the square at Cuzco, how his father bought the first donkey in Cuzco in 1557, how he was sent around to his father's neighbours with dishes of the first grapes that came to Cuzco and helped himself on the way, how he saw his father regaling his friends with asparagus and carrots but got none himself (lib. ix. caps. xviii., xix., xxv., xxx.), and how he played truant to see the first bullocks at work, yoked to an iron plough : "A whole army of Indians took me to see them, who came from all parts, astonished at a sight so wonderful and novel for them and for me. They said that the Spaniards were too idle to work, and that they forced those great animals to do their work for them. I remember all this very well, because my holiday with the bullocks cost me a flogging consisting of two dozen stripes : one dozen administered by my father, because I was not at school ; and the other dozen by the schoolmaster, because I had only had one dozen " (lib. ix. cap. xvii.).

graphical conditions. The valleys and platforms of the Andes did not favour the development of true pastoral life like the vast steppes of Scythia or the plains of lower Asia. The domestication of animals in ancient Peru was a powerful help to the development of a stable agricultural community, but no really pastoral stage of society was reached there. The llamas were kept in large flocks on pastures maintained by sedulous irrigation, just as the maize and potato crops were made to thrive.[1] It was an agricultural scene. There was nothing in it like the old patriarchal life on the plain of Mamre or by the waters of the Punjab. Here we get a clue to a feature of Peruvian society unlike anything else in the world. That society may be said to have constituted a nation. It was, indeed, a nation of very rudimentary type, but still in a

Attainment of nationality without the notion of private property

certain sense a nation. It was the only instance in ancient America in which a people attained to nationality in any sense ; and so far as history knows, it was the only instance in the world in which the

[1] It must be borne in mind that the vapour-laden trade winds from the Atlantic Ocean are robbed of their moisture by the cold peaks of the Andes, so that, while Brazil has a rainfall and consequent luxuriance of vegetation quite unequalled, on the other hand Peru is dry, in many places parched, and requires much irrigation. In this respect the conditions were not unlike those in our Rocky Mountain region.

formation of nationality, with the evolution of a distinct governing class, took place before there had been any considerable development of the idea of private property. The result, as we shall see toward the close of this chapter, was a state organized upon the principle of communistic despotism.

Let us first, however, observe some of the steps by which this rudimentary nationality was formed. The four tribes in which we _{The four} can first catch sight of the process _{tribes} were the Quichuas, situated about the headwaters of the river Apurimac, the Incas of the upper Yucay valley, and the Canas and Cauchis of the mountains between the site of Cuzco and Lake Titicaca. The first of these tribes gave the name Quichua to the common language of the Peruvian empire, the second gave the name Incas to the conquering race or upper caste in Peruvian society, while the names of the other two tribes lapsed into obscurity. These four tribes formed the nucleus of the Peruvian nationality. They were a race of mountaineers, short in stature, but strongly and lithely built, with features aquiline and refined, very soft skin, cinnamon complexion, fine black hair, and little or no beard. In the time of Manco Capac these tribes appear to have been made up of clans called *ayllus* or " lineages." His tribe, the Incas, established themselves in the elevated valley of

Cuzco, and from that point began to subdue the neighbouring kindred tribes. They did not confine themselves, like the Aztecs, to extorting tribute from the conquered people, but they effected a military occupation of the country, a thing which the Aztecs never did. Manco's three successors confined their attention chiefly to building Cuzco (cir. 1280–1300) and taking measures to consolidate their government. We may perhaps refer to this period the beginnings of that very remarkable military organization of society presently to be described. By this time the Canas and Cauchis had been brought entirely under Inca rule, and the fifth king, Capac Yupanqui, completed the subjugation of the Quichuas. The two following reigns seem to have been spent in work of internal organization ; and then under the eighth Inca, Viracocha, the work of imperial expansion fairly began. It is now that, as already observed, we come out into the daylight of history.

This eighth Inca had a somewhat notable name. The title of Inca, applied alike to all Names of the sovereigns, was simply the old the Incas tribal name, and continued to be applied to the descendants of the original tribe, who came to form a kind of patrician caste. The king was simply The Inca *par excellence*, very much as the chief of an Irish tribe was called The O'Neil. Of the epithets attached to this title, some, such as Manco and Rocca, may perhaps be true proper names, with the meaning lost, such as we do not find among any other people in ancient America ;[1] others, such as Lloque, " left-handed," are nicknames of a sort familiar in European history; the most common ones are laudatory epithets, as Tupac, "splendid," Yupanqui, "illustrious," Capac, " rich." The eighth Inca alone has a name identifying him with deity. Viracocha was the name of the sun-god or sky-god. It was very much as if the Romans, instead of calling their emperor Divus Augustus, had called him Jupiter outright.

The Inca Viracocha conquered and annexed the extensive country about Lake Titicaca, inhabited by a kindred people usually Conquest of called Aymaras, whose forefathers, the Aymaras; perhaps, had built the cyclopean walls at Tiahuanacu. Viracocha's son and successor, Urco, met with misfortunes. North of the Quichua country were two powerful groups of kindred tribes, the Chancas and Huancas, extending nearly to the equator, and beyond them were

[1] Markham, in Winsor's *Narr. and Crit. Hist.*, i. 231. It may be, however, that they are simply archaic words to which *we* have lost the clue, — which is a very different thing. It is quite doubtful, therefore, whether this should be cited as a slight exception to my former statement, vol. i. p. 83.

the Quitus, whose country reached to the confines of the Chibchas. While Viracocha was engaged in his conquests at the south, the Chancas overran the Quichua country, and shortly after Urco's accession they marched to the very gates of Cuzco ; but in a decisive battle, fought just outside the town, the invaders were totally defeated by Urco's brother, Yupanqui. Then Urco was deposed and his brother was elected to succeed him. Presently the Quichua country was won back, with the aid of its own people, who preferred the Inca rule to that of the Chancas. After a while this masterful Inca Yupanqui had conquered the whole Chanca country and that of the Huancas to boot. Next he turned his arms against the Chimus, a people of alien blood and speech, who occupied the Pacific coast from near the site of Lima northward to that of Tumbez.

These Chimus, whose name Humboldt thinks may have survived in that of the giant mountain Chimborazo,[1] were an interesting people, with a semi-civilization of their own, apparently quite different from that of the Incas. From Mr. Squier's archæological investigations[2] I am in-

[1] Humboldt, *Ansichten der Natur,* ii. 48.

[2] See Squier's *Peru : Incidents of Travel and Exploration in the Land of the Incas,* New York, 1877, pp. 135–192 ; see also Markham's valuable note in Winsor's *Narr. and*

clined to suspect that it may have been a semi-civilization of the Pueblo type, with huge communal houses. However this may Conquest of have been, the Inca Yupanqui con- the Chimus quered the Chimus. At his death the Inca sway extended from the basin of Lake Titicaca to the equator, and from the Andes to the coast; and when we compare the end of his reign with its beginning, it is clear that he fairly earned the epithet by which he was distinguished among the members of the Inca dynasty. He was the great hero of Peruvian history; and the name given him was Pachacutec, or "he who changes the world." The historian Garcilasso de la Vega was his grandson's grandson.

Under Tupac Yupanqui, son and successor of Pachacutec, the career of conquest was further extended. It was first necessary Conquest of to suppress a rebellion of the Ayma- the Quitus; ras. Then Tupac completed the conquest of the Quitus. So great a stretch of territory had been brought into subjection that it now seemed necessary to have a second imperial city from which to govern its northern portions. Accordingly Tupac founded the city of Quito, saying: "Cuzco must be the capital of one part of my empire and Quito of the other."[1] Then,

Crit. Hist., i. 275–278; not often do we find more food for the historian packed into three pages.

[1] Cieza, pt. ii. cap. lvi.

returning southward, he brought all the coast valleys under his sway, including the valley of Pachacamac, " where was the very ancient and sacred temple of the Yuncas, which he wished very much to see. . . . Many Indians say that the Inca himself spoke with the Devil who was in the idol of Pachacamac, and that he heard how the idol was the creator of the world, and other nonsense, which I do not put down, because it is not worth while."[1] The Inca, says Cieza, did not molest this temple, but built a

and of Chili

house of the Sun in the neighbourhood. After returning to Cuzco, he subjected some more barbarous tribes in the Charcas country southeast from Lake Titicaca, and then invaded Chili and penetrated as far as the river Maule, in almost 34° south latitude.

The conquest of Chili as far as this point was completed by Tupac's son, Huayna Capac, who was then called to the northward by a rebellion of the tribes about Quito. The absorption of

Rebellion at Quito suppressed

Inca strength in conquest at one end of this long territory was apt to offer opportunities for insurrection at the other end. In an obstinate battle near Quito the rebels were defeated with great slaughter. Many hundreds of prisoners were taken. " Very few were able to hide themselves. Near the banks of a lake the Inca ordered them all to be be-

[1] Cieza, pt. ii. cap. lviii.

headed in his presence, and their bodies to be thrown into the water. The blood of those who were killed was in such quantity that the water lost its colour, and nothing could be seen but a thick mass of blood. Having perpetrated this cruelty, . . . Huayna Capac ordered the sons of the dead men to be brought before him, and, looking at them, he said, *Campa manan pucula tucuy huambracuna*, which means, 'You will not make war upon me, for you are all boys now.' From that time the conquered people were called 'Huambracuna' to this day, and they were very valiant. The lake received the name it still bears, which is *Yahuarcocha*, or 'the lake of blood.' "[1] The last years of Huayna's long reign were spent in Quito. Upon his death in 1523 his eldest legitimate son, Huascar, succeeded him, and presently there broke out the civil war between Huascar and his bastard brother, the usurper Atahualpa, which lasted until the Spaniards arrived upon the scene.

The territory subject to Huayna Capac in 1523 extended from near Popayan, Dimensions north of the equator, to the river of the empire Maule in Chili, a distance of nearly 2700 miles.

[1] Cieza, pt. ii. cap. lxvii. One is reminded of Bajazet's wholesale massacre of French prisoners after the battle of Nicopolis in 1396, of which there is a graphic description in Barante, *Histoire des ducs de Bourgogne de la maison de Valois*, 7e éd., Paris, 1854, tom. ii. p. 198.

If the Spaniards had not interfered, the next enemies would have been the Chibchas on the north and the invincible Araucanians on the south. The average breadth of this Peruvian empire was from 300 to 350 miles, so that the area was more than 800,000 square miles, about equal to the united areas of Austria-Hungary, the German Empire, France, and Spain, or to the area of that part of the United States comprised between the Atlantic Ocean and the Mississippi River. If we contrast with this vast territory the extent of Montezuma's so-called empire, about equivalent to the state of Massachusetts or the kingdom of Würtemberg, we cannot but be struck with the difference. The contrast is enhanced when we remember that the Aztec confederacy did not effect a military occupation of the country over which its operations extended, nor did it undertake to administer the government of conquered pueblo-towns; it simply extorted tribute. Now the conquests of the Incas went much farther than this; they undertook, and to some extent effected, a military occupation and a centralized administration of the whole country. In this work their success was naturally most complete among the four original tribes about Cuzco; probably less complete among the Aymaras, still less among the Chimus and other coast tribes, and least at the two extremities in Quito and Chili.

"The grand aim and glory of the Incas," says Garcilasso, "was to reduce new tribes and to teach them the laws and customs of the children of the Sun."[1] The Incas imposed their language upon each conquered tribe,[2] until it came to

The Incas sought to assimilate conquered peoples

be spoken in all parts of their territory, often side by side with the local tongues, somewhat as Hindustani is spoken throughout the greater part of British India, side by side with Bengali, Guzerati, Punjabi, etc. The Incas, moreover, to the best of their ability abolished cannibalism and other savage customs wherever they found them, and introduced their own religious ceremonies and festivals.[3] They appointed governors (curacas) for all places.[4] They established garrisons at various points in order to secure their conquests;[5] and they built military roads, with storehouses at suitable intervals where provisions and arms could be kept.[6] In connec-

[1] Garcilasso, lib. vii. cap. xviii.

[2] Id., lib. vii. cap. i. ; Cieza, pt. ii. cap. xxiv.

[3] Garcilasso, lib. vi. cap. xvii. ; lib. viii. caps. iii., vii. ; and *passim*.

[4] Id., lib. v. cap. xiii.

[5] Garcilasso, lib. vi. cap. xvi. ; Cieza, pt. ii. caps. ix., xxii.

[6] Garcilasso, lib. v. cap. viii. ; Cieza, pt. i. cap. lx.

tion with these stations were barracks where the troops could find shelter. These roads, which radiated from Cuzco to many parts of the Inca's dominions, were about twenty-five feet in width, and almost as level as railroads, which in that rugged country involved much cutting through rocks and much filling of gorges. The central The military highway from Quito to Cuzco, which roads was finished by Huayna Capac, and was connected with a similar road extending from Cuzco southward, is described with enthusiasm by Cieza de Leon, whose accuracy cannot lightly be questioned. "The great road from Quito to Cuzco, which is a greater distance than from Seville to Rome, was as much used as the road from Seville to Triana, and I cannot say more.[1] . . . I believe that since the history of man has been recorded, there has been no account of such grandeur as is to be seen in this road, which passes over deep valleys and lofty mountains, by snowy heights, over falls of water, through live rocks, and along the edges of furious torrents. In all these places it is level and paved, along mountain slopes well excavated, by the mountains well terraced, through the living rock cut, along the river banks supported by walls, in the snowy heights with steps and resting places, in all parts clean swept, clear of stones, with post- and store-

[1] Cieza, pt. ii. cap. lvii.

132

houses and temples of the Sun at intervals.
Oh! what greater things can be said of Alexander, or of any of the powerful kings who have
ruled in the world, than that they had made
such a road as this, and conceived the works
which were required for it! The roads constructed by the Romans in Spain . . . are not
to be compared with it." [1] These roads facili-
tated the transmission of political and military
intelligence. At intervals of a league and a half,
says Polo de Ondegardo, there stood small
relay houses, each "adapted to hold
two Indians, who served as postmen, The couriers
and were relieved once a month, and they were
there night and day. Their duty was to pass
on the messages of the Inca from Cuzco to
any other point, and to bring back those of
the governors, so that all the transactions and
events of the empire were known. When the
Inca wished to send anything to a governor, he
said it to the first *chasqui* [courier], who ran at
full speed for a league and a half, and passed
the message to the next as soon as he was
within hearing, so that when he reached the
post the other man had already started." [2] The

---

[1] Cieza, pt. ii. cap. lxiii.

[2] " Report by Polo de Ondegardo," in Markham's *Narratives of the Rites and Laws of the Yncas*, London, 1873,
p. 169 (Hakluyt Society). The original MS. is in the
National Library at Madrid, and has, I believe, not yet been

Spaniards made use of this system of couriers, and were thus able to convey letters from Cuzco to Lima, a distance of nearly four hundred miles, in three days.[1] Such a system for written despatches would of course do very well ; but one is inclined to wonder how a verbal message, transmitted through a dozen or fifty mouths, should have retained enough of its original shape to be recognizable. For all except the very simplest messages the *quipus* must have been indispensable.

published. Ondegardo was a learned lawyer who came to Peru in 1547 with Gasca, and was afterwards " corregidor " or chief magistrate of Cuzco. His brief document is of much value.

[1] Ondegardo adds that these couriers were used to bring up fresh fish from the sea to Cuzco. A similar but ruder system of couriers was used in Mexico (Bandelier, in *Peabody Museum Reports*, vol. ii. p. 696). Something similar existed in ancient Persia (Herodotus, viii. 98), only there they used horses, as well as swift dromedaries (Strabo, xv. p. 724 ; Diodorus, xvii. 80 ; Quintus Curtius, vii. 2, 11–18). Marco Polo (lib. ii. cap. 26) describes the relays of mounted couriers in China in the thirteenth century. The carrying of dainties for the table from the coast to Cuzco was nothing to what was done for the Fatimite caliph Aziz, in the tenth century, according to Makrizi, iv. 118, quoted by Colonel Yule. As the caliph craved a dish of Baalbec cherries, his vizier " caused 600 pigeons to be despatched from Baalbec to Cairo, each of which carried attached to either leg a small silk bag containing a cherry ! " Yule's *Marco Polo*, vol. i. p. 392.

Remarkable as were these roads, and the arrangements connected with them, the limitations under which the Peruvians worked might be seen as soon as there was a river or a broad and deep ravine to be crossed. Here the difference between civilization and middle-barbarism comes out forcibly. The Incas could command enough human brawn and muscle to build cyclopean masonry; but as they did not understand the principle of the arch,[1] they could not build stone bridges, nor had they sufficient knowledge of carpentry and engineering to make bridges of wood. Their ingenuity was therefore driven to assert itself by stretching Rope bridges huge osier ropes across from side to side of the river or chasm, and laying upon the ropes a flooring of transverse planks. The sides of these swaying bridges were protected by a slight rope railing. Llamas with their burdens could be driven across such bridges, as mules can be driven across them to-day; but they are not comfortable places for people with unsteady nerves, and in a high wind they are unsafe.[2]

This extensive system of roads would of it-

[1] Garcilasso, lib. v. cap. xxii. ; lib. vii. cap. xxix.

[2] The picture of the rope bridge over the Apurimac River, still in use, which may be seen in Squier's *Peru*, p. 545, is enough to give one a turn of vertigo. For a description of this and other bridges in the Inca period, see Garcilasso, lib. iii. cap. vii.

self indicate a military empire that had passed beyond the mere stage of tribal confederation. A similar indication is furnished by the remarkable system of military colonies (*mitimaes*) established by the great Inca Pachacutec,[1] or perhaps

Military colonies
by his father Viracocha Inca. It was a custom peculiarly incident to the imperfect rudimentary development of nationality, and reminds one strongly of what was formerly to be seen in Assyria. The ancient kings of Babylon and Nineveh used to transfer a considerable part of a conquered population from their old homes to a new habitat in some distant part of the empire, in order to break up local patriotism and diminish the tendency to revolts. Sometimes such a population was transferred in block, and some other population put in its place; but more often it was broken into

[1] " Although some Indians say that the *mitimaes* were planted from the time of Viracocha Inca, those may believe it who please to do so. For my part I took such pains to ascertain the facts, that I do not hesitate to affirm the colonizing system to have been instituted by [Pachacutec] Inca Yupanqui." Cieza de Leon, ed. Markham, pt. ii. cap. xxii. The system is more likely to have grown up gradually than to have been invented all at once. Mr. Bandelier suggests that possibly there may have been a rude germ of it in Mexico, in the occasional repeopling of an abandoned pueblo by colonists of Nahuatl race, as in the case of Alahuitzlan, related by Father Duran (cap. xlv.) and Tezozomoc (cap. lxxiv.). — *Peabody Museum Reports*, vol. ii. p. 140.

small bodies and scattered. It was thus that
Tiglath-Pileser and Sargon of Nineveh carried
off the ten tribes of Israel,[1] and that a part of
the people of Judah were kept in exile by the
waters of Babylon until the great Cyrus released
them.[2] Now this same system of deportation
was extensively practised by the Incas, and for
the same reason. For example, Tupac Yupanqui removed from the islands of Lake Titicaca
their entire population, and scattered it in different places; he replaced it on the islands by
people taken from forty-two tribes in various
parts of his dominions.[3] When the same Inca
founded the city of Quito he peopled it with
mitimaes, largely from the regions near Cuzco
and likely to be loyal. Huayna Capac did the
same sort of thing in Chili. In many cases
chiefs and other important men among these
transported populations received especial marks
of favour from the Inca and were taught to
regard their fortunes as dependent upon him.
Strangers from all quarters, moreover, were
brought to Cuzco and assigned their several

---

[1] Rawlinson's *Ancient Monarchies*, 2d ed., London, 1871,
vol. ii. p. 152; 2 Kings xviii. 9–11. Similar things were
now and then done by the Romans; see Dio Cassius, liv. 11;
Florus, iv. 12.

[2] Ewald's *History of Israel*, vol. iv. pp. 263, 274; Rawlinson, *op. cit.* vol. iii. p. 385.

[3] Garcilasso, lib. viii. cap. vi.

quarters there, so that the city was a kind of epitome of the Inca's dominions.[1]

Now the features of Peruvian polity thus far enumerated — the imposing of a new language and religion upon conquered tribes, the appointment of governors (usually if not always of the Inca blood), the maintenance of garrisons, the system of military roads, and the wholesale deportation of peoples — are all features attendant Incipient na- upon the incipient development of tionality nationality through conquest and fusion of tribes and the breaking down of primitive tribal institutions. There were points of genuine analogy between this development in Peru and in Assyria. This kind of incipient nationality is of very low type. It is held together not by a national spirit of patriotism, but by the systematic coercion exercised by the ruling tribe, which has been developed into what is practically a ruling caste. Oriental history affords plenty of examples of the ease with which countries under such conditions are sometimes conquered. It is only necessary for the invader to strike down the sovereign and get control of the machinery of government, and the thing is done; the subject tribes simply exchange one master for another, or if here and there a tribe rebels, it is rather to regain its

[1] Instructive notices of the *mitimaes* may be found in Cieza, pt. i. cap. xciii.; pt. ii. caps. xiii., xxii., lii., lvi., lxii.

original independence than to restore the state of things immediately preceding the catastrophe. Sometimes it succeeds in its attempt, but often the new master, wielding the same resources as the old one, or even greater, reduces it again to submission.

In this rudimentary form of nationality, where anything like the application of representative government to nation-making is utterly above and beyond the range of men's thought, the only shape which government can assume is military despotism, exercised either by a royal family or by a caste. The despotic government of ancient Peru seems to have partaken of both these characters; it was exercised by a caste in which a particular family was preëminently sovereign. The Incas, as already observed, were originally a conquering tribe; and they remained superimposed upon the conquered peoples as an upper caste. Garcilasso tells us that " the Incas were free from the temptations which usually lead to crime, such as passion for women, envy and covetousness, or the thirst for vengeance ; because if they desired beautiful women, it was lawful for them to have as many as they liked ; and any pretty girl they might take a fancy to, not only was never denied to them, but was given up by her father with expressions of extreme thankfulness that an Inca should have condescended to take

The Inca caste

her as his servant. The same thing might be said of their property; for as they never could feel the want of anything, they had no reason to covet the goods of others; while as governors they had command over all the property of the Sun and of the Inca; and those who were in charge were bound to give them all that they required, as children of the Sun, and brethren of the Inca. They likewise had no temptation to kill or wound any one either for revenge or in passion; for no one ever offended them. On the contrary, they received adoration only second to that offered to the royal person; and if any one, how high soever his rank, had enraged any Inca, it would have been looked upon as sacrilege and very severely punished."[1] Of course some allowances must be made in accepting these statements; such sweeping generalizations always require more or less qualification; and it is not likely that there ever existed a society of which this description of Garcilasso's would have been literally accurate. But after making due allowances, it remains quite clear that his Incas constituted a distinct caste, and were regarded by the mass of people as beings of a superior order. They were not only an upper caste, but they were a ruling caste, and furnished for every part of the empire governors allied to one another by a keen sense of kinship.

[1] Garcilasso, lib. ii. cap. xv.

The chief of this Inca caste, called *par excellence* The Inca, was no doubt the descendant and representative of the ancient chiefs of the Inca tribe. Just how far the different attributes of royalty were united in his person and office, it is not easy to say. With regard to the highest legislative and judiciary powers, our authorities do not make it perfectly clear how far they were exercised by the Inca solely, or by the Inca in connection with a council. That there was a council is unquestionable, and that it was a development from the council of the primitive Inca tribe is in a high degree probable; but we are insufficiently informed as to the extent of its powers. From sundry statements, however, it may be inferred that these powers were considerable, and that the Inca was perhaps not quite so full-blown a despot as some of Mr. Prescott's authorities declared him to be. The statement that, if he had taken it into his head to put to death a hundred thousand Indians, his decree would have been executed without a murmur, has a strong smack of hyperbole.[1] On the other hand, we are told that before deciding upon any

> *The Inca sovereign and council*

---

[1] "Su palabra era ley, i nadie osaba ir contra su palabra ni voluntad: aunque obiese de matar cient mill Indios, no havia ninguno en su reino que le osase decir que no lo hiciese." *Conquista i poblacion del Peru*, MS., apud Prescott, *Conq. of Peru*, book i. chap. i.

measure of importance, the council was always consulted ; upon this point, says Cieza de Leon, all his informants were agreed.[1] As to the crucial question, however, how far the Inca's authority was effectively limited by the council, Cieza leaves us in the dark. Garcilasso refers to " Tupac Yupanqui and all his council" ordaining that two of the royal concubines should be legitimized and regarded as true queens, in order to provide against a possible failure in the succession, because the heir apparent, Huayna Capac, had no children by his first and legitimate queen.[2] Here the consent of the council, in a measure of prime importance, is evidently assumed to be essential. Still more significant is the brief mention made by Cieza of the deposition of the Inca Urco.[3] This ruler's military conduct had been disastrous. The invading Chancas had, in spite of him, arrived within sight of Cuzco, when they were defeated with prodigious slaughter by his brother, afterward famous as Pachacutec Yupanqui. After the victory there was earnest discussion within the city. Cieza does not mention the council by name, but except the council there was no authoritative body in which such a discussion could take place. Cieza's description throughout implies

The deposition of Urco

[1] Cieza, pt. ii. cap. xxvi.
[2] Garcilasso, lib. viii. cap. viii.
[3] Cieza, pt. ii. cap. xlvi.

that the proceedings were regular, and that the decision was at once accepted as final. It was decided that the unworthy Urco should not be allowed to enter the city, and that the fringed and feathered crimson cap, or *borla*, which served as the Inca diadem, should be taken from him and bestowed upon his victorious brother. In spite of Urco's protests this was done. It is further said that Urco's lawful queen, who had borne him no children, forthwith abandoned him, and, coming into Cuzco, became the lawful queen of Pachacutec.[1] All these proceedings seem to me consistent and probable, and they

---

[1] Cieza does not tell us what became of the deposed and forsaken king. " I say no more concerning Inca Urco, because the Indians only refer to his history as a thing to laugh at."

Garcilasso tells a different story. He places the invasion of the Chancas two generations earlier, in the reign of Urco's grandfather, Yahuar-huaccac. That Inca, says Garcilasso, fled from Cuzco, and his son Viracocha Inca defeated the invaders, whereupon the son dethroned the father, but allowed him to live in a comfortable palace in the pleasant Yucay valley (lib. v. cap. xviii.–xx.). But in this story also, the act which dethrones the father and enthrones the son is the act of " the court, which was the head of the kingdom, to avoid scandals and civil wars, and above all because there was no use in resisting, so that all that the prince desired was agreed to." Nothing could be more significant. The victorious prince is all-powerful in the council, but still the action, to be lawful, must be the action of the council. This preserves the reminiscence of despotism in the making, at a time when despotism was practically completed.

clearly indicate that the power of deposing and degrading the king, and filling his place by the prince next in the customary order of succession, was retained by the Inca council at Cuzco, as it was retained by the *tlatocan* at the city of Mexico, and could be exerted in cases of emergency.

On the whole, I am inclined to the opinion that the reigning Inca had practically acquired control of judicial, administrative, and legislative affairs through his paramount influence in the council; and that this is one reason why such meagre information about the council has come down to us. The Inca was, in all probability, much more a king than Agamemnon, — more like Rameses the Great.

One is the more inclined to this opinion because of the excessive development of sacerdotal supremacy in the Inca. As already observed, in the order of historic evolution the king is primarily the military chief; next he becomes chief priest, and in virtue of this combination of exalted functions, he acquires so much influence as to appropriate to himself by degrees the other functions of government, judicial, administrative, and legislative.[1] Now the Inca, originally the

The Inca was a "god-king" head war-chief of the Inca tribe, came naturally to be military head of the Inca empire. As to his sacerdotal functions he came to be something more than

[1] See above, vol. i. p. 128.

chief priest; his position was that of vice-deity, analogous to what Herbert Spencer calls a god-king. To illustrate this properly a few words must be devoted to an account of the Inca religion.

This religion was a comparatively high form of polytheism, in which ancestor-worship co-existed with worship of the Sun; and now and then some idea crudely suggestive of monotheism found expression, as in the remark attributed by Father Blas Valera to the Inca Tupac Yupanqui, that the Sun, who goes on his unvarying round like a tethered beast, must be obeying the mandates of an unseen power.[1] In the mind of the Inca this unseen power was probably Pachacamac, whose name means " Creator of the World." " All the theology of the Incas," says Garcilasso, " was in- Pachacamac cluded in the word *Pachacamac*." They believed that things must have been made somehow by somebody, but beyond that point they did not carry their speculations, for they had little science and still less theology, and " knew not how to raise their minds to invisible things." [2] In all Peru there was but one temple conse-

[1] The same remark was attributed by Father Acosta to Tupac's son, Huayna Capac. See Garcilasso, lib. viii. cap. viii. ; lib. ix. cap. x. Cf. *Myths and Myth-Makers*, pp. 169–171.

[2] Garcilasso, lib. ii. cap. xxv.

crated to Pachacamac. It was on the coast, some distance south of the site of Lima. It was a very old temple, standing on the top of a small hill and built of adobe brick. The interior walls were covered with figures of wild beasts. Within was an idol endowed with oracular powers, and its priests, when consulted, went off into paroxysms like the Cumæan Sibyl.[1] To the valley of Pachacamac came pilgrims with their offerings from all quarters to consult the oracle. It seems to have been a relic of the old idolatrous religion of the coast people, which the sagacious Tupac Yupanqui, instead of destroying it, converted to the uses of a more spiritual religion, somewhat as early Roman missionaries cleansed pagan temples and turned them into Christian churches.[2] The

[1] At Phœbi nondum patiens, immanis in antro
Bacchatur vates, magnum si pectore possit
Excussisse Deum.   Tanto magis ille fatigat
Os rabidum, fera corda domans, fingitque premendo.
Ostia jamque domus patuere ingentia centum
Sponte sua, vatisque ferunt responsa per auras.

Virg., *Æn.*, vi. 77.

[2] Cieza's remarks are entertaining.   He says that "the devil Pachacamac" was much pleased with the arrangement, and "showed great satisfaction in his replies, seeing that his ends were served both by the one party and the other, while the souls of the unfortunate simpletons remained in his power. Some Indians say that this accursed demon Pachacamac still talks with the aged people.   As he sees that his authority and credit are gone, and that many of those who once served him

146

general policy of the Incas, however, was to suppress idolatry among the peoples annexed to their dominions.[1] Garcilasso declares most positively that the Inca people "worshipped no other gods but the Sun, although there are not wanting persons who state the contrary."[2] The reverence for tutelar domestic deities, the spirits of deceased ancestors, Garcilasso would probably not have regarded as a real exception to his general statement, any more than, as a Catholic, he would have recognized the reverence for patron saints as an evanescent phase of polytheism. The public worship was Sun-worship. Some reverence was paid Sun-worship to the moon, the three brightest planets, and the Pleiades, but this was but accessory to the adoration of the orb of day. This worship was celebrated chiefly at four great festivals at the solstices and equinoxes of each year.[3] At these

have now formed a contrary opinion, he declares that he and the God of whom the Christians preach are one, and thus with other false and deceitful words induces some to refuse the water of baptism" (pt. i. cap. lxxii.). There was nothing of the comparative mythologist about Cieza !

[1] Garcilasso, lib. vi. cap. x. ; lib. viii. cap. iii.
[2] Garcilasso, lib. iii. cap. xx.
[3] For the method in which the Peruvians measured the year and determined the solstices and equinoxes by means of the shadows cast by towers, see Garcilasso, lib. ii. cap. xxii. They used the solar year, and intercalated a period at the end of the lunar year to bring it up to the solar. This period

festivals there were sacrifices of "sheep," *i. e.*
llamas or alpacas, and their lambs ; of rabbits
and birds used for food; of maize and other
vegetables, of the strength-sustaining herb *coca*,[1]
of the exhilarating *chicha*, or maize beer,[2] and
of fine cloths. " They burnt these things as a
thank-offering to the Sun for having created
them for the support of man."[3] As for human
sacrifices, Garcilasso assures us, and with evident knowledge of the subject, that
No human
sacrifices
there was nothing of the sort under
the Incas. In the times before the Inca supremacy, and among many of the peoples whom
the Incas conquered, there were human sacrifices accompanied by cannibalism ;[4] but both

they called "finished moon." See Markham's note, to
Garcilasso, vol. i. p. 179.

[1] The dietetic and medicinal uses of this valuable narcotic,
especially useful to mountaineers, are described in Garcilasso,
lib. viii. cap. xv.; and Cieza, pt. i. cap. xcvi.; cf. Johnston,
Chemistry of Common Life, vol. ii. pp. 116–135 ; Bibra,
Die Narkotischen Genussmittel und der Mensch, pp. 151–174.

[2] The maize beer is described in Garcilasso, lib. viii. cap.
ix. The Peruvians were sturdy tipplers ; the quantity of
beer they consumed, says our author (lib. vi. cap. iii.), "is
a thing almost incredible." After the Spaniards introduced
barley, the natives made beer from it (Cieza, pt. i. cap. xl.) ;
but the *chicha* is still in common use. See Squier's *Peru*, p.
126 *et passim*.

[3] Garcilasso, lib. ii. cap. viii.

[4] Compare Dr. Haug's remarks on the prevalence of

these practices were sternly suppressed by the Incas. Their abolition he would date as far back as the time of Manco Capac,[1] which was equivalent to " a time whereof the memory of man runneth not to the contrary." If some Spanish writers assert that there were human sacrifices in Peru, it shows that they do not exercise proper discrimination. Within the vast limits of the Inca dominion there were included a number of peoples with whom such sacrifices had long been customary, and it might well be that the Incas had not completely succeeded everywhere in stamping out the abomination. Garcilasso mentions a writer who described human sacrifices " in Peru ; " but it was in a place more than twelve hundred miles north of Cuzco, *i. e.* in a region recently conquered and imperfectly reorganized. " I am a witness," says the good Garcilasso, " to having heard my father and his contemporaries frequently compare the states of Mexico and Peru ; and in speaking of these sacrifices of men, and of the practice of eating human flesh, they praised the Incas of Peru because they neither practised nor permitted such acts, while they execrated the Mexicans for doing both the one and the other in the city in

human sacrifices in Vedic times and their abandonment by the Brahmans, in Muir's *Sanskrit Texts*, vol. i. p. 11.

[1] Garcilasso, lib. i. cap. xx.

so diabolical a fashion." [1]   Little if any doubt is now left that Garcilasso was quite right, and that among the burnt-offerings to the Sun on his great festal days there were no human creatures.

The duties and ceremonies of this Sun-worship were in charge of quite a hierarchy of ministering priests and confessors, sacrificers, hermits, and soothsayers, at the head of all the Villac Umu, "chief soothsayer" or high priest, and above him the Inca. [2] The soothsayers, like the Roman augurs, divined by the flight of birds or by inspecting the entrails of animals sacrificed. The ministering priests received confessions and served as the mouthpieces of oracles. The hermits dwelt in solitary places, and were, in some instances if not always, organized into a kind of celibate

The priest-hood

---

[1] Garcilasso, lib. ii. cap. viii. Mr. Prescott (*Conquest of Peru*, book i. chap. iii.) was inclined to admit that human sacrifices were performed, though very rarely, under the Incas, and quoted five contemporary authorities (including Cieza) against Garcilasso. But Mr. Markham has shown that Cieza and others were misled by supposing that the words *yuyac* and *huahua* signified " men " and " children," whereas, as applied to the victims of sacrifice, these words signified " adult beasts " and "lambs." Mr. Markham also quotes seven other important contemporary authorities (not mentioned by Mr. Prescott) in support of Garcilasso ; so that the question appears to be settled in his favour. See Winsor, *Narr. and Crit. Hist.*, i. 237, 238.

[2] The priesthood is described by Mr. Markham, in Winsor, *Narr. and Crit. Hist.*, i. 240.

monastic brotherhood with a chief hermit at the head. To these remarkable coincidences with various customs in the Old World may be added the special coincidence with ancient Egypt in mortuary customs. In Peru as in Egypt the bodies of the dead, swathed and wrapped in complicated fashion, were preserved as mummies, and sundry treasures and utensils were buried with them.[1]

Not the least interesting of these coincidences was the keeping of the sacred fire. Each year at the autumnal equinox a new fire was kindled by collecting the sun's rays on a burnished mir-

---

[1] Compare Cieza de Leon, pt. i. cap. lxiii. with Maspero's *Egyptian Archæology*, chap. iii. "Many of these ceremonies," says Cieza, "are now given up, because these people are learning that it suffices to inter the bodies in common graves, as Christians are interred, without taking anything with them other than good works. In truth, all other things but serve to please the Devil, and to send the soul down to hell the more heavily weighted." In several passages Cieza speaks of the custom of burying widows alive with their husband's mummy as if it were a common custom in Peru. It was undoubtedly common among many of the peoples conquered by the Incas, but it was not an Inca custom, and they did what they could to suppress it. A very high contemporary authority, known as "the anonymous Jesuit," declares that "in none of the burial-places opened by the Spaniards in search of treasure were any human bones found, except those of the buried lord himself." Markham, in Winsor, *Narr. and Crit. Hist.*, i. 237. Specimens of the mummies may be seen at the Peabody Museum in Cambridge.

ror, and this fire was kept alive through the year by consecrated maidens (*aclla-cuna*) analogous to the Roman vestal nuns. These vestals lived in convents presided over by matrons (*mama-cuna*). If the fire happened to go out it was an evil omen. If a nun broke her vow of chastity she was buried alive,[1] just as in Rome. But as compared with the Peruvian system of vestals, the Roman system seems either like a dwindled survival of something similar, or perhaps a parallel case of development arrested at an earlier stage. It was a much more extensive affair in Peru than in Rome, and its meaning is in many respects more obvious. In Rome there were six priestesses of Vesta, who were treated with most signal deference.[2] In Peru an *aclla-cuna* was treated with much deference, as a kind of superior being, but the number of them was very large. There were about 1500 of these vestals in the *aclla-huasi*, or "nuns'-house" at Cuzco, and in all parts of the kingdom a temple of the Sun generally had

The vestal nuns

[1] Garcilasso, lib. iv. cap. iii. According to Zarate (*Conquista del Peru*, ii. 7), the woman's paramour was burned alive.

[2] "They were emancipated from the *patria potestas* and became *sui juris*; . . . a lictor cleared the way before them; a seat of honour was reserved for them at the public shows; the fasces of a prætor or consul were lowered to them; and if they met a criminal on his way to execution he was reprieved." Ramsay, *Roman Antiquities*, p. 163.

such a convent attached to it. . Their vow of
perpetual celibacy meant that they were the
Sun's wives ; whence it was quite natural that
the punishment for infidelity should be burial
in the dark grave out of the offended husband's
sight. As wives of the Sun, they had certain
household duties. They baked cakes and
brewed beer for the great sacrificial festivals
of the winter solstice and the vernal equinox.
They also wove cloth of fine cotton and vicuña
wool, and made clothes for their husband the
Sun; but as the celestial spouse, so abundantly
cared for, could not come down from the sky
to take these clothes, the Inca took and wore
them. We are thus prepared for the information that the Inca, as representative   They were
of the Sun, was husband of all these   concubines
consecrated women. The convents   for the Inca
were not equivalent to Eastern harems, for the
Inca did not visit them. But he sent and took
from them as many concubines as he wished ;
those who were not thus taken remained vir-
gins.[1] It was absolutely required that the nuns
at Cuzco should be of pure Inca blood ; and
as every reigning Inca had two or three hundred
enumerated children,[2] the race seemed to be in
no danger of dying out.

[1] Many interesting details concerning these vestals are given
in Garcilasso, lib. iv. caps. i.–vii.

[2] How many more he may have had cannot be reck-

The theory of the Inca's person, upon which these customs were based, regarded him as the human representative or incarnation of the solar deity. He was the Sun, made flesh and dwelling among men. Such dignity was greater than that of mediæval Pope or Emperor ; it was even greater than that of the Caliph, who was a Mussulman pope and emperor combined ; and this is in harmony with the view that the Inca's rule was practically absolute. As for instances of monarchs with power strictly unlimited, like the king in a fairy-tale, they are not easy to find anywhere in history.

Great pains were taken to keep the lineage of this august person as narrowly definite as
possible. The Inca could have but one legitimate wife, and it was imperatively required that she should be his full sister, — the child of the same father by the same mother.[1] The children of the Inca by this incestuous marriage were thus as completely and narrowly royal in blood as possible,

The Inca's legitimate wife

oned. Apparently any woman in the Inca's dominions might at any time be summoned to be his concubine, and felt honoured and exalted by the summons. According to Garcilasso, his great-grandfather Tupac Yupanqui had 200 children in his family (lib. viii. cap. viii.) ; and his great-uncle Huayna Capac had from 200 to 300 (lib. ix. cap. xv.).

[1] This one legitimate wife was called *Coya,* equivalent to queen. See Garcilasso, lib. iv. cap. ix. ; Cieza, pt. ii. cap. lxix.

and the eldest son was the legitimate heir to the kingdom.[1] If the Inca had no children by his eldest sister, he married the second, and the third, and so on, until a legitimate heir was born to him. Only such an heir could be legitimate. The Inca's two or three hundred children by the vestals, of pure Inca blood, were counted as legitimate, but could not inherit the kingship. His children by ordinary women were mere bastards, and counted for nothing, although they were respected as nobler than common people.

Such notions of caste, of distinction between noble and ignoble blood, such extreme deification of the military head of the community, would have been inconceivable in any part of aboriginal America except Peru. In purely tribal society there is no such thing as caste, no such thing as monarchy. Caste and monarchy are results of the partial fusion of tribal societies through conquest. The conquering tribe becomes the ruling caste, its head war-chief becomes the semi-divine monarch. Nowhere except in Peru had there been enough conquest and fusion to produce any such results. The

Society had undergone further development in Peru than elsewhere in America

---

[1] In its origin this rule was probably a device for keeping the " royal succession in the male line, where otherwise succession through females prevailed." See Spencer, *Principles of Sociology*, vol. ii. p. 346.

Mexican *tlacatecuhtli* afforded an instance of primitive kingship developed almost as far as was possible in a purely tribal society ; he was a priest-commander, almost but not quite equivalent to the early Greek *basileus*, or priest-judge-commander. If the conquering career of the Aztec confederacy had gone on unchecked until the present time, it would probably have effected a military occupation of the whole Mexican territory, with garrisons in the principal pueblo-towns; the *calpixqui*, or tax-gatherers, would probably have developed into permanent satraps or governors, like the Peruvian *curacas ;* the Aztec tribe might very likely have developed into a ruling caste, supported entirely by the labour of the subjected peoples ; and the Aztec " chief-of-men " might well have become exalted into a despot like Xerxes or Tupac Yupanqui ; while the Aztec tribal council would have come to be an evanescent affair seldom mentioned by historians, like the council at Cuzco.

Thus the governmental development in ancient Peru was such as to indicate that society must, at least in some respects, have passed beyond the tribal stage as exemplified elsewhere throughout aboriginal America. We have other indications of a similar kind. There are reasons for believing that the primitive clan system was to a very considerable extent broken up.

Upon such points, indeed, our information is meagre and unsatisfactory. The ethnologist and the archæologist have not done so much for us in Peru as they have done in North America. There is much need in this field for work like that of Morgan, Cushing, and Bandelier. It would be interesting to know, for example, how far the great communal house or fortress, of the pueblo type, may have been common in Peru. One would gladly see the remarkable ruins at Caxarmarquilla[1] and at Chimu,[2] near Truxillo, explored with especial reference to this question. If it should turn out, however, that these and other structures in the coast region are the remains of ancient pueblos, it would still be unsafe to infer too hastily that the state of society implied by them was like that which prevailed nearer to Cuzco. It is probable that before the Inca conquests the entire coast region, from the Isthmus of Darien to Chili, was the seat of a semi-civilization in many respects like that of Mexico and Central America, in some respects cruder. These coast peoples were skilful irrigators and built huge structures of adobe brick ; they were cannibals, they sacrificed human beings to dog-headed idols, and they buried widows alive with their dead husbands. All such heathenish practices the conquering Incas,

Breaking up of the clan system

[1] Squier's *Peru,* p. 93.   [2] Id., pp. 143–164.

to the best of their ability, suppressed. If we were to infer, from the cannibalism practised by these peoples, that the Incas were likewise cannibals, we should make a grave mistake. It would clearly, therefore, be unsafe to infer, from any vestiges of communal living in this region, that the same sort of communal living formed any part of the Inca phase of society.

In this connection a certain passage in Garcilasso de la Vega is very suggestive. Eastward of the Andes, in a part of what is now Bolivia, lived a fierce race of barbarians called Chirihu-

The Chiri-
huanas
anas, — such cannibals that " if they come upon shepherds watching sheep [alpacas], they prefer one shepherd to a whole flock of sheep." In 1572 (*i. e.* in Garcilasso's own time, when he was thirty-two years old), the viceroy Don Francisco de Toledo undertook to invade the country of the Chirihuanas and chastise them into good behaviour. But their country, situated on the rainy side of the giant mountains, was a frightful maze of swampy forests, and Don Francisco was baffled, as in earlier days the great Inca Pachacutec had been baffled in the same enterprise. " The viceroy came back as a fugitive, having left behind all he had taken with him, that the Indians might be satisfied with their captures and leave him to escape. He came out by so bad a road that, as the beasts were unable to drag the litter in

which he travelled, the Spaniards and Indians
had to carry him on their shoulders. The Chirihuanas followed behind, with derisive shouts,
and cried out to the bearers to throw that old
woman [his highness, the viceroy !] out of the
basket, that they might eat her alive."

Now of these Chirihuanas Garcilasso goes on
to say that they learned from the Incas how to
make dwellings, in which they lived in common. There is a possible ambiguity   Their com-
about this sentence if it is carelessly   munal houses
read. From the context I understand it to mean,
not that the Incas taught them their communal
style of living, in which they resembled savages
and low barbarians generally; but that they
copied from neighbouring peoples under Inca
sway certain building arts which they applied to
their own purposes. Perhaps Garcilasso is mistaken in supposing that they learned their art
of building from the Incas; for on that point
he speaks as an antiquary. In the next sentence
he speaks as a contemporary. A Chirihuana
dwelling, he says, is a very large house, divided
into as many apartments as there are families;
these apartments, though small, are quite sufficient for people without much encumbrance in
the shape of clothes or household furniture;
and each great house may be called a village
(*pueblo*). Upon such a state of things Garcilasso looks with some disgust. "This is enough

to say about the brutal condition and manner
of life of the Chirihuanas, and it will be a great
marvel if we are able to draw them out of it." [1]

This is not the way in which the Inca historian would have mentioned pueblo-houses if
he had been familiar with them from boyhood.
He tells us, moreover, that the Peruvians of
whom he had personal knowledge, in Cuzco
and other cities, did not join their houses together, but each one stood by itself; on one
side was usually a large living room, on the
other were small chambers and closets.[2] The

[1] " Tambien aprendieron los Chirihuanas de los Incas à
hazer casas para su morada, no particulares, sino en comun :
porque hazen un galpon grandissimo, y dentro tantos aparta-
dijos quantos son los vezinos, y tan pequeños que no caben mas
de las personas y les basta porque no tienen axuar ni ropa de
vestir, que andan en cueros. Y desta manera se podra llamar
pueblo cada galpon de aquellos. Esto es lo que ay que dezir
acerca de la bruta condicion y vida de los Chirihuanas, que
sera gran marauilla poderlos sacar della." Garcilasso, lib. vii.
cap. xvii. (Lisbon, 1609). In his translation of this passage
Mr. Markham is evidently wrong as to the meaning of that
tricksome word *vezinos ;* here it clearly means families, not
individuals. Garcilasso surely did not mean to describe the
house as " divided into as many partitions as there are inhabitants."

[2] " Advertimos que los Indios del Peru . . . no trauauan
vnas pieças con otras, sino que todas las hazian sueltas cada
vna de porsi : quando mucho de vna muy gran sala o quadra
sacauan a vn lado, y a otro sendos aposentos pequeños que
seruian de recamaras," lib. vi. cap. iv.

inference, that the normal Peruvian household was a family and not a clan, is supported by the fact that in the remarkably symmetrical and artificial organization of society, about to be described, the unit of composition was not the clan, but the family averaging five or six persons.

It is quite in harmony with such a stage of family development that marriage was ordinarily indissoluble ;[1] that most men had but one wife, though in certain cases Monogamy polygamy was permissible ;[2] and that prostitutes were treated as outside the pale of society. They were obliged to live in huts in the fields, outside of the towns, and were called *pampay-runa*, or "women of the fields." They were treated by men "with extreme contempt. Women could not speak to them, on pain of receiving the same name, being shorn in public, declared as infamous, and repudiated by their husbands if married."[3]

[1] Report by Cristoval de Molina, in Markham's *Rites and Laws of the Yncas*, London, 1873 (Hakluyt Soc.), p. 54.

[2] "When any man had received a woman as his legitimate wife or *mamanchu*, he could not take another except through the favour of the Inca, which was shown for various reasons, either to one who had special skill in any art, or to one who had shown valour in war, or had pleased the Inca in any other way." Report by Polo de Ondegardo, in Markham, *op. cit.* p. 166.

[3] Garcilasso, lib. iv. cap. xiv. There is a *double entendre*

Such a development of the family indicates a great advance from the primitive type of clan or-

The indus-
trial army

ganization. But the extent to which the clan system had been broken up and superseded by a very peculiar and artificial system is illustrated in the industrial organization of the Peruvian people in their village communities. There everything was arranged as symmetrically as in the administration of departments, arrondissements, cantons, and communes in modern France; and such symmetry of arrangement is explicable only as the result of the action of a more or less thoroughly centralized government. This industrial organization in ancient Peru was really a military organization applied to industrial purposes; it was a system of army government extended through the whole framework of society. Families and villages were organized upon a deci-

in the word *pampayruna*; inasmuch as *pampa* means not only a field, but is also sometimes used to designate a public square, open to all comers, so *pampayruna* conveys the meaning of a public woman or strumpet. They were never called by their names, says Garcilasso, but only by this scornful epithet; *i. e.* they lost personality and were no longer entitled to personal names, but only to a common noun. The Incas preserved the tradition of a former state of comparative promiscuity, and with this former state, as well as with the loose sexual relations among neighbouring peoples, they contrasted the higher development of the family among themselves. Id., lib. i. caps. xiv., xv.

mal system, like companies and regiments. The average monogamous family of five persons was the unit. Ten such families made a *chunca*, ten *chuncas* made one *pachaca*, ten *pachacas* one *huaranca*, and ten *huarancas* one *hunu*, so that a *hunu* was a district with a population of about 50,000 persons.[1] Each of these decimal subdivisions had its presiding officer, who was responsible directly to his immediate superior and ultimately to the Inca. "The decurion was obliged to perform two duties in relation to the men composing his division. One was to act as their caterer, to assist them with his diligence and care on all occasions when they required help, reporting their necessities to the governor or other officer, whose duty it was to supply seeds when they were required for sowing; or cloth for making clothes; or to help to rebuild a house if it fell or was burnt down; or whatever other need they had, great or small. The other duty was to act as a crown officer, reporting every offence, how slight soever it might be, committed by his people, to his superior, who either pronounced the punishment or referred it to another officer of still higher rank."[2]

The land was divided into little areas called *tupus*, one *tupu* being enough to support a man

[1] Ondegardo, in Markham, *op. cit.* p. 155; Garcilasso, lib. ii. cap. xi.

[2] Garcilasso, lib. ii. cap. xii.

and his wife. As fast as children were born, "another *tupu* was granted for each boy, and half a *tupu* for each girl."[1] This land did not belong to the family or its head, but to the *chunca* or village community; and as the *chunca* was originally reckoned the equivalent of an *ayllu*, or "lineage," we have here a connecting link between this elaborate system and the earlier system of clan ownership which preceded it.[2] The *ayllu*, or fragment of an overgrown and disintegrated clan, was trimmed into a definite size, and thus survived as the *chunca* in the new decimal system. The *chunca* owned the land in the sense of occupying it, and at intervals of time there was a redistribution of it, in order to maintain equality, as among the ancient Germans and the modern Russians.[3] The produce of the land was divided into three shares, one for the Inca, one for the priesthood, one for the people. Every man who had been present at the sowing had his equal share of the people's third; if he had not been present at

Allotment of lands and produce

[1] Garcilasso, lib. v. cap. iii.

[2] See Bandelier's remarks on Peruvian land-tenure, in *Peabody Museum Reports*, vol. ii. p. 423.

[3] Maine, *Village Communities*, London, 1871 ; Nasse, *The Agricultural Community in the Middle Ages*, London, 1872 ; Phear, *The Aryan Village in India and Ceylon*, London, 1880 ; Mackenzie Wallace's *Russia*, London, 1877 ; Laveleye, *Primitive Property*, London, 1878.

the sowing, it was because he was absent in the
Inca's service (as, for example, on a campaign),
and thus he had his share in the Inca's third ;
or else he had been employed in work about the
temples, and accordingly took his share from the
priesthood's third. There was no room for idlers
or for millionaires. There were special census
officers, statistics were strictly kept on the *quipus*, and allotments made accordingly. Irrigation and tillage were directed by the decurion, or
village overseer. If a village suffered from war,
or pestilence, or earthquake, assessments were
made upon more fortunate villages for repairing
the damage. On the whole it was the most
complete illustration of government socialism
that the historian can discover by looking backward.

One is quite prepared to learn that in such a
society as this there was very little division of
labour. "They had no special trades- Little or no
men, as we have, such as tailors, shoe- division of
makers, or weavers ; but each man labour
learnt all, so that he could himself make all
that he required. All men knew how to weave
and make clothes ; so that when the Inca gave
them wool, it was as good as giving them
clothes. All could till and manure the land
without hiring labourers. All knew how to
build houses. And the women knew all these

165

arts also, practising them with great diligence and helping their husbands." [1] A society in which division of labour had been considerably developed would not have lent itself so readily to such a monotonous and spiritless regimentation as that of the Incas. As already observed, this system, which seems to have been fully developed by the time that the extensive conquests began under Viracocha Inca, and which was imposed successively upon one conquered people after another, was really an application of military organization to industrial purposes, and was incompatible with advanced progress in industrial art. As Herbert Spencer observes, in considering what constitutes a true industrial society, we are concerned, " not with the quantity of labour but with the mode of organization of the labourers. A regiment of soldiers can be set to construct earthworks ; another to cut down wood ; another to bring in water ; but they are not thereby reduced for the time being to an industrial society. The united individuals do these things under command ; and, having no private claims to the products, are, though industrially occupied, not industrially organized." [2]

We are here brought back to the statement,

---

[1] Garcilasso, lib. v. cap. ix.

[2] Spencer, *Principles of Sociology*, vol. ii. p. 694, where the case of Peru is cited in point.

made some time since,[1] that in Peru the formation of nationality, with the evolution of a distinct governing class, took place before there
had been any considerable development of the
idea of private property; so that the result was
a state organized upon the principle of communistic despotism. It was a kind of industrial
army.

If we recur now to the tripartite division of
the produce of the land, we observe that it was
an army in which the lion's share of this produce was consumed in the support of the administration. One third of the crop was evenly
divided among the cultivators; two thirds really
went to the government in the shape of taxes.
Members of the Inca nobility and the priesthood, as non-producers, contributed nothing to
these taxes, but were supported out of that portion of them which remained after military and
other administrative outlays had been made.
The taxes were paid in crops, woollen or cotton cloth, shoes, weapons, coca, or in cables for
moving great stones.[2]

With this military organization of labour it
becomes possible to understand how such buildings as the Sacsahuaman fortress could have
been reared by people but slightly acquainted

[1] See above, p. 122.
[2] Garcilasso, lib. v. cap. vi. ; Cieza de Leon, pt. ii. cap.
xviii.

with the art of engineering. The marvellous and impressive feature in this cyclopean ar-

Cyclopean works

chitecture is simply its massiveness. We do not admire it as an expression of intellectual qualities, as we praise a Greek temple for its beauty, or a Gothic church for its sublimity. Not even as fine mason-work, in the modern sense of the term, does it appeal to us. It simply amazes us with its herculean exhibition of brute force. The Sacsahuaman fortress was built of unhewn stones, often quite irregular in shape and very unequal in size, so chosen as to fit together without mortar. The marvel of it is simply how the huge stones could have been dragged to the spot and hoisted into place. A certain Spanish priest asked Garcilasso " whether it was possible to put them in their positions without the aid of the Devil." [1] But the *amautas* doubtless told the truth when they said it was all done by an enormous expenditure of human brawn and sinew. Of one huge mon-olith, famous as the " tired stone " because " it became tired and could not reach its place," the *amautas* said that more than 20,000 Indians were employed in dragging it with stout cables. The conditions of the case were not so very un-

[1] Garcilasso, lib. vii. cap. xxviii. Mr. Markham, from his own measurements, gives some of the sizes of stones in the outer wall as fourteen feet by eight, fourteen by twelve, sixteen feet six inches by six feet one inch, etc.

like those under which the pyramids of Egypt were erected, though the architecture and mason-work of the latter are of far higher type and show much more range of thought than any ancient structures in the New World.[1] Communistic despotism So far as mere command of human labour went, the communistic despotism of Peru could do things similar in kind, though lesser in degree, to the despotism of the Pharaohs.

This industrial army succeeded, as we have seen, in carrying agriculture to a considerable degree of perfection. The extent to which every available spot of ground was utilized indicates a somewhat dense population, though it must be remembered that much of the area included within the Inca's dominions was wild land unsuitable for cultivation. Agriculture Gardens were carried up the mountain-sides on terraces, as in modern Italy. Mr. Markham says that the finest Sea Island cotton of our day is not superior to the best crops raised

[1] See Rawlinson's *History of Egypt*, vol. i. pp. 182–211. According to Herodotus (ii. 124, 125) the Great Pyramid consumed the labour of 100,000 men for thirty years. Such numbers must be understood with much latitude. The Egyptians had oxen, and, according to Herodotus, made use of inclined planes in working upon the pyramids. Possibly the Peruvians may have been able here and there to utilize the principle of the inclined plane. For some remarks on early Phœnician building, see Brown's *Poseidon*, pp. 21, 27.

under the Incas. The potato and maize crops were also very fine. If Thorfinn Karlsefni and his men had seen Peruvian maize-fields, they would not have fancied that such corn grew wild. As for the Peruvian wools, we are beginning to learn that in comparison with the vicuña all other material for clothing seems both cumbrous and coarse.[1]

The vicuña and the huanacu were the wild animals hunted by the Peruvians, but a very tame affair was this hunting as compared with galloping after the hounds in England. There was no chance for sport; everything in this industrial army must be done to order. Nobody was allowed to kill one of these animals, except at Government the periodical government hunts, in hunts which whole villages, led by their overseers, took part. The people surrounded their game and closed in on it, and then it was methodically disposed of,— some of the beasts released till next time, some shorn and then released, some killed for the table. A strict record of all this was kept on the *quipus* by the census officer, — a thing, says Polo de Ondegardo, "which it would be difficult for me to believe if I had not seen it." [2] The huanacu

[1] The Spaniards were not long in learning the merits of the vicuña's fleece. Blankets made of it were sent to Spain for the bed of Philip II. ; see Garcilasso, lib. vi. cap. i.

[2] Markham's *Rites and Laws of the Yncas*, p. 165. Mr.

wool was divided among the people, but the
vicuña wool was reserved for those of Inca
blood.

Of these wools, as well as of the cottons, fine
cloth was woven and dyed of various hues,[1] and
ornamental tapestries were wrought and embroidered. Gold was obtained with
ease and in great quantity by washing   Arts
the sands of the rivers in the province of Car-
avaya. Blast furnaces were used for smelting
silver. Gold and silver were valued for their
beauty, and reserved for the Inca or for use in
the temples, and dishes, vases, and trinkets innumerable were made of them. But there was
no currency or money of any kind.[2] All trade
was simple barter, but in using scales and esti-
mating certain goods by weight, the Peruvians
were more advanced than the people of Mexico. In their implements of war and husbandry,
which were fashioned in bronze, they were far
superior to the Aztecs. In the pottery, which
was made in great abundance, the superiority
was perhaps less marked. In certain arts and

Darwin has pointed out how the selection of certain of these
animals for slaughter and others for release and further breed-
ing was so managed as to improve the race. *Variation of
Animals and Plants under Domestication*, vol. ii. p. 208.

[1] For the excellent fast vegetable dyes, see Garcilasso,
vol. i. p. 319, Markham's note.

[2] Garcilasso, lib. v. cap. vii.; lib. vi. caps. i., ii.

inventions they had not advanced so far as the people of Mexico ; their *balsas*, or rafts,[1] for example, were rude contrivances compared to the nimble Mexican canoes.

If we compare the culture of ancient Peru, as a whole, with that of the Mexicans and Mayas, we cannot fail to be struck with the contrast. In some points it was further removed from savagery by nearly the full length of an ethnical period. The cardinal points of superiority were the further development of the monogamous General family, the advance from tribal consummary federation toward rudimentary nationality, the progress into a more spiritual form of polytheism with the abandoning of human sacrifices and cannibalism, the domestication of animals and further development of agriculture, the improvement in roads, and the prevailing use of bronze for weapons and tools. This further progress from savagery was, however, attended with some disadvantages. In becoming nationalized, the Inca government had stiffened into despotism,[2] as was sure to be the

[1] Garcilasso, lib. iii. cap. xvi.

[2] As contrasted with the Peruvians, the tribes of Mexico and Central America thus possessed an advantage somewhat analogous to that of the Germans whom Tacitus knew over the Romans of his own time with whom he so suggestively compared them. They retained plasticity, whereas the society

case with all nations formed before the comparatively modern development of the ideas of legal contract and political representation ; and, as we have seen, the peculiar form of this despotism was communistic because it grew up among a people whose ideas of private property were still very imperfectly developed.

In point of humaneness and refinement the people of Peru were unquestionably superior to the Mayas and Mexicans. Their criminal code was severe, and now and then we read of wholesale beheadings for treason, or of prisoners being burned alive ;[1] but in civilized Europe one need go back scarcely a century to find the guillotine busy in Paris, and scarcely more than a century to witness an *auto de fe* in Spain, — not of criminals, but of useful and meritorious free-thinkers. On the whole, for a society in most respects within the middle period of barbarism, for a society less advanced intellectually than the Egyptians of the Old Empire, it would appear that the Inca society was remarkable for mildness and humanity. It

governed by the Incas had become rigid. The greatest of all the inherited advantages which English-speaking people to-day enjoy is the fact that our ancestral Teutonic society retained its tribal mobility and plasticity of organization to so late a period in history that it was able to profit to the fullest extent by Roman civilization without being swamped by Roman imperialism.

Humaneness

[1] Garcilasso, lib. iii. cap. iv.

was not cursed, like Mexico, with the daily spectacle of men and women torn open and cut into pieces. It looked upon such people as the Chibchas as ferocious barbarians, and it would have justly entertained a similar opinion of the people of Uxmal and Tezcuco if it had known anything about them. The pages of Cieza de Leon bear frequent testimony to the clemency and moderation of the Incas in many of their dealings with vanquished peoples; and one point, upon which he speaks emphatically, is quite startling in its unlikeness to what was common in ancient society. Soldiers were forbidden to pillage, under penalty of death, and this rule was enforced.[1]

With regard to intellectual culture, as exhibited in literary production, the Peruvians were at a disadvantage compared to the peoples north of the Isthmus of Darien. The data for a comparison are meagre indeed. There was some written literature, as we have seen, among the

Intellectual culture Mexican and Maya-Quiché peoples, but very little of it remains in a decipherable state. Such of it as is still accessible to the modern reader is, of course, rude and primitive in thought and sentiment. The Nahuatl hymns collected by Dr. Brinton, in his " Rig-Veda Americanus," are quite childlike as compared to the hymns of the great Rig-Veda

[1] Cieza, pt. ii. cap. xxiii.

174

of the Aryans. Of Peruvian thought, as expressed in poetry, we know even less than of Mexican. The Incas had bardic recitals and theatrical exhibitions; and one ancient Inca drama, entitled " Ollanta," has come down to us.[1] It is a love story, with the scene laid in the time of the great Inca Pachacutec; it would make a pleasant scene upon the stage, and is undeniably a pretty poem. We have already mentioned the special class of *amautas*, or " wise men," differentiated from the priesthood, whose business it was to preserve historic traditions and literary compositions. But unfortunately the Peruvian method of recording admitted of no considerable development in such sort of work. It led nowhere. Now and then we see animals, such as starfishes, which have started on a path of development that can lead only a very little way. In that queer spiny radiated structure there are nothing like the possibilities of further evolution that there are in the soft, loosely segmented, and mobile worm; and so the starfish stays where he is, but from the worm come insects and vertebrates. So with their knotted and twisted cords the Peruvians could keep rude records for a time, but in such

---

[1] *Ollanta: an Ancient Ynca Drama.* Translated from the original Quichua by Clements R. Markham, London, 1871 ; later editions are those of Zegarra (Paris, 1878) and Middendorf (Leipsic, 1890) ; the last is the most accurate.

a method there were no future possibilities. One might sooner expect to see systems of higher arithmetic and algebra developed with Roman instead of Arabic numerals, than to see a true literature developed with *quipus* instead of hieroglyphs. Until the Incas had either devised some better method or learned it from other people, their literary period would have had to wait. But the Mexicans, and still more the Mayas, with their hieroglyphics, had started on the road that leads by natural stages to that grand achievement of the human mind, supreme in its endless possibilities, the achievement which more than any other marks the boundary line between barbarism and civilization, between the twilight of archæology and the daylight of history, — the phonetic alphabet, the A B C.

Here we may bring to a close this brief sketch of the Inca society, one of the most curious and instructive subjects to which the student of history can direct his attention. In the next chapter we shall see the elements of weakness in that primitive form of nationality, characterized by conquest with imperfect fusion, well illustrated by the ease with which a handful of Spaniards seized and kept control over the dominions of the Incas.

X

THE CONQUEST OF PERU

THE chain of circumstances that led to the discovery and conquest of Peru, like the chain that led to the conquest of Mexico, had its origin in the island of Hispaniola, and was closely connected with the calamitous work of colonizing the Isthmus of Darien. In July, 1509, Diego Columbus, bringing with him his vice-queen Maria de Toledo, came out to San Domingo, to enter upon the government and colonization of such countries as had been discovered by his father, as well as of such as might be discovered by himself or his appointed captains. Such at least was his own theory of the situation, but the Crown took a different view of it. As we have seen, Diego had already set on foot a lawsuit against the Crown to determine the extent of his rights and privileges, and matters were to come to such a pass that in four years an attempt was to be made to invalidate his father's claim to the discovery of the Pearl Coast. We have already made some mention of that attempt and its failure, in the

Relations of
the Admiral
Diego Co-
lumbus to
the Crown

great judicial inquiry usually known in this connection as the *Probanzas*. The result of that
inquiry was entirely favourable to Columbus,
but anything like practical control over the
affairs of Terra Firma had already been virtually taken out of Diego's hands. We have seen
that the immediate result of the third voyage
of Columbus, in which the rich Pearl Coast was
discovered, was the sending of an expedition by
his enemy Fonseca to the same region. This
was the expedition of 1499, commanded by
Alonso de Ojeda, and from that time forth
Ojeda was closely associated with this coast,
made further explorations there, and was appointed governor of the small island of Coqui-
bacoa. La Cosa and Vespucius, also, who had
been Ojeda's pilots in 1499, did further work
in this neighbourhood. We have seen these two
great navigators, in 1505 and 1507, exploring
the Gulf of Darien and the Atrato River, where
they had hoped to find a passage to the Moluccas. Instead of such a passage they found
gold in the river-beds. After their return we
have seen Vespucius made Pilot Major of Spain,
and La Cosa made "alguazil mayor," or high constable, of a colony about to be founded at Darien.
Now if King Ferdinand had been well disposed
toward Diego Columbus and his claims he would
naturally have entrusted this important enterprise to his uncle Don Bartholomew, about

whose ability and integrity there could be no question. But the relations of the Crown to the Columbus claims made any such ap- Provinces of pointment impossible, and the gov- Terra Firma ernorship was given to the brave but granted to Ojeda and incompetent Ojeda. About the same Nicuesa time Diego de Nicuesa, another court favourite like Ojeda, but better educated and of finer mould, applied for the same position, and King Ferdinand arranged the matter by creating two provinces, one for each favourite. The country between the gulfs of Urabá (Darien) and Maracaibo was to be the province for Ojeda, while the Veragua and Honduras coasts, from the Gulf of Urabá to Cape Gracias á Dios, were assigned to Nicuesa. The former province did not trench upon any territory discovered by Columbus, but the latter was chiefly made up of coasts first visited by him, and the appointment of Nicuesa was hardly less than an affront to the Admiral Diego.

Thus when the joint expedition was getting ready to start from Hispaniola, in the autumn of 1509, everything had been arranged as ingeniously as possible to hinder cordial coöperation. To the rivalry between the two governors was added the dislike felt for both by Diego Columbus. First, the two governors wrangled over the boundary line between their provinces, until La Cosa persuaded them to agree upon the Atrato River. Then came the more important question of supplies. To ensure a steady supply of food, the island of Jamaica was to be placed at the disposal of Ojeda and Nicuesa; but as that was an invasion of the rights of Diego Columbus, he would not consent to it. So they started without any established base of supply, trusting themselves to luck. A sudden arrest for debt detained Nicuesa, so that Ojeda got off about a week before him. Before reaching the Gulf of Urabá, at a place near the site of Cartagena, the rash Ojeda made up his mind to go ashore and catch a few slaves to be sent over to Hispaniola in payment for food. Against the advice of the veteran La Cosa he insisted upon going, with about seventy men, and La Cosa went with him to screen him from the effects of such hardihood, for he had found out that the Indians in that region used poisoned arrows. A few drops of poison sometimes quite neutralized the advantages of armour and crossbows and gunpowder. La Cosa and all the other Spaniards save two were slain; one of these two was Ojeda, who was picked up four or five days later and carried aboard ship just in time to save him from death by starvation. Nicuesa now arrived upon the scene with his ships, and, forgetting past quarrels, treated his unfortunate rival with much

Starting of the expeditions

Death of La Cosa

180

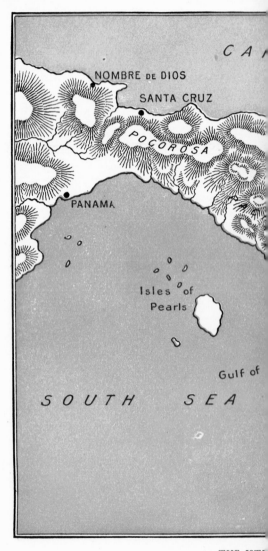

THE IST

CARIBBEAN SEA

SAN SEBASTIAN

SANTA MARIA DEL DARIEN

ACLA

CARETA

GRE

QUAREQUA

UMACO

quel

BIRU

Gulf
of
Uraba

DABAYBE

DARIEN

kindness and courtesy. After he had passed by, Ojeda stopped at the entrance to the Gulf of Urabá and began to build a rude town there which he called San Sebastian. The proceedings were soon checked by famine, and as a piratical fellow named Talavera happened to come along in a ship which he had stolen, Ojeda concluded to embark with him and hurry over to Hispaniola in quest of supplies and reinforcements. His party kept their ships, and it was agreed that if Ojeda should not return within fifty days they might break up the expedition and go wherever they liked. So Ojeda departed, leaving in temporary command an Estremaduran named Francisco Pizarro, of whom we shall have more to say.

Famine

The unfortunate commander never returned. After a voyage anything but agreeable in company with Talavera's ruffians, the stolen ship was wrecked on the coast of Cuba. In course of time Ojeda, sadly the worse for wear, got back to San Domingo, but long before that time his party had been scattered, and he had no means of making a fresh start. He died at San Domingo in abject misery, in 1515.

Death of Ojeda

While the shipwrecked Ojeda was starving on the coast of Cuba, a couple of ships, with horses, food, and ammunition, started from San Domingo to go to the relief of San Sebastian.

The commander was a lawyer, the Bachelor Martin Fernandez de Enciso, afterwards distin-guished as a historian and geogra-pher.[1] He was a kind of partner in Ojeda's enterprise, having invested some money in it. He was in many respects an estimable person, but hardly fitted for the work to which he had put his hand, for he was made of red tape, without a particle of tact about him. Among the barrels in Enciso's ship was one that contained neither bread nor gunpowder, but a handsome and penniless young cavalier who had contrived this way of escaping from his creditors. This was Vasco Nuñez de Balboa, who in spite of this undig-nified introduction is by far the most attractive figure among the Spanish adventurers of that time. After the vessel had got well out to sea Balboa showed himself, much to the disgust of Enciso, who could not abide such irregular pro-ceedings. He scolded Vasco Nuñez roundly, and was with some difficulty dissuaded from set-ting him ashore on a small desert island,—which apparently would not have been in the eyes of our man of red tape an irregular pro-ceeding! Arriving upon the site of Cartagena,

Expedition of Enciso

Appearance of Balboa

[1] His valuable work *Suma de Geografía, que trata de todas las partidas y provincias del mundo, en especial de las Indias,* was published at Seville in 1519. There were later editions in 1530 and 1546. It is now excessively rare.

Enciso met Pizarro, with the haggard remnant of Ojeda's party in a small brigantine. What business had these men here? thought this rigid and rigorous Enciso; they must be deserters and had better be seized at once and put in irons. With much ado they convinced him of the truth of their story. As the fifty days had expired without news of Ojeda, they had abandoned the enterprise. But now they were ready to follow Enciso, and all thus proceeded amicably together to the Gulf of Urabá. After some mishaps Balboa, who had formerly been on that coast with Bastidas and La Cosa, advised the party to choose the western shore of the gulf for their settlement, inasmuch as the Indians on that side did not use poisoned arrows. This sound advice was adopted, and the building of the town of Santa Maria del Darien was begun.

Enciso's overbearing temper soon proved too much for his followers and they resolved to depose him, but could not agree upon a successor. By crossing the gulf they had entered Nicuesa's province, and some thought that he ought therefore to become their commander, while some favoured Balboa, and a few remained loyal to Enciso. It was at length decided to elect Nicuesa, and until he should come Balboa remained the leading spirit of the little colony.

Enciso deposed by his men

It was now December, 1510. Nicuesa's story

183

had been an appalling record of famine and mutiny. Out of more than 700 men who had left
Hispaniola with him thirteen months
before, not more than 70 remained
alive at the little blockhouse which
they had built and called Nombre de Dios.
The Spanish adventurers in America need all
the allowances that charity can make for them,
and in rehearsing their deeds one is sometimes
led to reflect that their prolonged sufferings in
the wilderness must have tended to make them
as savage as wolves.[1] One sees this illustrated
in the melancholy fate of poor Nicuesa. That
kind-hearted gentleman had become maddened
by hardship until his harshness began to alarm
his men. His friend Colmenares, bringing food
from Hispaniola and a message of invitation
from the men at Darien, found him, " of all
lyuynge men most infortunate, in maner dryed
vppe with extreeme hunger, fylthye and horrible to beholde, with onely three score men . . .
lefte alyve of seven hundreth. They al seemed

---

1 " The more experience and insight I obtain into human
nature, the more convinced do I become that the greater portion of a man is purely animal. Fully and regularly fed, he
is a being capable of being coaxed or coerced to exertion of
any kind, love and fear sway him easily, he is not averse to
labour however severe ; but when starved it is well to keep
in mind the motto ' Cave Canem,' for a starving lion over
a raw morsel of beef is not so ferocious or so ready to take
offence." Stanley, *In Darkest Africa*, vol. i. p. 270.

to hym soo miserable, that he noo less lamented theyr case than yf he had founde them deade." [1] As soon as they had recovered strength enough to move about, they started in two caravels for Darien. Nicuesa's un- wonted harshness continued, and he was heard to utter a threat of confiscat- ing the gold which the men of Darien had found within his territory. This foolish speech sealed his fate. The other caravel, reaching Darien be- fore his own, warned the party there against him, and when he arrived they would not let him come ashore. With seventeen comrades left who would not desert him, the unfortunate Nicuesa put out to sea and was never heard of again.

Cruel treatment of Nicuesa by the men of Darien

This affair left Vasco Nuñez in undisputed command at Darien, and as he was thus the most conspicuous gainer from it, there was an opportunity for his enemies to cast upon him the blame for the cruel treatment of Nicuesa. On this grave charge, how- ever, he was afterward tried and ac- quitted by an unfriendly tribunal, and it seems clear that without opposing the decision not to receive Nicuesa as commander he tried his best to save him from harm. But his conduct to- ward the Bachelor Enciso was the very height of folly. Doubtless he found that martinet un- endurable, but what could be more unwise than

Balboa left in undisputed command

[1] *Decades of the Newe Worlde,* dec. ii. lib. iii.

first to imprison him and then to set him free on condition of leaving the colony in the first available ship? The angry Enciso went home to Spain and complained at court. Vasco Nuñez indeed tried to provide against such an adverse influence by sending his friend Zamudio to talk with King Ferdinand; but the trained advocate Enciso proved a better talker than Zamudio.

Balboa forthwith proceeded to explore the isthmus. He made an alliance with the chief Careta, who gave him his daughter in marriage. Then he added to the alliance a powerful chief named Comogre, whose town he visited with some of his men. This, it will be observed, was in 1512, before any rumour of the existence of Mexico had reached the ears of the Spaniards, and they were agreeably surprised at the sight of the house in which Comogre received them, which was much finer than any that they had hitherto beheld, and seemed to indicate that at length they were approaching the confines of Asiatic civilization. It was 150 paces in length by 80 feet in breadth, with finely wrought floors and ceiling, and, besides granaries, cellars, and living rooms, contained a kind of chapel where the bodies of deceased members of the clan were preserved as mummies.[1] The chief gave the Spaniards a large quantity of gold and seventy

[1] Peter Martyr, *De Orbe Novo*, Alcalá, 1516, dec. ii. lib. iii.

slaves. These Indians knew nothing of gold as a purchasing medium, but made it into trinkets, and they were sorely mystified at seeing the Spaniards melt it into bars or ingots, which they weighed with scales. A dispute, or, as Eden calls it, a "brabbling," arose among the Spaniards as they were weighing and dividing this gold. Then a son of Comogre got up and told the visitors that if they set so much value on this yellow stuff as to quarrel about it they had better go to a country where they could get more than enough for all. Over across the sierras there was a great sea, and far to the southward on the shore of this sea there was a land where gold was so plentiful that people used it instead of pottery for their bowls and cups. This was the first distinct and undoubted mention of the country of the Incas. Vasco Nuñez sent news of this speech to the Spanish court, accompanied by the king's share of the gold, one fifth of the amount ; but unfortunately the vessel was wrecked in the Caribbean Sea, and neither message nor gold found its way to King Ferdinand. It was not until the next spring that messengers reached the Spanish court, and then it was learned that Enciso had the king's ear, and legal proceedings against Vasco Nuñez were about to be begun.

Soon afterward, our adventurer received from the government in Hispaniola the appointment of captain-general over Darien. His satisfaction, however, was sadly clouded by the news from Spain, and he determined at once to cross the sierra, in the hope of finding the great sea and thus establishing a claim to favourable treatment. There was no use in waiting for reinforcements, for the same ship that brought fresh troops might bring an order for his dismissal and arrest. Early in September, 1513, accordingly, Balboa started across the isthmus with about 200 men and a small pack of bloodhounds. From Careta's territory he entered that of a cacique named Quarequa, who undertook to oppose his advance through that difficult country. But no sooner did it come to fighting than the Indians fled in wild terror from enemies who wielded thunder and lightning. Capturing some of these Indians and winning their confidence by kind treatment, Balboa used them as guides through the mountains. On the 25th of September, from one of the boldest summits in Quarequa's country, Balboa looked down upon the waste of waters which was afterwards shown to be the greatest ocean upon the globe.[1]

Discovery of the Pacific Ocean

Four more days of arduous toil brought the Spaniards down from the mountains to the shore

[1] Keats in his beautiful poem inadvertently puts Cortes in place of Balboa.

of the gulf which, because they reached it on Michaelmas, they named San Miguel. After launching out upon this rough sea in a small flotilla of canoes, and navigating a portion of it at the imminent risk of perishing in an equinoctial gale, Vasco Nuñez effected a landing upon its northern shore in the country of the chieftain Tumaco, whom he first defeated and then by kind treatment won his friendship. Tumaco confirmed the story of a rich empire far to the south, and produced a clay figure of a llama in illustration of some of his statements.

Further news of the golden kingdom

It was now high time to return to Darien with the tidings of what had been accomplished. Vasco Nuñez arrived there early in January, 1514, but too late for his achievement to effect such a result as he had hoped for. He might not unreasonably have expected to be confirmed in his governorship of the isthmus. But stories of the golden kingdom mentioned by Comogre's son had already wrought their effect in Spain. The victories of the French in Italy under the brilliant Gaston de Foix had alarmed King Ferdinand; an army for Italy had been collected and the command given to Gonsalvo de Córdova. But before this expedition started news came of the retreat of the French, and the king ordered Gonsalvo to disband his

Affairs in Spain

men.[1] Many of the gay cavaliers who had enlisted with fiery enthusiasm under the Great
Captain were thus thrown out of occupation, to
their intense disgust; when all at once there
came to Spain the report of an unknown sea
beyond the Terra Firma, and of a kingdom
abounding in wealth. There ensued one of the
bursts of excitement so common in that age of
marvels, and which the reading of Don Quixote
enables one to appreciate. On the word of an
unknown Indian youth, before it had been even
partially confirmed by Balboa's discovery of
the sea, these cavaliers were at once ready to
cross the Atlantic. If they were not to go to
Italy they would seek adventures in the Indies.
A fleet was accordingly fitted out, with accom-
modations for 1200 men, but at least 1500 contrived to embark. The admiral of the fleet and

Pedrarias   new governor of Terra Firma was a
Dávila   man over seventy years of age, named
Pedrarias Dávila, one of those two-legged tigers
of whom Spain had so many at that time. He
was a favourite at court, and his wife was a niece
of that Marchioness of Moya who had been the
friend of Queen Isabella and of Columbus.
For the next sixteen years Pedrarias was a leading figure in the Indies, and when he died the
historian Oviedo, in a passage of surpassing

[1] *Chronica del Gran Capitan*, lib. iii. cap. vii.; Mariana,
Historia de España, lib. xxx. cap. xiv.

quaintness, tried to compute how many souls of his murdered victims he would be called upon to confront at the Day of Judgment.[1] Oviedo was inclined to put the figure at 2,000,000. If we were to strike off a couple of ciphers, we should have a figure quite within the limits of credibility, and sufficiently terrible. It is hardly necessary to add that this green-eyed, pitiless, perfidious old wretch was an especial pet of Bishop Fonseca.

The arrival of this large force in Darien was the beginning of a self-sustaining colony. The collection of rude cabins called Santa Maria del Darien was made a "cathedral city," and Juan de Quevedo was appointed bishop. Gonsalvo Hernandez de Oviedo, afterwards famous as a historian, came out as inspector-general of the new colony. Gaspar de Espinosa was chief judge, and Enciso returned to the scene as chief con-stable. His first business was to arrest Vasco Nuñez, who was tried on various charges be-fore Espinosa, but was presently acquitted and set free. The news of his discovery and the arguments of admiring friends had begun to win favour for him at the Spanish court. For more

[1] Oviedo, *Historia de las Indias*, xxix. 34. This historian cherished a personal grudge against Pedrarias ; but all the other best authorities — Peter Martyr, Las Casas, Andagoya, Ben-zoni, Remesal — are in substantial agreement as to his atro-cious character.

than two years Vasco Nuñez contrived to avoid
a serious quarrel with the governor, whose jeal-

Jealousy be-
tween Pedra-
rias and Bal-
boa
ousy of him was intense, and made
all the more so by the comparisons
which men could not help drawing between the two. The policy of Pedrarias toward
the Indian tribes was the ordinary one of murder and plunder; in a few instances he chose
incompetent lieutenants who were badly defeated by the Indians; once he was defeated in
person; and such results could not but be contrasted with those which had attended the more
humane, honest, and sagacious management of
Balboa. In October, 1515, the latter wrote to
the king, complaining of the governor's cruel
conduct and its effect in needlessly alienating
the Indians; and it is impossible to read that
letter to-day [1] and not feel that Vasco Nuñez,
with all his faults, was a wise and true-hearted
man, with ample warrant for every word that he
said. But the king could not very well read
such a letter without some echoes of it finding
their way back to the New World. Matters grew
so stormy that Juan de Quevedo, the Bishop
of Darien, who was friendly to Balboa, thought
it necessary to negotiate a kind of treaty between him and the governor. Balboa was to be
sent, with a proper force, to visit the golden

[1] Balboa, *Carta dirigida al Rey*, 16 Octubre, 1515, in
Navarrete, *Coleccion de viages*, iii. 375.

kingdom at the South, and the bishop proposed to cement the alliance by a betrothal between Balboa and the daughter of Pedrarias. Doubtless the worthy clergyman, like most white men of his time, thought that an Indian wife counted for nothing. Vasco Nuñez did not think so. He was devotedly fond of the Indian girl and she of him, but as the other young lady was in Spain and her father in no great haste about the matter, Vasco Nuñez assented to this article in the treaty. Then he went off to Acla, a newly founded port on the Atlantic side of the isthmus, to engage in the herculean task of taking his ships piecemeal across the sierra to the point where they were to be put together and launched on the Pacific.[1] After many months of toil four ships, the first European keels to plough the great " Sea of the South," were ready to weigh anchor, and 300 men were ready to embark. Nothing was wanted but a little iron and pitch,

An expedition prepared to go in search of the golden kingdom

---

[1] Bishop Quevedo afterward reported to the Emperor Charles V. that "more than 500 Indians " perished under the hardships of this terrible undertaking ; but Quevedo's secretary told Las Casas that the real number of deaths was not less than 2000, a figure which the bishop refrained from stating, through fear of being accused of exaggeration. See Las Casas, *Historia de las Indias*, iv. 233. At the same time, says Las Casas, Balboa was no mere slave-driver. Whenever the hardest work was to be done he was foremost, taking hold with his own hands and everywhere aiding and cheering.

and the delay thus caused was to bring swift ruin upon Vasco Nuñez.

A rumour had just arrived that the king had superseded old Pedrarias and appointed a new governor for the Terra Firma. The rumour was not so much false as premature, for the complaints against Pedrarias had wrought some effect at court, and the appointment of Lope de Sosa was made in the course of the next year. This premature rumour had serious consequences. Now that things had advanced so far, Balboa was more disturbed than pleased, for being used to the frying pan he preferred it to the fire; a new governor might interfere and prevent his departure, and if it were not for that iron and pitch it would be prudent to sail at once. But since these articles were much wanted, let the small party sent back for them to Acla use some discretion and begin by ascertaining how much or how little truth there might be in the rumours. If the new governor should have arrived, perhaps it might be best to return as quietly and quickly as possible; but if Pedrarias should still be in power, then it were best to go in boldly and ask for the iron and pitch. Thus Balboa talked with two friends one summer evening on the rude veranda of a cabin which he

A fatal conversation had used for headquarters while the arduous shipbuilding had been going on. So far as Pedrarias was concerned, there does

not seem to have been a word of treason in the
conversation, but while they were talking in an
undertone it began to rain, and a sentinel, pacing
near headquarters, came up under the eaves for
shelter, and listened. From the fragments which
reached his ears he concluded that Balboa was
intending to throw off his allegiance to Pedrarias and set up a new government for himself;
and so, translating his crude inferences into
facts, this fellow contrived to send information
to La Puente, the treasurer at Acla, a man with
whom Vasco Nuñez had once had a little dispute about some money.

Now it happened that a man named Andres
Garavito,[1] having become enamoured of Balboa's Indian wife, had made overtures which
were indignantly repulsed by the woman, and
called forth stern words of warning from Vasco
Nuñez. The wretched Garavito thereupon set
out to compass Balboa's death. Having been
sent on some business to Acla, he told Pedrarias
that Balboa never meant to marry his daughter,
inasmuch as he cared for no one but the Indian
woman; moreover he was now about to go off
in his ships to the golden kingdom and gain

---

[1] The name is often written *Garabito*. The habitual confusion of these two labials in the Spanish language long ago
called forth from Julius Scaliger the epigram : —

> Haud temere antiquas Vasconia voces
> Cui nihil est aliud vivere quam bibere.
>
> *De Causis Linguæ Latinæ*, i. 14.

wealth in his own behoof with which to with-
stand and ruin Pedrarias. While the old man
Garavito's
treachery was cursing and raving over this story,
the party coming for iron and pitch
halted on the edge of the forest, and sent one
of their number into the town after nightfall to
make inquiries. It was this man's luck to be
arrested as a spy, but he sent word to his comrades, and they, coming into town, protested
their innocence so strongly and stated the true
object of their visit so clearly that the angry
governor was more than half convinced, when
all at once the treasurer La Puente came to see
him and told what he had heard from the sentinel. This sealed the fate of Vasco Nuñez.
The governor sent him a crafty letter, couched
in terms of friendship, and asking him to return
to Acla before sailing, as there were business
matters in which he needed advice. The un-
suspecting Balboa set forth at once to recross
the sierra. We are told that his horoscope had
once been taken by a Venetian astrologer, who
said that if he were ever to behold a certain
planet in a certain quarter of the heavens it
would mean that he was in sore peril, but if he
should escape that danger he would become the
greatest lord in all the Indies. And there is a
legend that the star now appeared one evening
to Vasco Nuñez, whereupon he told his attendants about the prophecy and mocked at it.

But as he drew near to Acla there came out a company of soldiers to arrest him, and the captain of this company was Francisco Pizarro, one of his old comrades who had served under him ever since the time when the lawyer Enciso was deposed from command. " How is this, Francisco Pizarro ? " said Balboa ; " it is not thus that thou wert wont to come forth to meet me." But he offered no resistance, and when put upon his trial he simply asked why, if he had really been meditating treason and deser- Balboa put tion, he should have come back so to death by promptly when called. A guilty man Pedrarias would have staid away. But it was no use talking.[1] The governor had made up his mind, and before the sun went down Vasco Nuñez and four of his friends had been tried, condemned, and beheaded.[2]

[1] "Valboa con giuramento negò, dicendo, che inquanto toccaua alla informatione che contra lui s' era fatta di solleuargli la gente che l' era à torto, e falsamente accusato, e che considerasse bene quello che faceua, e se lui havesse tal cosa tentata, non saria venuto alla presentia sua, e similmente del resto, si difese il meglio che puote ; ma dove regnano le forze, poco gioua defendersi con la ragione." Benzoni, *Historia del Mondo Nuovo*, i. 51, Venice, 1572.

[2] In the accounts of the Garavito treachery as given by Oviedo and Herrera, there is some confusion. Oviedo represents Garavito as having been arrested by Pedrarias and telling his base story in order to turn the governor's wrath away from himself. But as Sir Arthur Helps (*Spanish Conquest*, vol. i. p. 432) has pointed out, the discrepancy seems to have

Thus perished in the forty-second year of his age the man who but for that trifle of iron and pitch would probably have been the conqueror of Peru. It was a pity that such work should not have fallen into his hands, for when at length it was done, it was by men far inferior to him in character and calibre. One cannot but wish that he might have gone on his way like Cortes, and worked out the rest of his contemplated career in accordance with the genius that was in him. That bright attractive figure and its sad fate can never fail to arrest the attention and detain the steps of the historian as he passes by. Quite possibly the romantic character of the story may have thrown something of a glamour about the person of the victim, so that unconsciously we tend to emphasize his merits while we touch lightly upon his faults. But after all, this effect is no more than that which his personality wrought upon the minds of contemporary witnesses, who were unanimous in their expressions of esteem for Balboa

arisen from confounding Andres Garavito with his brother Francisco, who was one of the company sent for the iron and pitch and was faithful to Vasco Nuñez. The man who was arrested as a spy seems to have been Luis Botello, one of the four friends who were executed with Vasco Nuñez. See Pascual de Andagoya, *Relacion*, in Navarrete, *Coleccion de viages y descubrimientos*, iii. 405.

and of condemnation for the manner of his taking off.

Seven years passed before the work of discovering the golden kingdom was again seriously taken up. It was work of almost insuperable difficulty in the absence of a base of operations upon the Pacific coast of the isthmus; and, as we shall see, men's attention was distracted by the question as to the Molucca Islands. During this interval of seven years the conquest of Mexico was begun and completed, so far as the towns once tributary to the Aztec Confederacy were concerned. By 1524 the time had arrived when the laurels of Cortes would not allow other knights-errant to sleep, and then Balboa's enterprise was taken up by his old comrade Francisco Pizarro.

An interval

This man, like Cortes and Balboa, was a native of the province of Estremadura. He was an illegitimate son of Gonzalo Pizarro, an officer of good family, who had served in Italy under the Great Captain. As the mother of Cortes was a Pizarro, it has been supposed that there was relationship between the two families. Francisco Pizarro, whose mother was a young woman of humble station, was born somewhere between 1470 and 1478. Unlike Cortes, who had some scant allowance of university education, Pizarro had no school-

Francisco Pizarro

ing at all, and never learned to write his own name. His occupation in youth seems to have been that of a swineherd, though he may, according to one doubtful tradition, have accompanied his father in one or more Italian campaigns. His first distinct appearance in history was in Ojeda's expedition in 1509, when he was left in command of the starving party at San Sebastian, to await the arrival of the succours brought by Enciso. He served under Balboa for several years, was with that commander when he first saw the great South Sea, and happened — as we have seen — to be the officer sent out by Pedrarias to arrest him.

In 1515, two years before Balboa's fall, Pizarro took part in an expedition under Gaspar de Morales, sent by Pedrarias to explore the coasts of the Gulf of San Miguel. The expedition, as usual, was characterized by wonderful endurance of hardship on the part of the Spaniards and by fiendish cruelty toward the Indians. They invaded the territory of a warlike chief named Birú, on the southern shore of the gulf, and met with such a hot reception that, although victorious, they did not care to risk a second fight, but retreated to the isthmus. It was some years before the Spaniards got so far south again, and when they had occasion to refer to the unvisited territory beyond the Gulf of San Miguel they fell into

Origin of the name "Peru"

a habit of speaking of it as the *Birú* or *Perú* country. The golden kingdom, about which there had been so much talk, was said to be somewhere upon that coast, and in such wise it seems to have received its modern name.[1] Not long after Balboa's death Pedrarias learned that Lope de Sosa had at length been appointed governor in his place. It was unwelcome news. The old man had good reason to fear the result of an examination into his conduct. It might be held that in executing Balboa without allowing an appeal to the Crown he had exceeded his powers, and the Spanish court sometimes showed itself quite jealous of such encroachments upon its royal prerogative of revision and pardon. There were, moreover, numerous instances of judicial robbery and murder that could easily be brought home to their perpetrator. Accordingly Pedrarias thought it wise to put the mountains between himself and the Atlantic coast, so that in case of necessity he might do just what he had beheaded Vasco Nuñez for doing, — quit the dangerous neighbourhood and set up somewhere for himself.

Lope de Sosa appointed to supersede Pedrarias

This prudent resolve led to the founding of Panama by Pedrarias in August, 1519. Later

---

[1] See Andagoya's *Narrative,* translated by Markham, London, 1865, p. 42 ; also Winsor, *Narr. and Crit. Hist.,* ii. 505.

in the same year the opposite port of Nombre de Dios was founded, and a rude road through the wilderness, connecting these two places, was begun. When Lope de Sosa arrived at Darien in May, 1520, with 300 men, Pedrarias happened to be on the spot, but was favoured with one of those inscrutable providences that are so apt to come to the rescue of such creatures. Before setting foot on shore the new governor was suddenly taken sick and died in his cabin. This left Pedrarias in office. The newly arrived *alcalde*, before whom his examination was to take place, published notices and summonses in due form for thirty days; but no man was hardy enough to enter complaint against him so long as he still remained invested with the insignia of power. The crafty old governor could thus look on smiling while a certificate that no one accused him was despatched on its way to Spain. Then he retired to Panama, which forthwith became the base for operations along the Pacific coast.

Sudden death of Lope de Sosa

This stroke of fortune gave Pedrarias a new lease of undisputed power for nearly seven years. Meanwhile, as the judge Espinosa was involved along with him in the risk attendant upon the case of Balboa, he had sent that pearl of magistrates to take command of Balboa's little fleet and therein seek safety in a fresh voyage of discovery. As Magel-

Espinosa's voyage in Balboa's ships

lan's voyage had not yet been made and the existence of a broad ocean south and west of the Isthmus of Darien was still unknown,[1] the Spaniards upon the isthmus still supposed themselves to be either in eastern Asia or at no great distance from that continent; and accordingly Espinosa, instead of sailing southward in search of the golden kingdom, turned his prows westward, apparently in the hope of settling the vexed question as to the Spice Islands. This would have required a voyage of nearly 11,000 English miles. After accomplishing some 500 miles, as far as Cape Blanco, in what is now the state of Costa Rica, Espinosa returned to the isthmus late in 1519.

Just at that time the controversy over the Moluccas was occupying a foremost place in the public attention. It was on the 10th of August, 1519, that Magellan started on his epoch-making voyage. Earlier in that year one   Gil Gonzalez of Balboa's pilots, Andres Niño, was   Dávila at the Spanish court, urging that the ships of his late commander might be sent to find the Spice Islands. On the 18th of June a royal order was issued, authorizing such an expedition and entrusting the command of it to Gil Gonzalez Dávila, a man of high reputation for ability and integrity.

[1] It must be remembered that Balboa could not see across the ocean.

How fortunate it was for Magellan that his theory of the situation led him far away to the southward, subject indeed to trials as hard as ever man encountered, but safe from the wretched intrigues and savage conflicts of authority that were raging in Central America! Had he chosen the route of Gil Gonzalez he would have begun by encountering obstacles more vexatious, if not more insuperable, than those of the lonely and barren sea. When Gil Gonzalez arrived at Acla in the spring of 1520 and demanded the ships that had been Balboa's, Pedrarias refused to give them up. The death of Lope de Sosa confirmed the old man in this contumacy; so that nothing was left for Gil Gonzalez but to build and equip ships for himself. A flotilla, constructed with incredible toil, was destroyed by worms and weather. The dauntless Gil Gonzalez built a second, consisting of four small vessels, and early in 1522 he set sail for the coveted Moluccas. After eighteen months he returned to Panama, loaded with gold, after having discovered the coast of Nicaragua as far as the bay of Fonseca. As he crossed the isthmus, Pedrarias, in a frenzy of greed, Troubles of sent officers to arrest him, but he Gil Gonzalez eluded them and got safely to Hispaniola. There he was authorized to return and take possession of Nicaragua. This time he approached it from the north by way of the Honduras coast, in order to avoid the isthmus and its dangerous governor. But among the vices of Pedrarias listlessness and sloth were not included. He laid claim to Nicaragua by reason of the prior voyage of Espinosa, and had already despatched Francisco Hernandez de Córdova,[1] with a considerable force, to occupy that country. Córdova's second in command was Fernando de Soto, a young man whom we shall meet again more than once in the course of our story. Gil Gonzalez, marching down from the north, encountered Soto and defeated him, but was afterwards obliged to retire before Córdova's superior force. Retreating into Honduras, Gil Gonzalez was captured by Cristóval de Olid, whom Cortes had sent from Mexico to occupy that country. A wild scramble ensued, — every man for himself and the devil take the hindmost. Córdova threw off his allegiance to Pedrarias, but in an incredibly short time that alert octogenarian had come to Nicaragua and the severed head of the insubordinate lieutenant, thrust aloft upon a pole, was baking in the sun. Olid threw off his allegiance to Cortes, and was presently assassinated, probably with the complicity of Gil Gonzalez, who forthwith tried to

---

[1] He must not be confounded with his namesake Francisco Hernandez de Córdova, the discoverer of Yucatan, mentioned above, p. 30. The latter, it will be remembered, died of his wounds on returning from his ill-starred voyage in 1517.

come to an understanding with the conqueror of Mexico as to the boundary between their respective provinces. At this juncture Gil Gonzalez was seized by some of Olid's friends and sent to Spain to be tried for murder. Arriving at Seville in 1526, the strength of this much-enduring man suddenly gave way, and he died of hardship and grief.

His death

The voyage of Magellan, revealing the breadth of the ocean between America and Asia, destroyed the illusion as to the nearness of the Moluccas; and the discovery of Nicaragua convinced the Spaniards on the Isthmus of Darien that there was no use in sending expeditions to the westward, inasmuch as the way was closed and the ground preoccupied by the conquerors of Mexico. Their attention was thus turned decisively to the southward, whence fresh rumours of the wealth of the Incas had lately reached their ears. In 1522 Pascual de Andagoya crossed the Gulf of San Miguel and gathered much information concerning the golden kingdom. A voyage of discovery to the southward was projected, and as Andagoya was completely disabled by an attack of acute rheumatism, Pizarro formed a partnership with a couple of his friends, Almagro and Luque, and Pedrarias entrusted to them the enterprise. Diego Almagro, a man of unknown parentage, was probably not less than

Attention again turned to the golden kingdom

fifty years old. Of fiery but generous disposition, he had the gift of attaching men to his fortunes, but there is little to be said in praise of his intelligence or his character. As compared with Cortes and Balboa, or with the humane and virtuous Andagoya, both Pizarro and Almagro were men of low type. The third partner, Fernando de Luque, a clergyman, at Panama, was associated in the enterprise as a kind of financial agent, contributing funds on his own account and also on that of the judge Espinosa.

The distance to the land of the Incas was much greater than had been supposed, and the first expedition, which started in 1524, returned in a very dilapidated state, having proceeded as far as the mouth of the river San Juan, scarcely one third of the way to Tumbez. On the second expedition, in 1526, Pizarro landed most of his men at the San Juan, while he sent his pilot Bartholomew Ruiz forward in one of the two ships, and Almagro in the other went back to Panama for reinforcements and provisions. Ruiz, after crossing the equator[1] and

Pizarro and Almagro start in search of the golden kingdom

---

[1] In Mr. Markham's chapter on the Conquest of Peru in Winsor's *Narrative and Critical History*, vol. ii. p. 507, Ruiz is said to have been "the first European to cross the equator on the Pacific Ocean." Magellan had crossed it five years before from south to north. *Aliquando dormitat bonus Homerus.*

coming within sight of the snow-clad summit of Chimborazo, returned to Pizarro with some native Peruvians whom he had captured on a sailing-raft. The story of the grandeur of the Inca kingdom was confirmed afresh by these men.

These things were going on while Pedrarias was wielding his headsman's axe in Nicaragua. Death of Pedrarias About this time he was really deposed from his government at Panama, but by dint of skilful chicanery he succeeded in keeping possession of Nicaragua for four years more, committing cruelties worthy of Nero, until his baleful career was ended by a natural death in 1530.

Having obtained from the new governor, Pedro de los Rios, fresh men and supplies, Almagro returned to the San Juan, where he found his comrades nearly dead with hunger. Explorers and military men will all agree that it is not easy to carry on operations at a distance of a thousand miles from one's base. In those dreary expeditions each step in advance necessitated a step backward, and the discouragement must have been hard to endure. On the third start the adventurers coasted nearly down to the equator and were finding more frequent symptoms of civilization upon the shores they passed, when at length it became necessary to send back again to Panama. Again Pizarro halted, this time upon the little island of Gallo, until his partner should return. After many weeks of misery spent under the drenching tropical rain, the starving men descried a white sail in the offing; but it was not Almagro. The governor, disgusted at such a prolonged wild-goose chase, had detained that commander, and sent a ship with strict orders to bring back Pizarro and all his men. For the most part the weary creatures had lost heart for their work, and were eager to go. But the dog- *The scene at Gallo* ged Pizarro, whose resolution had kept stiffening with each breath of adversity, refused to budge. Drawing an east and west line upon the sandy beach with the point of his long sword, he briefly observed that to the south of that line lay danger and glory, to the north of it ease and safety; and, calling upon his men to choose each for himself, he stepped across. Sixteen staunch men followed their commander;[1]

[1] The names of the sixteen have been preserved, and may be found, with brief biographical notices, in Winsor, *op. cit.* ii. 510. Among them, fortunately, was the daring and skilful pilot Ruiz. A second was the Cretan artillery officer, Pedro de Candia, whose son was afterwards, at Cuzco, a schoolmate of Garcilasso de la Vega, the historian. Garcilasso relates the incident with much precision of detail. Sir Arthur Helps is inclined to dismiss it as theatrical and improbable. Perhaps he would regard Pedro de Candia's testimony as worthless anyway, in view of the old adage Κρῆτες ἀεὶ ψεῦσται. Seriously, however, the evidence (including that of

the rest embarked and went on their way. After they had gone Pizarro and his comrades made a raft and paddled to the island of Gorgona, where they lived on such shell-fish as they could find upon the shore, and now and then shot a passing bird.

When the ship arrived at Panama without them, Los Rios declared that he would leave such foolhardy creatures to their fate; but he was presently persuaded to send another ship, which found Pizarro and his party after they Discovery of had staid seven months upon Gor-Peru gona. The skill of the pilot Ruiz now came into play, and in this little ship the party made a voyage of discovery, landed at Tumbez, and admired the arts and wealth of one of the most important of the Inca's cities. Thence they continued coasting beyond the site of Trujillo, more than 600 miles south of the equator, when, having seen enough to convince them that they had actually found the golden king-

Pizarro's secretary Xeres) seems to be very good indeed, and as for the melodramatic character of the story, it must be borne in mind that the sixteenth century was a theatrical age, *i. e.* the sober realities of that time are theatrical material for our own. It is interesting and curious to see how differently Mr. Prescott regards Pizarro's act : " He announced his own purpose in a laconic but decided manner, characteristic of a man more accustomed to act than to talk, and well calculated to make an impression on his rough followers." *Conquest of Peru*, book ii. chap. iv.

dom, they returned to Panama, carrying with them live llamas, fine garments of vicuña wool, curiously wrought vases of gold and silver, and two or three young Peruvians to be taught to speak Spanish and serve as interpreters.

Enough had now been ascertained to make it desirable for Pizarro to go to Spain and put the enterprise upon a more independent footing. On his arrival at Seville in the summer of 1528, it was his luck to encounter the lawyer Enciso, who straightway clapped him into jail *Pizarro's visit* for a small debt which dated from the *to Spain* founding of Darien some eighteen years before. But the discoverer of Peru was now in high favour at court; so the man of red tape was snubbed, and Pizarro went on to Toledo to pay his respects to the emperor. The story of his romantic adventures made him the hero of the hour. He was ennobled by letters patent, and so were the comrades who had crossed the line with him at Gallo. He was appointed captain-general and *adelantado* of Peru, titles which he was to make good by conquering that country for thrifty Charles V.; and so in 1530 he returned to Panama, taking with him his four brothers and a small party of enthusiastic followers.

Of all the brothers Fernando was the eldest and the only legitimate son of his father. His character has perhaps suffered somewhat at the hands of historians through the sympathy that has been generally felt for the misfortunes of his enemy, the "under dog," Almagro. Fernando Pizarro was surely the ablest and most intelligent of the family. He had received a good education. To say that he was not more

The Pizarro brothers

harsh or unscrupulous than his brethren is faint commendation; but there were times when he showed signal clemency. Gonzalo and Juan Pizarro were full brothers of Francisco, but much younger; Martinez de Alcántara was son of the same frail mother by a different father. As soldiers all were conspicuous for bull-dog tenacity and ranked among the bravest of the brave.

It was with an ill grace that Almagro saw so many of his partner's family coming to share in

Seeds of strife

the anticipated glory and booty. He instantly recognized Fernando's commanding influence and felt himself in a measure thrust into the background. Thus the seeds of a deadly feud were not long in sowing themselves.

In December, 1531, the Pizarros started in advance, with about 200 men and 50 horses. When they arrived at Tumbez in the following spring, they learned that a civil war was raging. The conquering Inca, Huayna Capac, had died in 1523 and was succeeded by his lawful heir Huascar, son of his Coya, or only legitimate wife. The next in succession, according to Peruvian rules, seems to have been Manco, of whom we shall have more to say presently. But the late Inca had a son by one of his concubines, the daughter of a vanquished chief or tribal king of the Quitus; and this son Atahualpa had been a favourite with his father. When Huascar came to the throne, Atahualpa was made ruler of Quito, apparently in accordance with his father's wishes. Under no circumstances was Atahualpa eligible for the position of reigning Inca. He was neither the child of a Coya nor of a woman of pure Inca blood, but of a foreign woman, and was therefore an out and out bastard. About three years before the arrival of the Spaniards, however, Atahualpa, with the aid of two powerful chieftains, Quizquiz and Chalcuchima, left his own territory and marched upon Cuzco. The war which ensued was characterized by wholesale barbarity. At length Atahualpa's chieftains defeated and captured the Inca, and, entering Cuzco in triumph, massacred his family and friends as far as they could be found. But the Inca Huascar himself they did not put to death, for they realized that it might be necessary to use him as an instrument for governing the country.[1] Atahualpa put on the tasselled

Civil war in Peru and usurpation of Atahualpa

---

[1] Somewhat as Cortes used Montezuma ; see Garcilasso, *Comentarios reales,* pt. i. lib. ix. cap. xxxvi.

crimson cap, or Inca diadem, and proceeding on his way to Cuzco had arrived at Caxamarca, when couriers brought him news of the white and bearded strangers coming up from the sea, clad in shining panoply, riding upon unearthly monsters, and wielding deadly thunderbolts. The newcomers were everywhere regarded with extreme wonder and dread, but their demeanour toward the natives had been in the main friendly, as the Pizarros understood the necessity of enforcing strict discipline.

Arrival of the Spaniards

Plainly it was worth while to court the favour of these mysterious beings, and Atahualpa sent as an envoy his brother Titu Atauchi with presents and words of welcome. Pizarro had been reinforced by Fernando de Soto with 100 men and a fresh supply of horses; he had built a small fortress near the mouth of the Piura River, to serve as a base of operations; and late in September, 1532, he had started on his march into the interior, with about two thirds of his little force. Titu found him at Zaran, a village among the foothills of the Andes. When Garcilasso[1] tells us that the envoy humbled himself before Pizarro and addressed him as " son of Viracocha," he reveals the theory which the Peruvians doubtless held concerning the newcomers. Viracocha was

They were supposed to be "sons of Viracocha"

[1] *Comentarios reales*, pt. ii. lib. i. cap. xix.

MAP ILLUSTRATING THE CONQUEST OF PERU

the counterpart of Zeus, the sky-god, arising from the sea-foam, the power that gathers the clouds and delights in thunder. Like Apollo and other Greek solar deities he was conceived as fair in complexion with bright or golden hair. After the conquest of Peru the name *viracocha* passed into a common noun meaning "white man," and it is still used in this sense at the present day.[1] For the red man to call the white stranger a child of Viracocha might under some circumstances be regarded as a form of ceremonious politeness, or the phrase might even be a mere descriptive epithet; but under the circumstances of Titu's visit to Pizarro we can hardly doubt that the newcomers were really invested with supernatural terrors, that the feeling of the Peruvians was like that which had led the Mexicans at first to take it for granted that their visitors must be children of Quetzalcoatl. Upon any other supposition it does not seem possible to understand the events that followed.

After receiving and dismissing the envoy with assurances of friendship, Pizarro pushed on through the mountains and entered Caxamarca on the 15th of November. It was a town of about 2000 inhabitants.[2] The houses were

---

[1] Brinton, *Myths of the New World*, p. 180.

[2] It is well described in " A True Account of the Province of Cuzco," by Pizarro's secretary, Francisco de Xeres, in

chiefly of adobe-brick with thatched roofs, but some were built of hewn stones laid together without cement. Around the great Caxamarca open square, which might serve as market-place or mustering ground, were what the Spaniards called capacious barracks. Hard by was a temple of the Sun, with a convent of vestals charged with the care of the sacred fire. The town was overlooked by a circular tower of defence, girt with a rampart ascending spirally, somewhat, I fancy, as in old pictures of the tower of Babel. On a rising ground some two miles distant was encamped Atahualpa's army, — some thousands of Indians in quilted cotton doublets, with bucklers of stiff hide, long bronze-pointed lances and copper-headed clubs, as well as bows, slings, and lassos, in the use of which these warriors were expert. Toward nightfall Fernando Pizarro and Fernando de Soto, with five and thirty horsemen, went to visit the self-styled Inca in his quarters, and found him surrounded with chieftains and bedizened female slaves. After introducing themselves and inviting Atahualpa to a conference with their commander next day in the market-place, the cavaliers withdrew. On both sides the extreme of ceremonious politeness had been observed.[1]

Markham's *Reports on the Discovery of Peru*, London, 1872 (Hakluyt Society).

[1] Except for a moment when Soto's steed, at the malicious

Surely so strange an interview was never seen save when Montezuma ushered Cortes into the city of Mexico. Between the two cases there was an essential likeness. It is clear that Atahualpa and his men were paralyzed with superstitious dread, while the Spaniards on their part were well aware that according to all military principles they had thrust themselves into a very dangerous position. As they looked out that anxious night upon the mountain-slope before them, gleaming with innumerable watchfires, we are told that many were profoundly dejected. The leaders saw that there must not be a moment's delay in taking advantage of the superstitious fears of the Indians. They must at once get possession of this Inca's person. Here, of course, the Pizarros took their cue from Cortes. In repeating the experiment they showed less subtlety and more brutality than the conqueror of Mexico; and while some allowance must be made for differences in the situation, one feels nevertheless that the native wit of Cortes had a much keener edge than that of his imitators.

and prudent touch of his rider's spur, pranced and curvetted, to the intense dismay of half a dozen dusky warriors, whom Atahualpa, after the departure of the visitors, promptly beheaded for showing fright (Zarate, *Conquista del Peru*, ii. 4); an interesting touch of human nature! Garcilasso (pt. i. lib. ix. cap. xvi.) gives a vivid account of the uncontrollable agonies of terror with which the Peruvians regarded horses.

Atahualpa must have passed the night in quite as much uneasiness as the Spaniards. When he came next day strongly escorted into the market-place he found no one to receive him, for Pizarro had skilfully concealed his men in the neighbouring houses. Presently a solitary white man, the priest Valverde, came forth to greet the Inca, and proceeded — through one of the interpreters heretofore mentioned — to read him a long-winded disquisition on dogmatic theology and church history, beginning with the creation of Adam and passing stage by stage to the calling of St. Peter, and so on to the bull by which Alexander VI. had given the kingdom of the Incas (along with other realms too numerous to mention) to the Most Catholic King. In conclusion Atahualpa was summoned, under penalty of fire and sword, to acknowledge the papal supremacy and pay tribute to Charles V.[1] Of this precious rigmarole the would-be Inca probably fathomed just enough to be convinced that the mysterious strangers, instead of being likely to lend him aid, were an obstacle of unknown strength to be reckoned with ; and in a fit of petulant disappointment he threw upon the ground the Bible

Capture of Atahualpa

---

[1] There is a good abstract of this speech, with some eminently sound critical remarks, in Helps's *Spanish Conquest*, vol. iii. pp. 533–541. Compare the famous *Requerimiento* of Dr. Palacios Rubios, *id.*, vol. i. pp. 379–384.

which the priest had handed him. As soon as this was reported to Pizarro the war-cry "Santiago!" resounded, the ambushed Spaniards rushed forth and seized Atahualpa, and for two hours a butchery went on in which some hundreds of his bewildered followers perished.

The success of this blow was such as the wildest imagination could not have foreseen. Here at the crisis of the war the superhuman "sons of Viracocha" had come upon the scene and taken matters into their own hands. They held the person of the sacrilegious usurper Atahualpa, and men who had rashly come too near them had been slain with unearthly weapons, struck down as if by lightning. The people were dumb and helpless. The strangers treated Atahualpa politely, and such edicts as they issued through him were obeyed in some parts of the country.

His first thought was naturally for his liberation. Confined in a room twenty-two feet in length by seventeen in width, he made a mark upon the wall as high as he could reach with his hand, and offered as ransom gold enough to fill the room up to that height. Pizarro accepted the offer, and the gold began to be collected, largely in the shape of vases and other ornaments of temples. But it came in more slowly than Atahualpa had expected, and in June, 1533, the stipulated quan-

Ransom collected for Atahualpa

tity was not yet complete. In some towns the priests dismantled the sacred edifices and hid their treasures, waiting apparently for the crisis to pass. The utter paralysis of the people in presence of the white men was scarcely matched by anything in the story of Cortes. While the treasure was collecting, Fernando Pizarro, with twenty horsemen and half a dozen arquebusiers, made a journey of four hundred miles through the heart of the country to the famous temple of Pachacamac, and although they boldly dese-crated the sacred shrine they went and came unmolested![1] Soon after Fernando's return to Caxamarca, in April, Almagro arrived at that town, with his party of 150 soldiers and 84 horses. In June the enormous spoil of gold, equivalent to more than $15,000,000 in modern reckoning, besides a vast amount of silver, was divided among the children of the sky-god. Almagro's newly arrived men wished to share equally with the others, and as they were obliged

---

[1] The people believed that no one but the consecrated priests of Pachacamac could enter the shrine of the wooden idol without instantly perishing. So when Fernando Pizarro coolly walked in and smashed the "graven image," and had the shrine demolished, and made the sign of the cross as "an invincible weapon against the Devil," they concluded that he must be a god who knew what he was about, and with whom it would be unsafe to interfere. See Squier's *Peru*, p. 65; Markham, *Reports on the Discovery of Peru*, London, 1872, p. 83.

to content themselves with a much smaller portion, there was fresh occasion for ill-feeling between Almagro and the Pizarros.

Fernando Pizarro was now sent to Spain with the emperor's share of the plunder. Atahualpa placed more trust in him than in the others, and gave expression to a fear that his own safety was imperilled by his departure. The atmosphere seems to have been heavy with intrigue. From Cuzco the imprisoned Inca Huascar offered the Spaniards a treasure still larger than they had as yet received, on condition that they would set him free and support him against Atahualpa. The latter heard of this, and soon afterward Huascar was secretly murdered. At the same time the Spaniards, still uneasy and suspicious, as was natural, had reason to believe that Atahualpa was privately sending forth instructions to his chieftains to arouse their parts of the country. When one is driven to despair, one is ready to fight even against sky-gods. Pizarro saw that it would not do for a moment to allow such proceedings. A savage display of power seemed necessary; and so Atahualpa, having been brought to trial for conspiracy against the white men, for the murder of his brother, and for divers other crimes, even including idolatry and polygamy, was duly convicted and sentenced to be burned at the stake. On his consenting to accept bap-

Murder of the captive Inca Huascar by Atahualpa

tism the sentence was commuted for a milder one, and on the 29th of August, in the public square at Caxamarca, Atahualpa was strangled with a bowstring. At this time Fernando de Soto was absent; on his return he denounced the execution as both shameful and rash. As to the shamefulness of the transaction modern historians can have but one opinion. Personal sympathy, of course, would be wasted upon such a bloodthirsty wretch as Atahualpa; but as for the Spaniards, it would seem that perfidy could no farther go than to accept an enormous ransom from a captive and then put him to death. As a question of military policy, divorced from considerations of morality, the case is not so clear. The Spaniards were taking possession of Peru by the same sort of right as that by which the lion springs upon his prey; there was nothing that was moral about it, and their consciences were at no time scrupulous as to keeping faith with heretics or with heathen. They were guided purely by considerations of their own safety and success, and they slew Atahualpa in the same spirit that Napoleon murdered the Duke d'Enghien, because they deemed it good policy to do so. In this Pizarro and Almagro were agreed; Soto and a few others were of a different opinion, and it is not easy now to tell which

Atahualpa put to death by the Spaniards

side conceived the military situation most correctly.

In order to control the country Pizarro must control the person of the Inca, and that sovereign must understand that to conspire against the "sons of Viracocha" was simply to bring down sure and swift destruction upon himself. There was reason for believing that Atahualpa's usurped authority was not so willingly recognized by the country as that of the genuine Inca; and Pizarro had expressed an intention of bringing Huascar to Caxamarca and deciding between his claims and those of Atahualpa, when his purpose was frustrated by the assassination of the former. It thus appears that there was a valid political reason for holding Atahualpa responsible for the murder.

For the present Pizarro proclaimed Toparca, one of Atahualpa's sons, but the lad fell sick and died within a few weeks. Symptoms of anarchy were here and there manifested; in some towns there were riots, and distant chieftains prepared to throw off their allegiance. On the march to Cuzco, which began late in September, the Spaniards, now about 500 in number, were for the first time attacked. The assailants were 6000 Indians, led by Atahualpa's brother, Titu Atauchi, but the Spaniards beat them off without serious loss. Pizarro laid the blame of this attack upon the chieftain Chalcuchima, whom he had with him, and the Indian was accordingly burned at the stake for an example. A few days afterward, Manco, already mentioned as next to Huascar in the customary line of succession, came to the Spanish camp and made his submission in due form. It was a great and decisive triumph for Pizarro. He lost no time in proclaiming the new Inca under the style of Manco Capac Yupanqui, and on the 15th of November, 1533, the sovereign and his supernatural guardians made a solemn entry into Cuzco, where the usual inaugural ceremonies and festivities took place. It was the anniversary of Pizarro's entry into Caxamarca. In that one eventful year he had overthrown the usurper, and now, as he placed the crimson cap upon the head of the legitimate Inca, might it not seem that he had completed the conquest of the golden kingdom? Relying upon the superstitious awe which had helped him to such an astounding result, he ventured in the course of the next four months to set up a Spanish municipal government in Cuzco, to seize upon divers houses and public buildings for his followers, and to convert the temple of the Sun into a Dominican monastery.

The chieftain Quizquiz, with a portion of

The true Inca, Manco, makes his submission, and is inaugurated at Cuzco by Pizarro

Francisco Pizarro

Atahualpa's forces, held out against the new Inca, whereupon Almagro in a brief campaign drove him into the Quito territory and over-powered him. Meanwhile the news of all these wonderful events had reached the ears of Pedro de Alvarado in Guatemala, and not yet satiated with adventure, that cavalier, with 500 followers, sailed for the South American coast, landed in the bay of Caraques, and after a terrible march through the wilderness, in which one fourth of the number perished, he came up with Almagro at Riobamba. After some parley, as his men showed symptoms of deserting to Almagro, Alvarado came to the conclusion that it would be wiser not to inter-fere in this part of the world. He consented to be bought off for a good round sum, and went back to Guatemala, leaving most of his men to recruit the Spanish forces in Peru.

The arrival of Fernando Pizarro in Spain, with his load of gold and his tale of adventure, aroused such excitement as had hardly been felt since the return of Columbus from his first voy-age across the Sea of Darkness. Again Spaniards began flocking to the New World, and ships plied frequently between Panama and the shores of the Inca's country. For commercial purposes a seat of government on the coast was preferable to Cuzco, and ac-cordingly on the 6th of January, 1535, Francisco Pizarro founded the city of Lima. While he was busy in laying out streets and putting up houses his brother Fernando returned from Spain. Francisco had been created a marquis and the territory subject to his government had been described in the royal patent as extending southward 270 leagues from the river Santiago, in latitude 1° 20′ north. Provision had also been made for Almagro, but in such wise as to get him as far out of the way as possible. He was appointed governor of the country to the south of Pizarro's, with the title of marshal. Pizarro's province was to be called New Castile ; Almagro's, which covered Chili, or the greater part of it, was to be called New Toledo.

Thus with fair phrases Almagro was virtually set aside ; he was told that he might go and conquer a new and unknown country for himself, while the rich country already won was to be monopolized by the Pizarros. Theirs was the bird in the hand, his the bird in the bush ; and no wonder that his wrath waxed hot against Fernando. In this mood he insisted that at any rate the city of Cuzco fell south of the boundary line, and therefore within his jurisdiction. This was not really the case, though its nearness to the line afforded ground for doubt, and something might depend upon the way in which the distance from the river Santiago was measured. Almagro was

Almagro's disgust ; he starts for Chili

La conquista del Peru.

llamada la nueua Castilla. La ᷒l tierra por diuina vo
luntad fue marauillosamente conquistada en la felicif
sima ventura del Emperador y Rey nuestro señor: y
por la prudencia y esfuerço del muy magnifico y vale
roso cauallero el Capitan Francisco piçarro Gouerna
dor y adelantado de la nueua castilla: y de su herma
no Hernando piçarro: y de sus animosos capitanes
z fieles y esforçados compañeros. q̃ cõ el se hallaron

TITLE–PAGE OF BOOK ON THE CONQUEST OF PERU, 1534

a weak man, apt to be swayed by the kind of argument that happened to be poured into his ears for the moment. At first he was persuaded to abandon his claim to Cuzco, and in the autumn of 1535 he started on his march for Chili, with 200 Spaniards and a large force of Indians led by the Inca's brother Paullu, and accompanied by the high priest or Villac Umu. There were to be stirring times before his return.

Three years had now elapsed since the seizure of Atahualpa, and two since the coronation of Manco, and quiet seems to have been generally maintained. But the Inca's opinion as to the character and business of the white strangers must needs have been modified by what was going on. If at first he may have welcomed their aid in overthrowing the rival party and helping him to his throne, he could now see unmistakable signs that they had come to stay. Spaniards were arriving by the shipload; they were building towns, seizing estates and enslaving the people, despoiling temples, and otherwise comporting themselves as odious masters. Mere familiarity must have done something toward dispelling the glamour which had at first surrounded and protected them. Æsop's fox nearly died of fright on first seeing a lion, but by and by made bold to go up to him and ask him how he did. In an emergency it might be worth while to test the power of the new tyrants and see if they were really the sacred children of Viracocha. The departure of Almagro for Chili offered a favourable moment for an insurrection, and there is no doubt that the plans of the Inca and his friends were deliberately concerted. Almagro had not proceeded many days' march when Paullu and the Villac Umu deserted him with their Indians and hurried back toward Cuzco, while at the same time the Inca succeeded in escaping from the city. Now ensued the only serious warfare between Spaniard and Indian which the conquest of Peru involved. With astonishing suddenness and vehemence the rebellion broke out in many parts of the country, so that the communication between Cuzco and Lima was cut, and for some months the Spaniards in the one town did not know whether their friends in the other were alive or dead. Francisco Pizarro at Lima was fain to call for succour from Panama, Guatemala, and Mexico. The Inca occupied the great Sacsahuaman fortress overlooking Cuzco, and laid siege to the city, where Fernando was in command, with his brothers Gonzalo and Juan. For six months, from February to August, 1536, the siege was closely pressed. There were frequent and vigorous assaults, and how the little band of Spaniards contrived to maintain themselves against such

Manco plans an insurrection

The Spaniards besieged in Cuzco

228

terrible odds is one of the marvels of history. They not only held their own within the walls, but made effective sorties. Such prodigies of valour have rarely been seen except in those books of chivalry that turned Don Quixote's brain. Juan Pizarro was slain in an assault upon the fortress, but Fernando at length succeeded in taking it by storm. After a while the Inca began to find it difficult to feed so many mouths. As September approached, it was necessary, in order to avoid a famine, for large numbers to go home and attend to their planting. With his force thus reduced the Inca retired into the valley of Yucay, where he encountered Almagro returning from Chili. A battle ensued, and Manco was defeated with great slaughter.

Total defeat of the Inca

Almagro's men, after penetrating more than three hundred miles into Chili, and enduring the extremes of cold and hunger, without finding wealthy towns or such occasions for pillage as they expected, had at length begun to murmur, and finally they persuaded their leader to return and renew his claim to Cuzco. He arrived in time to complete the discomfiture of the Inca, and then appeared before that city. He was refused admission, and an agreement was made by which he promised to remain encamped outside until the vexed question of jurisdiction could be peaceably de-

Almagro returns and seizes Cuzco

termined. Some months of inaction passed, but at length, in April, 1537, Almagro was led to believe, perhaps correctly, that Fernando Pizarro was secretly strengthening the works, with the intention of holding the city against him. Almagro thereupon treated the agreement as broken, seized the city by surprise, and took Fernando and Gonzalo prisoners.

This act was the beginning of a period of eleven years of civil disturbance, in the course of which all the principal actors were swept off the stage, as in some cheap blood and thunder tragedy. For our purposes it is not worth while to recount the petty incidents of the struggle, — how Almagro was at one moment ready to submit to arbitration and the next moment refused to abide by the decision ; how Fernando was set at liberty and Gonzalo escaped ; how Almagro's able lieutenant, Rodrigo de Orgoñez, won a victory over Pizarro's men at Abançay,

Civil war; execution of Almagro; and final defeat of the Inca

but was totally defeated by Fernando Pizarro at Las Salinas and perished on the field ; how at last Fernando had Almagro tried for sedition and summarily executed. On which side was the more violence and treachery it would be hard to say. Indeed, as Sir Arthur Helps observes, " in this melancholy story it is difficult to find anybody whom the reader can sympathize much with." So far as our story of the conquest of Peru is concerned, we may observe the Spaniards once, in a leisure interval among their own squabbles, turning their attention to it ! After his victory at Abançay in July, 1537, Orgoñez completed the overthrow of the Inca Manco, scattered his army, and drove him to an inaccessible fastness in the mountains.

Almagro's execution was in July, 1538, and the next year Fernando Pizarro thought it prudent to return to Castile, with an enormous quantity of gold, and give his own account of the late troubles. But, as already observed, the Spanish government was liable to resent too summary measures on the part of its servants in the Indies, and much depended upon the kind of information it obtained in the first place. On this occasion it got its first impressions from friends of Almagro, and it fared ill with the other side. How Fernando Pizarro was received in Spain Fernando was kept under surveillance at Medina del Campo for more than twenty years, and was then allowed to go home to his estate in Estremadura, where he died in 1578, at the age, it is said, of one hundred and four years.

After his brother's departure the Marquis Pizarro had some further trouble with the Inca, who from time to time renewed a desultory warfare among the mountains. It was but a slight annoyance, however. Peru was really conquered, and Pizarro was able to send out expeditions to great distances. In March, 1540, Pedro de Valdivia set out for Chili and remained there seven years, in the course of which he founded Valparaiso (September 3, 1544) and other towns, and for the moment seemed to have conquered the country. Nevertheless it was here that the Spaniards encountered more formidable opposition than anywhere else in America. On Valdivia's return to his colony in 1549 its very existence was imperilled by the assaults of the Araucanians. These valiant Indians, led by their illustrious chieftains, Caupolican and Lautaro, maintained a warfare which has been celebrated in the famous epic poem of Alonso de Ercilla, who was one of the Spanish officers engaged.[1] In this struggle Valdivia perished. Other governors until the end of the century found the Araucanians unconquerable; and, indeed, even to the present day this aboriginal American people may boast, with the Montenegrins of the Balkan peninsula, that they have never bent their necks to the yoke of the foreigner.

To return to the Marquis Pizarro: in 1539 he put his brother Gonzalo in command over the province of Quito, which had been con-

Valdivia's conquest of Chili

[1] Ercilla, *La Araucana*, Madrid, 1776, 2 vols. 12°. Lope de Vega wrote a play on the same subject, " Arauco Domado," in his *Comedias*, tom. xx., Madrid, 1629.

quered by Benalcazar, and on Christmas of that year Gonzalo started to explore the cinnamon forests to the eastward. A memorable affair it was, and placed this Pizarro in a conspicuous place among men of incredible endurance. His little army of 350 Spaniards (attended at the outset by 4000 Indians) crossed the Andes and plunged deeper and deeper into the wilderness, until food grew scarce. Then, lured on by false re- *Expedition of Gonzalo Pizarro in search of El Dorado* ports of a rich and fruitful country ahead (mayhap, another golden kingdom! why not?) they pressed onward, with great exertion built a small vessel capable of carrying part of their company and their baggage, and so, partly on water, partly on land, made their way down the Napo River, one of the tributaries of the Amazon. Hearing now that the rich country was to be found at the confluence of the Napo with the greater river, Gonzalo sent Francisco de Orellana ahead with fifty men in the brigantine to gather supplies, and return. When Orellana reached the region in question he found scant sustenance there, and decided that it would be impossible to force his vessel back against the powerful current. It was easier to keep on down-stream and see if some golden kingdom might not be found upon its banks. So Orel- *Orellana's descent of the Amazon* lana basely left his comrades in the lurch, and sailed down the Amazon 4000 miles to its mouth, a most astounding exploit in the navigation of an unknown and very dangerous river. Escaping the perils of starvation, shipwreck, and savages, Orellana came out upon the ocean and made his way to the island of Cubagua, whence he went soon afterward to Spain, and succeeded in raising an expedition to return and make conquests in the Amazon country,[1] but his death and the remonstrances of Portugal frustrated this attempt.

One of Orellana's companions, who had boldly denounced as cowardly and treacherous his intention of deserting Pizarro, was left behind to starve in the forest, but contrived to keep himself alive till Gonzalo arrived at the mouth of the Napo, and found him, a mere skeleton. On learning his story it became evident that there was nothing to do but make the best of their way back to Quito. After one
Gonzalo's return to Quito of the most terrible marches recorded in history, a march in which more than two thirds of the company perished, Gonzalo brought the famished survivors into Quito in June, 1542, and there he was met by unwel-

---

[1] " The name of river of the Amazons was given to it because Orellana and his people beheld the women on its banks fighting as valiantly as the men. . . . It is not that there are Amazons on that river, but that they said there were, by reason of the valour of the women." Garcilasso (Markham's transl.), lib. viii. cap. xxii.

come news. During the two and a half years of his absence great changes had taken place.

For a time everything had gone prosperously with Francisco Pizarro. The rage for silver and gold had brought thousands of Spaniards into the country, and by taking advantage of the system of military roads and posts already existing, they were soon better able than the Incas had ever been to hold all that territory in complete subjection. Pizarro was fond of building and gardening, and took much interest in introducing European cereals and other vegetables into Peru. While he was engaged in such occupations his enemies were laying plots. His brother Fernando, on leaving the country, had warned him against the "men of Chili," as Almagro's partisans were called. But the marquis did not profit by the warning. A man of tact, like Cortes, would have won over these malcontents by extending to them judicious favours and making them feel it to be for their interest to come to his support. But Pizarro had neither the generosity nor the sagacity to adopt such a course, nor had he the prudence of his brother Fernando. He treated the men of Chili with rudeness and severity, and still was careless about guarding himself. To such straits, it is said, were some of these men reduced through persecutions that could be traced to Pizarro, that a dozen cavaliers, who happened to have their quarters in the same house, had only one cloak among them, which they used to take their turns in wearing, the cloaked man going out while the others staid at home.[1] After a while some of these ill-used men conspired to murder Pizarro, and on Sunday, June 26, 1541, nineteen of them, led by a very able officer named Juan de Rada, boldly made their way into the governor's palace at Lima just as he was finishing his mid-day dinner, and in a desperate assault, in which several of the conspir-

Assassination of Pizarro ators fell under Pizarro's sword, they succeeded in killing the sturdy old man, along with his half-brother Alcántara and other friends.[2] Almagro's illegitimate half-breed son, commonly called "Almagro the lad," was now proclaimed governor of Peru by the conspirators. But his day was a short one. It happened that Charles V. had sent out a learned judge, Vaca de Castro, to advise with Pizarro concerning the government of his province, and with characteristic prudence had authorized him in case of Pizarro's death to assume the government himself. Castro had just arrived at Popayan when he was met there by the news of the assassination. Finding himself sure of

[1] Herrera, dec. vi. lib. viii. cap. vi.

[2] The scene is most graphically described by Prescott, in his *Conquest of Peru*, book iv. chap. v.

the allegiance of some of Pizarro's principal
captains, as Benalcazar and Alonso de Alvarado,
he proclaimed himself governor, and *The "bloody*
in the battle of Chupas, September *plains of*
16, 1542, he defeated young Alma- *Chupas"*
gro, who was forthwith tried for treason and be
headed in the great square at Cuzco.

Gonzalo Pizarro loyally gave in his allegiance
to the new governor, and retired to his private
estate in Charcas, south of Lake Titicaca. The
troubles, however, were not yet over. In the
next chapter we shall see how Indian slavery
grew up in the New World, and how *The New*
through the devoted labours of Las *Laws, and*
the rebellion
Casas measures were taken for its *of Gonzalo*
abolition. It was in 1542 that Las *Pizarro*
Casas, after a quarter of a century of heroic effort,
won his decisive victory in the promulgation of
the edicts known as the " New Laws." These
edicts, as we shall see, resulted in the gradual
abolition of Indian slavery. If they had been
put into operation according to their first intent
they would have worked an immediate abolition,
and the act of confiscation would have applied
to nearly all the Spaniards in Peru. The New
Laws therefore aroused furious opposition, and
the matter was made still worse by the violent
temper of the new viceroy, Blasco Nuñez Vela,
who arrived in Lima early in 1544, charged
with the duty of enforcing them. From arbitrary

imprisonment Vela's violence extended to open and shameless murder, until at length the people rose in rebellion, and Gonzalo Pizarro came forth from his retirement to lead them. After a year of turbulence a battle was fought near Quito, January 18, 1546, in which poor, half-crazed Vela was defeated and slain, and Gonzalo became master of Peru.

But his triumph was short-lived. The Spanish government sent out a wily and smooth-tongued ecclesiastic, a military priest and member of the Council of the Inquisition, Pedro de la Gasca, armed with extensive powers for settling all the vexed questions. Gasca's most effective weapon was the repeal of those clauses of the New Laws which demanded the immediate abolition of slavery. These clauses were repealed, and preparations were made for the compromise hereafter to be described. But for these preliminaries Gasca would probably have accomplished little. As it was, his honeyed tongue found no difficulty in winning over the captains of Pizarro's fleet at Panama. They had been sent there to watch the situation, and, if necessary, to prevent Gasca from proceeding farther, or to bribe him to join Pizarro, or perhaps to seize him and carry him to Peru as a prisoner. But this crafty man, "this Cortes in priestly garments," as Sir Arthur Helps calls him, talked so well that the captains

Pedro de la Gasca

put the fleet at his disposal and conveyed him to Tumbez, where he landed June 13, 1547. It was still open to Pizarro to maintain that he had not taken up arms against the Crown, but only against a tyrannical viceroy and in defence of the emperor's loyal subjects. It was rather a difficult position, but Vela's conduct had been such as to lend it strong support, and had Gonzalo Pizarro been richer in mental resources he might have carried it off successfully. As it was, he had great and not unmerited confidence in his own military ability, and unwisely decided to hold out against Gasca.

For a moment events seemed to favour Pizarro. An able captain, Diego de Centeno, who through all these vicissitudes had remained loyal to the Crown, now captured Cuzco for Gasca; whereupon a campaign ensued which ended in the total overthrow of Centeno in the bloody battle of Huarina, near Lake Titicaca, October 20, 1547. This gleam of success was but momentary. Nowhere was the sword to be found that could prevail against Gasca's tongue. Such wholesale defection as suddenly ruined Gonzalo Pizarro has seldom been seen. When he en- *Defeat and* countered Gasca in person, on the *execution of Gonzalo Pi-* plain of Sacsahuana, April 9, 1548, *zarro* his soldiers began deserting by scores. As one company after another contrived to slip away and flee into the arms of the royalists, Gonzalo's quaint lieutenant, Carvajal, a weather-beaten veteran of the wars in Italy, kept humming with grim facetiousness the words of an old Spanish ditty : —

> Estos mis cabellos, madre,
> Dos á dos me los lleva el ayre.[1]

After a faint pretence of fighting, in which fifteen men were killed, Pizarro, finding himself without an army, quietly rode over to Gasca's camp and surrendered himself. On the following day he was beheaded, while old Carvajal, in his eighty-fifth year, was hanged and quartered, and this was the end of the sway of the Pizarros in the land of the Incas. All except Fernando died by violence. The victorious Gasca proved himself an adept in hanging and beheading, but accomplished little else. After his bloody assizes he returned to Spain in 1550, and was rewarded with a bishopric. In 1553 there was a brief epilogue of rebellion in Peru, under the lead of Hernandez Giron, who was beheaded in 1554.

A new era began under the able administra-

Arrival of Mendoza

tion of Andrea Hurtado de Mendoza, Marquis of Cañete, who came out in 1556. The conquest of Peru may with his

---

[1] As Helps renders it, "These my hairs, mother, two by two the breeze carries them away." *Spanish Conquest,* vol. iv. p. 258. The best description of Gonzalo's rebellion is the one given by Helps.

viceroyalty be pronounced complete; in other words, not only had the Indians been conquered, but their unruly conquerors were at last overcome, and into the country, thus reduced to order, more than 8000 Spaniards had come to stay.

Considering the story of the conquest of Peru as a whole, we cannot but be struck with the slightness of the resistance made by the people. Except for the spirited siege of Cuzco by the Inca Manco, there was no resistance worthy of the name. The conquerors turned temples into churches and enslaved the people, and yet in the midst of this large population a handful of Spaniards were able to squabble among themselves and kill each other with as little concern as if they had been in an empty country. Evidently this society in which governmental control had been so far developed at the expense of individualism was a society where it did not make much difference to the people what master they served. To conquer such a country it was only necessary to get control of the machinery of administration. I think it may have been a perception of this state of things that encouraged Atahualpa to make his attempt to overthrow the legitimate line of Incas. He doubtless hoped, with the aid of the men of

Some reasons why the conquest was so easily accomplished

Quito and other imperfectly conquered provinces, to get control of Cuzco and the system
of military posts and roads radiating therefrom,
believing that thus he could maintain himself
in power in spite of the fact that his birth dis-
qualified him for the position of supreme Inca.
His success would have been a revolution; and
it is instructive to see him trying to provide
against the opposition of the Inca caste by keeping the genuine Inca a captive in his hands instead of putting him to death. By thus control-
ling all the machinery of government, the captive
Inca included, Atahualpa evidently had no occasion to fear anything like popular insurrection.
Whether his scheme would have succeeded
must, of course, remain doubtful; but it is extremely curious to see the Spaniards at the critical moment step in and beat him at his own
game, without more than half understanding
what they were doing. In capturing Atahualpa
there is no doubt that Pizarro took his cue from
Cortes, but between the seizure of Atahualpa
and that of Montezuma the points of difference
were more important than the points of likeness. It is customary to speak of Atahualpa as
" the last Inca," and I suppose the fact is commonly forgotten that he was really only governor
of Quito, a victorious usurper who had just begun to call himself the Inca, but had not been
formally invested with that supreme dignity.

Garcilasso expressly declares that the people — by whom he means the members of his own Inca caste and their loyal dependents — were grateful to the white man for overthrowing the usurper who had first captured and finally murdered their true Inca Huascar. "They said that the Spaniards had put the tyrant to death as a punishment and to avenge the Incas; and that the god Viracocha, the father of the Spaniards, had ordered them to do it. This is the reason they called the first Spaniards by the name of Viracocha, and believing they were sons of their god, they respected them so much that they almost worshipped them, and scarcely made any resistance to the conquest."[1]

This explanation, from so high an authority as Garcilasso Inca, shows us clearly why resistance to the Spaniards did not fairly begin until three years after the seizure of Atahualpa; and then, when the legitimate Inca Manco headed the attack upon the Spaniards, not only had their numbers greatly increased, but they had already secured control of a great part of the governmental machinery, and to the mass of the people a mere change of masters was not a matter of vital importance.

After the decisive defeat of Manco Capac by Orgoñez in 1537, that Inca retired to an almost inaccessible fastness in the great fork of the

[1] Garcilasso, pt. i. lib. v. cap. xxi., Markham's translation.

Andes where the river Marañon takes its rise, and there he kept up a kind of court. From that point he now and then made a sudden de- Fate of the scent and attacked the Spaniards, but Inca Manco accomplished little or nothing. His end was a strange one, with a touch of the comical. When Juan de Rada and his party were crossing the great square at Lima, on their way to assassinate the Marquis Pizarro, one of the company, a certain Gomez Perez, was observed to step out of the way to avoid wetting his shoes in a puddle. " What ! " cried the fierce Rada, " here are we about to wade up to our knees in blood, and you are afraid of a pool of water ! Go home, you silly fop, you are no fit company for the like of us ! " After the over- throw of young Almagro at Chupas, this Gomez Perez, with others of that faction, took refuge at the Inca's little court in the mountains, where they were hospitably received. On the arrival of Blasco Nuñez Vela in 1544 there were nego- tiations between that viceroy and the Inca, which resulted in Manco's giving in his allegiance to the Emperor Charles V. Gomez Perez served as the Inca's messenger in these negotiations. He was an ill-mannered fellow, who took no pains to veil his contempt for " coloured men," and he was often rude to the Inca, who usually received his coarse words with quiet dignity. But one day, as the two were playing at nine-

pins some dispute arose, and the Spaniard became so abusive that Manco gave him a push,
exclaiming, " Go away, you forget with whom
you are speaking." Without another word
Gomez, who had one of the big balls in his
hand, hurled it at the Inca's head and killed
him on the spot.[1] At the sight of this outrage
the Indians who were present, watching the
game, fell upon Gomez and slew him. The
other Spaniards fled to their quarters, but the
enraged Indians set fire to the building, and
butchered them all as fast as they were driven
out by the flames. Thus ignominiously perished the wretched remnant of the Almagro
faction.

Manco was succeeded by his son Sayri
Tupac, who for fourteen years continued to
hold his court among the mountains. On the
arrival of the Marquis of Cañete, negotiations
were opened with this Inca, who con- End of the
sented to become a pensioner of the Inca dynasty
Spaniards. The valley of Yucay was given him,

[1] Garcilasso, *Comentarios reales*, pt. ii. lib. iv. cap. vii.
Mr. Prescott's account of this affair (*Conquest of Peru*, book
iv. chap. iii.) is slightly misleading. Mr. Markham (in
Winsor, *Narr. and Crit. Hist.*, vol. ii. p. 546) makes a
strange mistake in the date, and the context shows that it is
not a misprint ; he says that Manco " met his death in 1553,
after a disastrous reign of twenty years.'' Manco was
crowned in 1533, and his death occurred in 1544, and in
the eleventh year of his reign.

and there he lived from 1558 until his death in 1560. His brother and successor, Titu Cusi Yupanqui, returned to Manco's mountain lair, and held court there for eleven years, resuming his practical independence. When the viceroy Francisco de Toledo arrived, in 1571, he determined to put a stop to this sort of thing, and events soon furnished him with a pretext. A missionary friar having gone to visit Titu Cusi at his court, the Inca suddenly fell sick and died, whereupon the friar was seized and put to death for sorcery. Titu Cusi was succeeded by his brother Tupac Amaru, a mere lad. Now the viceroy Toledo sent an army into the mountains, which broke up the Inca's court, slew many chieftains, and captured the Inca Tupac Amaru. The unfortunate youth was taken to Cuzco, and beheaded in revenge for the friar's death, and this was the end of the Inca dynasty.

XI

LAS CASAS

IT is curious to reflect that with the first arrival of civilized Europeans in this New World there should have come that plague of slavery which was so long to pol- The plague lute and curse it, and from the com- of slavery plicated effects of which we shall not for long years yet succeed in fully recovering. Nor is it less curious to reflect how the fates of the continents America and Africa, with their red men and black men, became linked together, from the early time when Prince Henry of Portugal was making those exploring expeditions that prepared the way for the great discovery of Columbus. It was those expeditions upon the African coast that introduced slavery into the world in what we may distinguish as its modern form. For in the history of slavery there have been two quite distinct periods. The ancient slave was the prisoner captured in war, the $αἰχμά-λωτος$, in the picturesque phrase of the Greeks, which has been somewhat freely rendered as "fruit of the spear." We have observed that in the lower stage of barbarism captives are

247

tortured to death ; in the middle stage they are sacrificed to the gods, but as agriculture devel-

Ancient sla-
very

ops and society becomes settled they are more and more used as slaves ; and in the upper stage of barbarism a complete system of slave-labour is developed. Doubtless this course of things was attended with some advantages in its day. Ancient slavery was a help in the coalescence of tribes into nations, and to enslave the captive was not quite so cruel as to roast him alive or cut him to pieces. With the advance of civilization ancient slavery slowly grew milder in type. The slaves of a Greek or a Roman were white men like himself, so that the element of race antipathy was absent. By slow degrees European slaves acquired customary rights and privileges and often became freemen.[1]

---

[1] For a brief characterization of Roman slavery see Gibbon's *Decline and Fall*, chap. ii., with Guizot's and Milman's notes. The cruelties inflicted upon slaves in the days of the Roman republic were frightful, but in the general and remarkable improvement of Roman law in point of humanity under the emperors, the condition of the slaves was notably ameliorated. One among countless testimonies to the mildness of slavery in the fifth century of the Christian era is furnished by an interesting conversation which took place in the year 448 between the Roman historian Priscus and a certain versatile Greek who had become enamoured of wild life and was engaged in the service of the terrible Attila. Priscus says the Romans treat their slaves much more kindly than the Hunnish king treats the free warriors that follow his banner

In general, after making all due allowances, the face of the Christian Church was resolutely set against slavery, so that later wars and conquests created only such modified forms of it as serfdom and villenage. By the fifteenth century ancient slavery was dead in England, and moribund on the continent of Europe, when all at once and most unexpectedly modern slavery came into existence. In this modern system slavery became an extensive Modern slavery branch of commerce. Men of weaker race, despised as heathen with red or black skins, were hunted and caught by thousands, and sold in places where there was a demand for cheap labour. There were features in this modern system as hideous as the worst features of the ancient system. And curiously enough, just as

and divide the spoils of war. They deal with them as friends or brothers, teach them the Scriptures, nurse them tenderly in sickness, and are not allowed to inflict upon them cruel punishment ; moreover, it is a common and highly esteemed practice to give them freedom either by last will and testament, or by deed during the master's lifetime. See Bury's *Later Roman Empire*, vol. i. p. 219. On the general subject, see Wallon, *Histoire de l'esclavage dans l'antiquité*, Paris, 1847, 3 vols. ; Denis, *Histoire des théories et des idées morales dans l'antiquité*, Paris, 1856, tom. ii. pp. 55–218 ; Friedländer, *Mœurs romaines du règne d'Auguste à la fin des Antonins*, Paris, 1865, tom. i. pp. 288–292 ; Ozanam, *History of Civilization in the Fifth Century*, London, 1868, vol. ii. pp. 36–43.

the progress of discovery in Africa had originated this wholesale traffic in men, the discovery of America opened up an immense field where there was soon to be a great and growing demand for cheap labour.

In 1441 Prince Henry's master of the robes, Antonio Gonçalvez, in a voyage along the Morocco coast, captured a few Moors and carried them to Portugal.[1] The next year these Moors begged Gonçalvez to take them back to Morocco, and offered him a ransom in the shape of negro slaves. On hearing of this, Prince Henry told Gonçalvez by all means to exchange the Moors for negroes, because the former were obstinate infidels who would not give up their Mahometan faith, whereas the black men, being simply heathen, might more easily be persuaded to espouse Christianity.[2] Gonçalvez accordingly sailed, set free his Moors, and returned to Portugal with a small cargo of negro slaves. This transaction, in the year 1442, seems to have been the beginning of slavery in its especially modern form. After this many shiploads of negroes were brought to Lisbon, and Prince Henry, in receiving his royal fifth of the proceeds of these

Its beginnings

[1] See above, vol. i. p. 372.

[2] To doubt the sincerity of such an argument is to misunderstand Prince Henry and the age in which he lived.

expeditions, was known to take slaves along with buffalo hides and gold dust.

A graphic description of the arrival of a company of these poor creatures, brought by Lançarote in the year 1444, is given by an eye-witness, the kind-hearted Portuguese chronicler Azurara. " The other day," he says, " which was the eighth of August, very early in the morning by reason of the heat, the mariners began to bring to their vessels, and ... to draw forth those captives .... Azurara's narrative whom, placed together on that plain, it was a marvellous sight to behold, for amongst them there were some of a reasonable degree of whiteness, handsome and well made ; others less white, resembling leopards in their colour ; others as black as Ethiopians, and so ill-formed, as well in their faces as in their bodies, that it seemed to the beholders as if they saw the forms of a lower world. But what heart was that, how hard soever, which was not pierced with sorrow, seeing that company : for some had sunken cheeks, and their faces bathed in tears, looking at each other ; others were groaning very dolorously, looking at the heights of the heavens ... and crying out loudly, as if asking succour from the Father of nature ; others struck their faces with their hands, throwing themselves on the earth ; others made their lamentations in songs, according to the customs of their country, which, although we could not understand their language, we saw corresponded well to the height of their sorrow. But now . . . came those who had the charge of the distribution, and they began to put them apart one from the other, in order to equalize the portions; wherefore it was necessary to part children and parents, husbands and wives, and brethren from each other. Neither in the partition of friends and relations was any law kept, only each fell where the lot took him. . . . And while they were placing in one part the children that saw their parents in another, the children sprang up perseveringly and fled unto them; the mothers enclosed their children in their arms and threw themselves with them upon the ground, receiving wounds with little pity for their own flesh, so that their offspring might not be torn from them! And so, with labour and difficulty, they concluded the partition, for, besides the trouble they had with the captives, the plain was full of people, as well of the town as of the villages and neighbourhood around, who on that day gave rest to their hands the mainstay of their livelihood, only to see this novelty." [1]

---

[1] I quote from the version given by Sir Arthur Helps, in his *Spanish Conquest*, vol. i. pp. 37–39, since it would be impossible to improve upon it. The original text is in Azurara, *Chronica do descobrimento e conquista de Guiné*, Paris, 1841, pp. 132–134. This chronicle was completed

There we have the infernal picture, very much as it was to be seen four hundred years later in our own country, as so many of us can still remember. But for the discovery of America this traffic in human beings would doubtless have been greatly limited in extent and duration. The conditions of European agriculture and mining were not such as to create a market for them. Natural economic laws would have prevented slavery from thriving in Europe, as they prevented it in New England. But in the subtropical regions of the New World slavery grew up quickly and sturdily, as foul weeds sprout in a congenial soil. At first it was a slavery of red men, and Columbus himself played an important part in establishing it. When Columbus came to Hispaniola on his second voyage, with 17 ships and 1500 followers, he found the relations between red

in 1453. Azurara goes on to give another side to the picture, for being much interested in the poor creatures he made careful inquiries and found that in general they were treated with marked kindness. They became Christians, and were taught trades or engaged in domestic service ; they were also allowed to acquire property and were often set free. This, however, was in the early days of modern slavery and in the period of Prince Henry and his ideas. At a later date, when Portuguese cruisers caught negroes by the hundred and sold them at Seville, whence thev were shipped to Hispaniola to work in the mines, there was very little to relieve the blackness of the transaction.

men and white men already hostile, and in order to get food for so many Spaniards, foraging expeditions were undertaken, which made matters worse. This state of things led Columbus to devise a notable expedient. In some of the neighbouring islands lived the voracious Caribs. In fleets of canoes they would swoop upon the coasts of Hispaniola, capture men and women by the score, and carry them off to be cooked and eaten. Now Columbus wished to win the friendship of the Indians about him by defending them against these enemies, and so he made raids against the Caribs, took some of them captive, and sent them as slaves to Spain, to be taught Spanish and converted to Christianity, so that they might come back to the islands as interpreters, and thus be useful aids in missionary work. It was really, said Columbus, a kindness to these cannibals to enslave them and send them where they could be baptized and rescued from everlasting perdition; and then again they could be received in payment for the cargoes of cattle, seeds, wine, and other provisions which must be sent from Spain for the support of the colony. Thus quaintly did the great discoverer, like so many other good men before and since, mingle considerations of religion with those of domestic economy. It is apt to prove an unwholesome mixture. Columbus proposed such an arrange-

Beginnings of Indian slavery under Columbus

ment to Ferdinand and Isabella, and it is to their credit that, straitened as they were for money, they for some time refused to accept it.

Slavery, however, sprang up in Hispaniola before any one could have fully realized the meaning of what was going on. As the Indians were unfriendly and food must be had, while foraging expeditions were apt to end in plunder and bloodshed, Columbus tried to regulate matters by prohibiting such expeditions and in lieu thereof imposing a light tribute or tax upon the entire population of Hispaniola above fourteen years of age. As this population was dense, a little from each person meant a good deal in the lump. The tribute might be a small piece of gold or of cotton, and was to be paid four times a year. Every time that an Indian paid this tax, a small brass token duly stamped was to be given him to hang about his neck as a voucher. If there were Indians who felt unable to pay the tribute, they might as an alternative render a certain amount of personal service in helping to plant seeds or tend cattle for the Spaniards.

Tribute

No doubt these regulations were well meant, and if the two races had been more evenly matched, perhaps they might not so speedily have developed into tyranny. As it was, they were like rules for regulating the depredations of wolves upon sheep. Two years had not elapsed before the alternative of personal service was demanded from whole villages of Indians at once. By 1499 the island had begun *Reparti-* to be divided into *repartimientos*, or *mientos* shares. One or more villages would be ordered, under the direction of their native chiefs, to till the soil for the benefit of some specified Spaniard or partnership of Spaniards; and such a village or villages constituted the *repartimiento* of the person or persons to whom it was assigned. This arrangement put the Indians into a state somewhat resembling that of feudal villenage; and this was as far as things had gone when the administration of Columbus came abruptly to an end.

It will be remembered that in 1502 the Spanish sovereigns sent to Hispaniola a governor *Ovando's* selected with especial care, a knight *treatment of* of the religious order of Alcántara, *white men* named Nicolas de Ovando. He was a small, fair-haired man of mild and courteous manners, and had an excellent reputation for ability and integrity. We are assured on the most unimpeachable authority that he was a good governor for white men. As to what was most needed in that turbulent colony, he was a strict disciplinarian, and had his own summary way of dealing with insubordinate characters. When he wished to dispose of some such incipient Roldan he would choose a time to invite him to dinner, and then, after some polite and interested talk, whereby the guest was apt to feel highly flattered, Ovando would all at once point down to the harbour and blandly inquire, "In which of those ships, now ready to weigh anchor, would you like to go back to Spain?" Then the dumbfoundered man would stammer, "My Lord, my Lord," and would perhaps plead that he had not money enough to pay his passage. "Pray do not let that trouble you," said this well-bred little governor, "it shall be my care to provide for that." And so without further ceremony the guest was escorted straight from dinner-table to ship.[1]

But this mild-spoken Ovando was capable of strange deeds, and the seven years of his administration in Hispaniola were so full of horror that I never can read his name without a shudder. His methods with Indians may be illustrated by his treatment of Anacaona, wife of that chieftain Caonabó who had been sent to Spain.[2] Ovando heard that the tribe, in which this woman exercised great authority, was meditating another attack upon the Spaniards, and he believed that an ounce of prevention was worth a pound of

Ovando's treatment of red men

[1] Las Casas, *Historia de las Indias*, tom. iii. p. 204.
[2] See above, vol. ii. p. 173.

cure. His seat of government was at the town of San Domingo, and Anacaona's territory at Xaragua was 200 miles distant. Ovando started at once with 300 foot soldiers and 70 horse. On reaching Xaragua he was received in a friendly manner by the Indians, who probably had no wish to offend so strong a force. Games were played, and Ovando proposed to show the Indians a tournament, at which they were much pleased, as their intense fear of the horse was beginning to wear off. All the chieftains of the neighbourhood were invited to assemble in a large wooden house, while Ovando explained to them the nature of the tournament that was about to take place. Meanwhile the Spanish soldiers surrounded the house. Ovando wore upon his breast the badge of his order, a small image of God the Father,[1] and as he stood talking with the chiefs, when he knew the preparations to be complete, he raised his hand and touched the image. At this concerted signal the soldiers rushed in and seized the chiefs, and bound them hand and foot. Then they went out and set fire to the house, and the chiefs were all burnt alive. Anacaona was hanged to a tree, several hundred Indians were put to the sword, and their country was laid waste. Ovando then founded a town in Xaragua, and called it

1 " Un Dios Padre en abito blanco." Marquez, *Tesoro militar de Cavallería*, p. 24, apud Helps, vol. i. p. 207.

the City of Peace, and gave it a seal on which was a dove with an olive branch.[1]

But this was nothing to what happened in Ovando's time. There were such atrocities as would seem incredible were they not recounted by a most intelligent and faithful witness who saw with his own eyes many of the things of which he tells us. Bartolomé de Las Casas was born in Seville in 1474.[2] His family, one of the

---

[1] An account of the affair is given in Herrera, dec. i. lib. vi. cap. iv., and with a pictorial illustration in Las Casas, *Indiarum devastationis et excidii narratio*, Heidelberg, 1664, p. 11. Herrera observes that the queen did not approve of Ovando's proceedings, and expressed an intention of investigating the affair, but the investigation was never made. Very likely Ovando's patron Fonseca, who cynically avowed that he cared not how many Indians perished, may have contrived to prevent it.

[2] The life of Las Casas is beautifully and faithfully told by Sir Arthur Helps, in his *History of the Spanish Conquest in America*, London, 1855–61, in 4 vols., a book which it does one's soul good to read. The most recent and elaborate biography is by Don Antonio Fabié, *Vida y escritos de Fray Bartolomé de Las Casas*, Madrid, 1879, in 2 vols. See also Llorente, *Vie de Las Casas*, prefixed to his *Œuvres de Las Casas*, Paris, 1822, tom. i. pp. ix–cx ; Remesal, *Historia de Chyapa y de Guatemala*, Madrid, 1619. References may also be found in Oveido, Gomara, Herrera, Torquemada, and other historians. One should above all read the works of Las Casas himself, concerning which much information may be obtained from Sabin's *List of the Printed Editions of the Works of Fray Bartolomé de Las Casas, Bishop of Chiapa*, New York, 1870. The book contains also a notice of the

noblest in Spain, was of French origin, descended from the viscounts of Limoges.[1] They were already in Spain before the thirteenth century, and played a distinguished part in the conquest of Seville from the Moors by Ferdinand III. of Castile, in 1252. From that time forward, members of the family were to be found in positions of trust, and among their marked traits of character were invincible courage and spotless integrity. By birth and training Bartholomew was an aristocrat to the very tips of his fingers. For the earlier part of his life dates can hardly be assigned, but the news of the triumphant return of Columbus from his first voyage across the Sea of Darkness may probably have found him

Birth and family of Las Casas

MSS. — The *Life of Las Casas*, by Sir Arthur Helps, London, 1868, consists of passages extracted from his larger work, and suffers seriously from the removal of the context.

[1] Argote, *Nobleza de Andalucia*, fol. 210. According to Llorente (*Vie de Las Casas*, p. xcviii) a branch of the Seville family returned to France. Don Carlos de Las Casas was one of the grandees who accompanied Blanche of Castile when she went to France in the year 1200, to marry the prince, afterward Louis VIII. From this nobleman was descended Napoleon's faithful chamberlain the Marquis de Las Cases. The migration of the French family to Spain probably antedated the custom of giving surnames, which was growing up in the eleventh and twelfth centuries. The name Las Casas was of course acquired in Spain, and afterward the branch of the family which had returned to France changed the spelling to Las Cases.

at the university of Salamanca, where for several years he studied philosophy, theology, and jurisprudence, and obtained a licentiate's degree. His father, Don Francisco de Las Casas, accompanied Columbus on the second voyage, and returned to Seville in 1497 with a young Indian slave whom Columbus had given him. It was on this occasion that Isabella asked, with some indignation, " Who has empowered my admiral thus to dispose of my subjects?" The elder Las Casas gave the Indian to his son, who soon became warmly interested in him and in his race; and as the father retained an estate in Hispaniola, the son came out with Ovando in 1502 and settled in that island.[1] He was then twenty-eight years old. Little is known of his first occupations there, except that he seems to have been more or less concerned in money-making, like all the other settlers. But about 1510 he was ordained as a priest. He seems to have been the first Christian clergyman ordained in the New World. He was a person of such immense ability and strength of character that in whatever age of the world he had lived he would undoubtedly have been one of its foremost men. As a man of business he had rare

[1] According to Llorente, the elder Las Casas accompanied Columbus on his first voyage in 1492, and Bartholomew was with him on his third voyage in 1498, but this has been disproved. See Humboldt, *Examen critique*, tom. iii. p. 286.

executive power; he was a great diplomatist and an eloquent preacher, a man of Titanic energy, ardent but self-controlled, of unconquerable tenacity, warm-hearted and tender, calm in his judgments, shrewdly humorous, absolutely fearless, and absolutely true. He made many and bitter enemies, and some of them were unscrupulous enough; but I believe no one has ever accused him of any worse sin than extreme fervour of temperament. His wrath could rise to a white heat, and indeed there was occasion enough for it. He was also very apt to call a spade a spade and to proclaim unpleasant truths with pungent emphasis. But his justice is conspicuously displayed in his voluminous writings. He was one of the best historians of his time, and wrote a most attractive Spanish style, quaint, pithy, and nervous,— a style which goes straight to the mark and rings like true metal.[1] It is impossible to doubt

His character and writings

---

[1] I do not mean to be understood as calling it a *literary* style. It is not graceful like that of great masters of expression such as Pascal or Voltaire. It is not seldom cumbrous and awkward, usually through trying to say too much at once. But in spite of this it is far more attractive than many a truly artistic literary style. There is a great charm in reading what comes from a man brimful of knowledge and utterly unselfish and honest. The crisp shrewdness, the gleams of gentle humour and occasional sharp flashes of wit, and the fervid earnestness in the books of Las Casas, combine to make them very delightful. It was the unfailing sense of humour, which

the accuracy of his statements about the matters
of fact which were within the range of his personal knowledge. His larger statistics, as to the
numbers of the Indian populations extermi-
nated, have been doubted with good reason ;
statistics are a complicated affair, in which it is
easy to let feelings make havoc with figures.[1]
But with regard to particular statements of fact
one cannot help believing Las Casas, because
his perfect sincerity is allied with a judgment so
sane and a charity so broad as to constrain our
assent. He is almost always ready to make allowances, and very rarely lets his hatred of sin blind
him to any redeeming qualities there may be in
the sinner. It was he that said, in his crisp way,
of Ovando, that he was a good governor, but not

is so often wanting in reformers, that kept Las Casas from developing into a fanatic. The judicious words of Humboldt in
another connection will apply very well to the style of Las
Casas : in speaking of it, "il ne s'agit pas de discuter ce
qu'on appelle vaguement le mérite littéraire d'un écrivain. Il
s'agit de quelque chose de plus grave et de plus historique.
Nous avons considéré le style comme expression du caractère,
comme reflet de l'intérieur de l'homme. . . . C'est chez
les hommes plus disposés à agir qu' à soigner leur diction,
chez ceux qui demeurent étrangers à tout artifice propre à
produire des émotions par le charme du langage, que la liaison
si long-temps signalée entre le caractère et le style se fait sen-
tir de préférence." *Examen critique*, tom. iii. p. 240.

[1] The arithmetic of Las Casas is, however, no worse than
that of all the Spanish historians of that age. With every one
of them the nine digits seem to have gone on a glorious spree.

for Indians. What Las Casas witnessed under the administration of Ovando and other governors, he published in 1552, in his " Brief Relation of the Destruction of the Indies," a book of which there are copies in several languages, all more or less rare now.[1] It is one of the most gruesome books ever printed.

We have seen how by the year 1499 communities of Indians were assigned in *repartimiento* to sundry Spaniards, and were thus reduced to a kind of villenage. Queen Isabella The royal had disapproved of this, but she was orders of 1503 persuaded to sanction it, and presently in 1503 she and Ferdinand issued a most disastrous order. They gave discretionary power to Ovando to compel Indians to work, but it must be for wages. They ordered him, moreover, to see that Indians were duly instructed in the Christian faith, provided that they must come to mass " as free persons, for so they are." It was further allowed that the cannibal Caribs, if taken in actual warfare, might be sold into slavery. Little did the sovereigns know what a legion of devils they were letting loose. Of course the doings in Hispaniola always went

[1] I have never seen any of the English versions. Sabin mentions four, published in London in 1583, 1656, 1687, and 1699. *List of the Printed Editions*, etc., pp. 22–24. The edition which I use is the Latin one published at Heidelberg, 1664, small quarto.

the full length of the authority granted from Spain, and generally went far beyond. Of course the Indians were compelled to work, and it was not for wages ; and of course, so long as there was no legal machinery for protecting the natives, any Indian might be called a cannibal and sold into slavery. The way in which Ovando carried out the order about missionary work was characteristic. As a member of a religious order of knights, he was familiar with the practice of *encomienda*, by which groups of novices were assigned to certain preceptors to be disciplined and instructed in the mys- *Encomiendas* teries of the order. The word *encomienda* means "commandery" or "preceptory," and so it came to be a nice euphemism for a hateful thing. Ovando distributed Indians among the Spaniards in lots of 50 or 100 or 500, with a deed worded thus : "To you, such a one, is given an *encomienda* of so many Indians, and you are to teach them the things of our holy Catholic Faith." In practice the last clause was disregarded as a mere formality, and the effect of the deed was simply to consign a parcel of Indians to the tender mercies of some Spaniard to do as he pleased with them. If the system of *repartimientos* was in effect serfdom or villenage, the system of *encomiendas* was unmitigated slavery.

Such a cruel and destructive slavery has seldom, if ever, been known. The work of the

Indians was at first largely agricultural, but as many mines of gold were soon discovered they were driven in gangs to work in the mines. There was a rush of Spaniards to Hispaniola, like the rush of all sorts and conditions of white men in recent times to California and Australia, and we know well what kind of a population is gathered together under such circumstances. For a graphic description of it we may go to Charles Reade's " Never too Late to Mend." And here we must take care not to identify too indiscriminately the Spaniards, as such, with the horrors perpetrated in Hispaniola.

Effects of the discovery of gold

It was not in the character of Spaniards so much as in the character of ruffians that the perpetrators behaved, and there have been ruffians enough among people who speak English. If the worst of these slave-drivers was a Spaniard, so too was Las Casas. Many of the wretches were the offscourings of camps, the vile refuse of European wars ; some of them were criminals, sent out here to disencumber Spanish jails. Of course they had no notion of working with their own hands, or of wielding any implement of industry except the lash. With such an abundant supply of cheap labour an Indian's life was counted of no value. It was cheaper to work an Indian to death and get another than to take care of him, and accordingly the slaves were worked to death without mercy. From time to time the Indians rose in rebellion, but these attempts were savagely suppressed, and a policy of terror was adopted. Indians were slaughtered by the hundred, burned alive, impaled on sharp stakes, torn to pieces by blood-hounds. In retaliation for the murder of a Spaniard it was thought proper to call up fifty or sixty Indians and chop off their hands. Little children were flung into the water to drown, with less concern than if they had been puppies. In the mingling of sacred ideas with the sheerest devilry there was a grotesqueness fit for the pencil of Doré. Once, " in honour and reverence of Christ and his twelve Apostles," they hanged thirteen Indians in a row at such a height that their toes could just touch the ground, and then pricked them to death with their sword-points, taking care not to kill them quickly. At another time, when some old reprobate was broiling half a dozen Hideous Indians in a kind of cradle suspended cruelties over a slow fire, their shrieks awoke the Spanish captain who in a neighbouring hut was taking his afternoon nap, and he called out testily to the man to despatch those wretches at once, and stop their noise. But this demon, determined not to be baulked of his enjoyment, only gagged the poor creatures. Can it be, says Las Casas, that I really saw such things, or are they hideous dreams? Alas, they are no dreams;

" all this did I behold with my bodily mortal eyes." [1]

This tyranny went on until the effect was like that of a pestilence. The native population rapidly diminished until labour grew scarce, and it was found necessary in Hispaniola to send and kidnap Indians from other islands, and to import from Seville negroes that had been caught by the Portuguese in Africa. The first slave-hunters that went to the Lucayan Islands beguiled the simple natives with pretty stories and promises, and thus enticed them on board their ships. Some thousands of Lucayans were taken to Hispaniola, and there is a touching story of one of these poor fellows, who cut down and hollowed out a pithy tree, and lashed to it smaller stems till he had made a good staunch raft. He stuffed it with corn and calabashes of fresh water, and then with two friends, a man and a woman, he put to sea one dark night, and they paddled toward the north star.[2] After many anxious days and nights they had gone more than 200 miles and were coming near to their own land, when

[1] " Todo esto yo lo vide con mis ojos corporales mortales." *Hist. de las Indias*, tom. iii. p. 96.

[2] Herrera, *Historia de las Indias*, Madrid, 1601, tom. i. p. 228. As Sir Arthur Helps observes, " there is somewhat of immortality in a stout-hearted action, and though long past it seems still young and full of life : one feels quite anxious now, as if those Indians were yet upon that sea, to know what becomes of them." *Spanish Conquest*, vol. i. p. 226.

all at once their hearts were sickened at the sight of a Spanish cruiser in the offing, and presently they were stowed beneath its deck and carried back in black despair to the land of bondage. No less pathetic is the story of the cacique Hatuey in Cuba, who had heard that the Spaniards were coming over from Hispaniola and hit upon an ingenious expedient for protecting his people. Taking a big lump of gold he called his clan-chiefs together, and said: Behold, this is the god of the white men; wherefore let us dance to it and reverence it, that if peradventure they come hither, it may tell them to do us no harm; and so these simple barbarians adored the piece of yellow metal and danced around it, and sought to win its favour.[1]

In 1509 Ovando was recalled, and went home, a poor man, leaving as his last act the larger part of his property to found a hospital for needy Spaniards. Under his successor, Diego Columbus, there was little improvement. The case had become a hard one to deal with.

[1] Herrera, *op. cit.* tom. i. p. 293. This propitiation of the white man's yellow god did not avail to save the unfortunate cacique. Soon after their arrival in Cuba the Spaniards caught him, and he was burned alive at the stake. As he was writhing amid the flames, a priest held up a cross before him and begged him to " become a Christian " so that he might go to heaven. The half-roasted Indian replied that if there were Christians in heaven he had no desire to go to any such place. See Las Casas, *Indiarum devastationis et excidii narratio*, p. 16.

There were now what are called " vested rights," the rights of property in slaves, to be respected. Antonio Montesino But in 1510 there came a dozen Dominican monks, and they soon decided, in defiance of vested rights, to denounce the wickedness they saw about them. So one Sunday in the year 1511 Father Antonio Montesino preached a great sermon in the church at San Domingo, from the text, " I am the voice of one crying in the wilderness." His words, says the chronicler, were " very piercing and terrible." He told his dismayed hearers that they were living in mortal sin, and their greed and cruelty were such that for any chance they had of going to heaven they might as well be Moors or Turks !

Startling words, indeed, to Spanish ears, — to be told that they were no better than Mahometans ! The town was in an uproar, and after the noon dinner a deputation of the principal citizens went to the shed which served temporarily as a monastery, and angrily demanded an apology from Father Antonio. The prior's quiet reply was that Father Antonio's sentiments were those of the Dominican community and would on no account be retracted. The infuriated citizens then said that unless a different tone was taken in the pulpit next Sunday the monks had better pack up their goods for a sea voyage. That would be easily done, quoth the prior, and verily, says Las Casas, with his sly humour, it was so, for all they had on earth would have gone into two small trunks.[1]

Next Sunday the church was thronged with Spaniards from far and near, for the excitement was fierce. Mass was performed, and then, amid breathless silence, Father Antonio stepped into the pulpit and preached a still more terrible sermon; threatened his hearers with eternal torments, and declared that the monks would refuse confession to any man who should mal-treat his Indians or engage in the slave-trade. Glorious Antonio Montesino ! first of preachers on American soil to declare war to the knife against this gravest of American sins !

Loyalty to the church was too strong among Spaniards for any violence to be offered to these monks, but the citizens made complaint to King Ferdinand. His wife Isabella, dying six years before these events, had left to him in her will one half of the income to be got from The king's the Indies during his lifetime. After position Isabella's death the crown of Castile had passed to their daughter Joanna, and Ferdinand for a while, restricted to his own kingdom of Aragon, had little to do with American affairs. But after a couple of years, Joanna having become

[1] These events are related with full details by Las Casas, *Hist. de las Indias*, tom. iii. pp. 365–380.

insane, Ferdinand had become regent of Castile, and was thus lord over America, and as half the American revenue, which was chiefly gold from the mines, was to come to him, the colonists in Hispaniola looked to him to defend their vested interests. The citizens of San Domingo got hold of an unworthy member of the Franciscan order, and sent him to Spain to complain against the Dominicans; and Antonio Montesino went over himself to forestall the Franciscan monk. Antonio saw the king and made a deep impression upon him, so that a conclave of learned priests was assembled, and various plans of relief and reform were discussed. Nothing was really accomplished, except that some seeds of reform were sown, to bear fruit at a later season.

Meanwhile the good Montesino had gained an ally upon the scene of action worth a dozen kings. Las Casas was by natural endowment a many-sided man, who looked at human affairs from various points of view. Under other circumstances he need not necessarily have developed into a philanthropist, though any career into which he might have been drawn could not have failed to be honourable and noble. At

Las Casas at first a slave-owner

first he seems to have been what one might call worldly minded. But the most interesting thing about him we shall find to be his steady intellectual and spirit-

ual development ; from year to year he rose
to higher and higher planes of thought and feeling. He was at first a slave-owner like the rest,
and had seen no harm in it. But from the first
his kindly sympathetic nature asserted itself, and
his treatment of his slaves was such that they
loved him. He was a man of striking and
easily distinguishable aspect, and the Indians in
general, who fled from the sight of white men,
came soon to recognize him as a friend who
could always be trusted. At the same time,
however, as a good man of business he was disposed to make money, and, as he tells us, " he
took no more heed than the other Spaniards to
bethink himself that his Indians were unbe-
lievers, and of the duty that there was on his
part to give them instruction, and to bring them
to the bosom of the Church of Christ." He
sympathized with much that was said by Montesino, but thought at first that in his unquali-
fied condemnation of the whole system of slavery that great preacher was going too far. We
must not be wanting in charity toward slave-
holders. It is hard for a man to extricate himself from the entanglements of ideas and situa-
tions prepared for him before he was born. The
heart of Las Casas, however, was deeply stirred
by Montesino, and he pondered much upon
his words.

In the same year that those memorable sermons were preached, Diego Columbus made up his mind to conquer and colonize Cuba, and he sent Velasquez for that purpose. Las Casas presently followed. The usual tale of horrors had begun, but he succeeded in doing much to improve the situation. For the time he was the only priest on the island. The tremendous power of the church was personified in him, and he used it unflinchingly in defence of the Indians. When the island was regarded as conquered, Velasquez proceeded to give *encomiendas* of Indians to his friends, and a large village was given as an *encomienda* to two partners, of whom

Conversion of Las Casas one was Las Casas. It was the duty of Las Casas to say mass and now and then to preach, and in thinking of his sermon for Pentecost, 1514, he opened his Bible, and his eye alighted upon these verses in the 34th chapter of Ecclesiasticus : —

" The Most High is not pleased with the offerings of the wicked : neither is he pacified for sin by the multitude of sacrifices.

" The bread of the needy is their life ; he that defraudeth him thereof is a man of blood.

" He that taketh away his neighbour's living slayeth him ; and he that defraudeth the labourer of his hire is a shedder of blood."

As he read these words a light from heaven seemed to shine upon Las Casas. The scales fell from his eyes. He saw that the system of slavery was wrong in principle. The question whether you treated your slaves harshly or kindly did not go to the root of the matter. As soon as you took from the labourer his wages the deadly sin was committed, the monstrous evil was inaugurated. There must be a stop put to this, said Las Casas. We have started wrong. Here are vast countries which Holy Church has given to the Spaniards in trust, that the heathen may be civilized and brought into the fold of Christ; and we have begun by making Hispaniola a hell. This thing must not be suffered to grow with the growth of Spanish conquest. There was but one remedy. The axe must be put to the root of the tree. Slavery must be abolished.

Las Casas began by giving up his own slaves. He had reason enough to know that others might not treat them so well as he, but he was not the man to preach what he did not practise. His partner, Pedro de Renteria, was a man of noble nature and much under his influence, so that there was no difficulty there. Then Las Casas went into the pulpit and preached to his congregation that their souls were in His first danger so long as they continued to proceedings hold their *encomiendas* of Indians. "All were amazed," he says; "some were struck with compunction; others were as much surprised to hear it called a sin to make use of the Indians,

. 275

as if they had been told it were sinful to make use of the beasts of the field."

Too many were of this latter mood, and finding his people incorrigible, Las Casas sold what worldly goods he had left, and went to Spain to lay the case before King Ferdinand. First he visited Bishop Fonseca, as the most important member of the Council for the Indies. His reception From this coarse man, with his cyn-by Fonseca ; ical contempt for philanthropists, Las Casas got such a reception as might have been expected. It will be remembered that Ovando was one of Fonseca's creatures. When Las Casas told how 7000 children had cruelly perished in Hispaniola within three months, he doubtless overstated the case, and clearly Fonseca did not believe him. He answered roughly, "Look here, you droll fool, what is all this to me, and what is it to the king?" This fairly took our poor priest's breath away. He only exclaimed, "O great and eternal God! to whom, then, is it of any concern?" and so he turned upon his heel and left the room.

On arriving at Seville, he learned that the king had just died, January 23, 1516. Ferdinand's daughter Joanna, queen of Castile and heiress to the throne of Aragon, was still insane, and both thrones descended practically to her illustrious son Charles, a boy of sixteen, who was then in Flanders. For the present the great

Cardinal Ximenes was regent of Spain, and to him went Las Casas with his tale of woe. From the cardinal he obtained ready and and by Cardinal Ximenes cordial sympathy. It was a fortunate circumstance that at this juncture brought two such men together. Las Casas knew well that the enslavement of Indians was not contemplated in the royal orders of 1503, except so far as concerned cannibals taken in war; but the evil had become so firmly established that at first he hesitated about the policy of using this line of argument. He prudently shaped his question in this wise : " With what justice can such things be done, whether the Indians are free or not ? " Here, to his joy, the cardinal caught him up vehemently. " With no justice whatever : what, are not the Indians free ? who doubts about their being free ? " This was a great point gained at the start, for it put the official theory of the Spanish government on the side of Las Casas, and made the Spaniards in America appear in the light of transgressors. The matter was thoroughly discussed with Ximenes First attempts and that amiable Dutchman, Cardinal at reform Adrian, who was afterwards Pope. A commission of Hieronymite friars was appointed to accompany Las Casas to the West Indies, with minute instructions and ample powers for making investigations and enforcing the laws. Ximenes appointed Las Casas Protector of the

277

Indians, and clothed him with authority to impeach delinquent judges or other public officials. The new regulations, could they have been carried out, would have done much to mitigate the sufferings of the Indians. They must be paid wages, they must be humanely treated and taught the Christian religion. But as the Spanish government needed revenue, the provision that Indians might be compelled to work in the mines was not repealed. The Indians must work, and the Spaniards must pay them. Las Casas argued correctly that so long as this provision was retained the work of reform would go but little way. Somebody, however, must work the mines ; and so the talk turned to the question of sending out white labourers or negroes.

Here we come to the statement, often repeated, that it was Las Casas who first introduced negro slavery and the African slave-trade into the New World. The statement is a good specimen of the headlong, helter-skelter way in which things get said and believed in this super-

The popular notion about Las Casas and negro slavery ficial world. As first repeated, there was probably an agreeable tinge of paradox in representing the greatest of philanthropists as the founder of one of the vilest systems of bondage known to modern times. At length it has come to pass that people who know nothing about Las Casas, and have absolutely no other idea associated with his

name, still vaguely think of him as the man
who brought negro slaves to America as substitutes for Indians, — the man who sacrificed
one race of his fellow-creatures to another, and
thus paid Peter by robbing Paul.

There could not be a grosser historical blun-
der than this notion, and yet, like most such
blunders, it has arisen from a perversion of
things that really were said if not done. In
order to arrive at historical truth, it is not enough
to obtain correct items of fact ; it is necessary to
group the items in their causal relations and to
estimate the precise weight that must be accorded
to each in the total result. To do this is often
so difficult that half-truths are very commonly
offered us in place of whole truths ; and it
sometimes happens that of all forms of falsehood
none is so misleading as the half-truth.

The statement about Las Casas, with which
we are here concerned, properly divides itself
into a pair of statements. It is alleged, in the
first place, that it was Las Casas who first suggested the employment of negroes as substitutes
for Indians ; and in the second place, that the
origin, or at any rate the steady development,
of negro slavery in America was due to this
suggestion. These are two different propositions
and call for different comments.

With regard to the first, it is undoubtedly
true that Las Casas at one time expressed the

opinion that if there must be slave-labour, the enslavement of blacks might perhaps be toler-

What Las Casas said

ated as the smaller of two evils, inasmuch as the negroes were regarded as a hardier race than the Indians and better able to support continuous labour. At one time the leading colonists of Hispaniola had told Las Casas that if they might have license to import each a dozen negroes, they would coöperate with him in his plans for setting free the Indians and improving their condition. When Las Casas at the Spanish court was confronted with the argument that there must be somebody to work the mines, he recalled this suggestion of the colonists, and proposed it as perhaps the least odious way out of the difficulty. It is therefore evident that at that period in his life he did not realize the wickedness of slavery so distinctly in the case of black men as in the case of red men. In other words, he had not yet outgrown that mediæval habit of mind which regarded the right to "life, liberty, and the pursuit of happiness," and other rights, not as common to all mankind, but as parcelled out among groups and classes of men in a complicated way that to our minds, on the eve of the twentieth century,

Mediæval and modern conceptions of rights

has become well-nigh unintelligible. It was the great French writers of the eighteenth century who first gave distinct expression to the notion of "unalienable

280

rights," with which mankind has been endowed by the Creator. This notion has become so familiar to our minds that we sometimes see the generalizations of Rousseau and Diderot, or whatever remains sound in them, derided as mere platitudes, as if it had never been necessary to preach such self-evident truths. But these " platitudes " about universal rights were far enough from being self-evident in the sixteenth century. On the contrary, they were extremely unfamiliar and abstruse conceptions, toward which the most enlightened minds could only grope their way by slow degrees.[1] In Las Casas it is interesting to trace such a development. He had gradually risen to the perception of the full wickedness of slavery in the form in which he had become familiar with it; but he had not yet extended his generalizations, as a modern thinker would do, to remote cases, and in order to gain a point, the supreme importance of which he keenly felt, he was ready to make concessions. In later years he blamed himself roundly for making any such concessions. Had

Gradual development of the modern conception in Las Casas

---

[1] As Mr. John Morley observes, " the doctrine of moral obligations toward the lower races had not yet taken its place in Europe." *Diderot and the Encyclopædists*, London, 1880, p. 386. Mr. Morley's remarks on the influence of Raynal's famous book, *Histoire des deux Indes* in this connection, are admirable.

he "sufficiently considered the matter," he would not for all the world have entertained such a suggestion for a moment; for, said he, the negroes "had been made slaves unjustly and tyrannically, and the same reason holds good of them as of the Indians." [1]

With regard to the second of the statements we are considering, the question arises how far did this suggestion, for which Las Casas afterward so freely blamed himself, have any material effect in setting on foot the African slave-trade or in enlarging its dimensions? The reply is that it had no such effect whatever. As for the beginnings, negroes had been carried to Hispaniola in small numbers as early as 1501; and in the royal instructions drawn up at that time for Ovando, he was forbidden to take to the colony Moors, Jews, new converts from Islam or Judaism, monks not Spanish, and the children of persons burned at the stake for heresy, but he might take negro slaves.[2] Official documents prove that at various times between 1500 and 1510 negroes were sent over to work in the mines, but not in large numbers.[3] As for the extensive development of negro slavery in the West Indies, it did not begin for

His momentary suggestion had no traceable effect upon negro slavery

---

[1] Las Casas, *Hist. de las Indias*, tom. iv. p. 380.
[2] Navarrete, *Coleccion de viages*, tom. ii. doc. 175.
[3] Herrera, *Hist. de las Indias*, tom. i. pp. 274–276.

many years after that period in the career of Las Casas with which we are now dealing, and there is nothing to show that his suggestion or concession was in any way concerned in bringing it about. If, on the other hand, instead of confining our attention to this single incident in his life, the importance of which has been egregiously exaggerated, we consider the general effect of his life-work, that effect was clearly adverse to the development of the African slave-trade. For if the depopulation of the New World had continued, which Las Casas did so much to check, it cannot be doubted that the importation of negroes to Spanish America would have been immeasurably greater than it has been. The African slave-trade would have assumed much larger proportions than it has ever known, and its widely ramifying influence for evil, its poisonous effects upon the character of European society in the New World, whether Spanish or English, would probably have surpassed anything that we can now realize. When the work of Las Casas is deeply considered, we cannot make him anything else but an antagonist of human slavery in all its forms, and the mightiest and most effective antagonist, withal, that has ever lived. Subtract his glorious life from the history of the past, and we might still

His life-work did much to diminish the volume of negro slavery and the spiritual corruption attendant upon it

be waiting, sick with hope deferred, for a Wilberforce, a Garrison, and a Lincoln.

In all the work at the Spanish court the Bishop of Burgos tried by every means in his power to impede and thwart Las Casas, and agents of the colonists gained the ears of the Hieronymite friars, so that matters were very imperfectly mended, and the next year, after a stout fight, Las Casas returned to Spain to find the great cardinal on his death-bed. The loss of this powerful ally was a serious misfortune for Las Casas. He was not long, however, in Charles V. winning the esteem of Charles V. The and Las Casas young king greatly liked him, and his grave face always lighted up with pleasure whenever he happened to meet " Master Bartholomew," as he used to call him. Las Casas now tried to enlist white emigrants for the West Indies, to labour there ; but the task of getting Spaniards to work, instead of making slaves work for them, was not an encouraging one. At length, however, he devised a scheme which seemed likely to work. He undertook to select fifty Spaniards for whose characters he could vouch, to subscribe 200 ducats each and go with him to found a colony upon the mainland. That the Indians might distinguish between these men and any other Spaniards they had ever seen, they were to wear a peculiar uniform,

white with a coloured cross. If their work should
prose he intended to ask the Pope to recognize them as a religious fraternity, A noble
like those of the Middle Ages, which scheme
had been of such inestimable value as civilizing
agencies. He promised to make it an enterprise which should justify itself by paying its
own way and yielding a steady revenue to the
Crown. If he could not cure the evils in the
islands, he could at least set the example of a
new colony founded on sound principles, and
might hope that it would serve as a centre for
the diffusion of a higher civilization in the New
World.

In pursuance of this scheme Las Casas obtained from Charles V. a grant of territory
about Cumaná on the Pearl Coast. There were
three years of hard work in these preliminaries,
hindered at every step by the malignant intrigues of Bishop Fonseca. At length, in 1520,
the Protector of the Indians returned to Hispaniola, and in 1521 he was ready for the Pearl
Coast. Some Dominicans had already founded
a small monastery there, and from them Las
Casas could always look for cordial assistance.
But Satan had not been asleep while The mischief
these things were going on. In the that one miserable sinner
neighbouring island of Cubagua, fish- can do
ing for pearls, was a young man named

Alonso de Ojeda,[1] concerning whom Las Casas says, with truth, "that if he had not been born, the world would have lost nothing." Ojeda wanted slaves, and thought it a bright idea to catch a few on the mainland and pretend they were cannibals. He took a notary with his party in order to catechise some chiefs and have such answers taken down as could be made to convict them of cannibalism.[2] But having no paper about him he stopped at the Dominican monastery and asked for a sheet, which was given him. Ojeda presently changed his mind, abandoned his catechising project as uncertain and tedious, and adopted some other device. A few miles down the coast he fell in with some Indians, attacked them under circumstances of foulest treachery, slew a great many, and carried off the rest in his vessel. Now the Indians were always deeply impressed with the way in which white people communicated intelligence to one

[1] Llorente (*Œuvres de Las Casas*, tom. i. p. 139) confounds him with the Alonso de Ojeda whose career we have already traced down to his death in 1515, five years before the time of the events we are now narrating. Curiously enough, on another page of the same volume (p. xlv) Llorente warns the reader not to confound the two, but thinks that this younger sinner may perhaps have been the son of the other. I suspect this is a mere guess.

[2] The reader will observe that some slight progress seems to have been made, since these legal formalities were deemed necessary.

another by means of mysterious bits of paper.
Some Indians had seen the innocent monk give
the piece of paper to Ojeda, and so, as the news
of his evil deeds flew along the coast, they naturally concluded that the Dominicans must be
his accomplices. So they not only contrived to
kill the worthless Ojeda the next time he
touched upon the coast, but they set fire to the
monastery and massacred the monks. And so
fiercely was their wrath now kindled against all
Spaniards that soon after the founding of the
colony of Las Casas at Cumaná, on an occasion
when — fortunately for him — some business
had called him back to Hispaniola,
they attacked the little colony in over- *Destruction*
whelming numbers, and destroyed it. *of the little*
colony
Those who escaped their javelins were fain to
flee to the neighbouring islands and thence to
San Domingo. Their incipient village was
burned to the ground, and not a white man
was left on the Pearl Coast.

Seven years had now elapsed since that memorable Pentecost of 1514, seven years of cease-
less toil and sore perplexity, and now, just as
the way was beginning to seem clear toward
some tangible result, everything was ruined by
the villainy of one scurvy knave. There is reason to suppose that Las Casas may have somewhat overtaxed his strength. His nerves were
strained beyond endurance, and when he heard

the news of this terrible blow, he fell, for the first and only time in his life, into a fit of profound despondency. Perhaps, said he, in prophetic language, " the Spaniards are not to be saved from the commission of great wickedness and from decay of their power." Perhaps God had for some inscrutable purpose decreed that the Indians must be destroyed. Perhaps there was in his own soul some lurking sin which made him unworthy to be God's instrument for righting these grievous wrongs.[1] The Dominican monastery at San Domingo was no longer a mere shed. In its pleasant garden would Las Casas sit motionless hour after hour, absorbed in meditation upon these heart-rending mysteries of the Divine Providence. The good monks improved the situation by persuading Las Casas to join their order. He became a Dominican in 1522, and remained there at the monastery for eight years, leading the life of a close student, acquiring a profound knowledge of patristic and mediæval theology, becoming expert in

Grief of Las Casas; he becomes a Dominican monk

[1] " The dignity and greatness of his cause were so predominant in the mind of Las Casas as to leave no room for influences merely personal. It does not appear that he ever expected gratitude from the Indians ; nor did the terrible disaster which he suffered at Cumaná leave, apparently, the slightest rancour in his mind." Helps, *Spanish Conquest*, vol. iv. p. 334.

the sinuosities of scholastic logic, and writing history such as the world could ill afford to spare.

During these eight years the Spanish empire in America was rapidly expanding. When Las Casas entered the monastery, Cortes had lately captured the great Mexican pueblo and overthrown the Aztec Confederacy. Then Pedro de Alvarado conquered Guatemala, while Pedrarias and his captains devastated Nicaragua like a typhoon or a plague. *Spanish conquests, and resulting movements* Now in 1530 the Pizarros and Almagro were just starting on their final and decisive expedition for the conquest of Peru. Old Pedrarias had just died at somewhere about his ninetieth year. The horrors of Hispaniola had been repeated in Nicaragua. We may suppose that this had much to do with arousing the Dominicans of Hispaniola to renewed activity. Las Casas tells us very little about himself at this conjuncture. Indeed, his history of the Indies brings us down no farther than 1522. But we learn from Antonio de Remesal — an excellent authority for this part of his career — that he emerged from his seclusion in 1530, went over to Spain, and obtained from Charles V. a decree prohibiting the enslavement of Indians in the countries which Pizarro and Almagro were expected to conquer.[1] On returning to Hispa-

[1] Remesal, *Historia de Chiapa*, Madrid, 1619, p. 103.

niola, Las Casas was sent to the new Dominican monastery in Mexico, there to take companions and proceed to Peru, for the purpose of proclaiming the imperial decree and founding a monastery there. For some reason the latter purpose was not carried out. The decree was proclaimed, but it proved impossible to enforce it. For three or four years Las Casas was kept busy in Nicaragua, putting a curb upon the rapacity and cruelty of the new governor. Meanwhile a friend of his was appointed Bishop of Guatemala, and thither Las Casas repaired early in 1536. A Dominican monastery, founded there somewhat prematurely, had been unoccupied for six or seven years, and Las Casas and three of his companions now took possession of it. There the first thing they did was to acquire a knowledge of the Quiché language spoken by the natives of Guatemala, a language not without some interesting native literature which modern scholarship has discovered and edited.[1] So zealously did these four monks work that it was not long before they could talk quite fluently in Quiché, and they soon found occasion

The little monastery in Guatemala

[1] See Brasseur de Bourbourg, *Bibliothèque Mexico-Guatémalienne ; Popol Vuh, le Livre Sacré des Quichés ;* and for the literature of a neighbouring people in Guatemala, see Brinton's *Annals of the Cakchiquels,* Philadelphia, 1885.

to put this rare accomplishment to a practical use.

While in the monastery at San Domingo, Las Casas had written his famous Latin treatise *De unico vocationis modo*, or the only proper method of calling men to Christianity. In these years of trial his mind had been growing in clearness and grasp. He had got beyond all sophistical distinctions between men of one colour and faith and men of another, — a wonderful progress for a Spaniard born eight years before the Moor was driven from Granada. He had come to see what was really involved in the Christian assumption of the brotherhood of men; and accordingly he maintained that to make war upon infidels or heathen, merely because they are infidels or heathen, is sinful; and that the only right and lawful way of bringing men to Christ is the way of reason and persuasion. To set forth such a doctrine at that time and still keep clear of the Inquisition required consummate skilfulness in statement. This little book was never printed, but manuscript copies of the original Latin and of a Spanish translation were circulated, and called forth much comment. The illustrations drawn from American affairs exasperated the Spanish colonists, and they taunted Las Casas. He was only a vain theorizer, they said; the gospel of peace would be all very well in a world already perfect, but in our world the only practicable gospel is the gospel of kicks and blows. Go to, let this apostle try himself to convert a tribe of Indians and make them keep the peace ; he will soon find that something more is needed than words of love. So said the scoffers, as they wagged their heads.

A challenge

Las Casas presently took them at their word. The province of Tuzulutlan, just to the north of Guatemala and bordering upon the peninsula of Yucatan, was called by the Spaniards the " Land of War." It was an inaccessible country of beetling crags, abysmal gorges, raging torrents, and impenetrable forest. In their grade of culture the inhabitants seem to have resembled the Aztecs. They had idols and human sacrifices,and were desperate fighters. The Spaniards had three times invaded this country, and three times had been hurled back in a very dilapidated condition. It could hardly be called a promising field, but this it was that Las Casas chose for his experiment.[1]

The Land
of War

Let us note well his manner of proceeding, for there are those to-day who maintain that the type of character which Victor Hugo has sketched in Monseigneur Bienvenu is not calculated to

[1] A full account of the work of Las Casas in Tuzulutlan is given in Remesal's *Historia de Chiapa,* lib. iii. cap. ix.–xi., xv.–xviii.

GULF OF

San Juan de Ulloa

COATZACUALCO

TA

MITLA

SOCONUSCO

SOUTH SEA

TUZULUTLAN, O

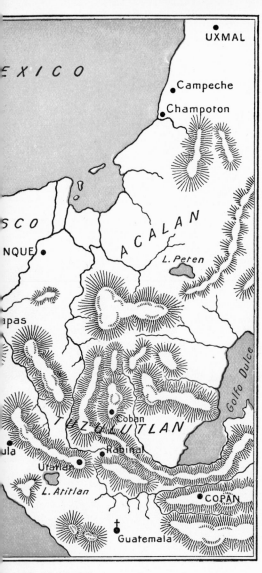

"LAND OF WAR"

achieve success in the world. The example of Las Casas, however, tends to confirm us in the opinion that when combined with The highest type of man-hood sufficient intelligence, that type of character is the most indomitable and masterful of all. And in this I seem to see good promise for the future of humanity. The wisdom of the serpent, when wedded to the innocence of the dove, is of all things the most winning and irresistible, as Las Casas now proceeded to prove.

Alvarado, the fierce governor of Guatemala, was absent in Spain. Las Casas talked with the temporary governor, Alonzo de Maldonado, and the result of their talk was the following agreement, signed May 2, 1537. It Diplomacy of Las Casas was agreed that "if Las Casas, or any of his monks, can bring these Indians into conditions of peace, so that they should recognize the Spanish monarch for their lord paramount, and pay him any moderate tribute, he, the governor, would place those provinces under his majesty in chief, and would not give them to any private Spaniard in *encomienda*. Moreover, no lay Spaniard, under heavy penalties, except the governor himself in person, should be allowed for five years to enter into that territory." [1] Ojedas and other such sinners were now, if possible, to be kept at a distance. No doubt Mal-

[1] Helps, *Spanish Conquest*, iii. 337.

donado smiled in his sleeve when he signed his name to this agreement. Of course it could never come to anything.

Thus guaranteed against interference, the good monks went to work, and after a due amount of preliminary fasting and prayer they began by putting into Quiché verses an epitome of Christian doctrine simple enough for children to apprehend, — the story of the fall of man, the life and death of Christ, the resurrection of the dead, and the final judgment. It is a pity that these verses have not been preserved, but no doubt Las Casas, whose great heart knew so well how to touch the secret springs of the Indian mind, knew how to make the story as attractive and as moving as possible. The verses were nicely balanced in couplets, so as to aid the memory, and were set to music so that they might be chanted to the accompaniment of the rude Indian instruments. Then the monks found four Indian traders, who were in the habit of travelling now and then through the " Land of War " with goods to barter. They spent many weeks in winning the affection of these Indians and teaching them their sacred poem, explaining everything with endless patience, until the new converts knew it all by heart and felt able to answer simple questions about it. When the monks felt sure that the work was

Preparations for a peaceful invasion of the Land of War

Ancient Nahuatl Flute Melodies.

thoroughly done, they despatched the four traders on their missionary errand to the pueblo of the most powerful cacique in that country, taking care to provide them with an ample store of mirrors, bells, Spanish knives, and other stuff attractive to barbarians.

When the traders arrived at their destination they were hospitably received, and, according to custom, were lodged in the tecpan.[1]

How an entrance was effected

They were zealous in their work, and obeyed their instructions faithfully. After vending their wares as usual, they called for some Mexican drums or timbrels, and proceeded to chant their sacred couplets.[2] They were well

---

[1] See Bandelier, in *Peabody Museum Reports*, vol. ii. p. 673.

[2] As a specimen of the kind of music likely to have been employed on this occasion, I give a page of ancient Nahuatl flute melodies, taken from Dr. Brinton's *The Güegüence; a Comedy Ballet in the Nahuatl-Spanish Dialect of Nicaragua*, Philadelphia, 1883. In the introduction to that interesting work there is a section on the music and musical instruments of the natives of Nicaragua, who were and are an outlying branch of the great Nahua people. From statements of Oviedo, Father Duran, Benzoni, and other old writers, further illustrated by the investigations of modern travellers, Dr. Brinton has made a learned and valuable essay. If the reader who is familiar with the history of music will take the trouble to compare the melodies here cited from page xxxiv of Dr. Brinton's work with the melodies from the Güegüence itself, given by Dr. Brinton on page xl, he will recognize at once that the latter have been produced under Spanish influences, while the

received. Indians uttering such strange sweet
words must have seemed miraculously inspired,
and so the audience thought. For several days
the performance was repeated, and the traders
were beset with questions. After a while they
drew pictures of the tonsured monks, and said
that they learned these mysteries from these
holy men, who, although white men, were not
like other Spaniards, for they spent their lives
in doing good, they had no wives, they treated
all women with respect, they cared nothing for
gold, and they taught that the time had come
for abolishing human sacrifices. The cacique
became so interested as to send his younger
brother back to Guatemala with the Indian
traders, charging him to watch the Dominicans
narrowly, and if he should find them answering
to the description that had been given of them
he might invite them to visit Tuzulutlan.

former show no trace of such influence and are undoubtedly
genuine aboriginal music. The reader will observe the monot-
ony and the limited range of the melodies here cited, and can
imagine the lugubrious but perhaps not wholly unpleasant effect of such tunes when chanted in the open air to the accompaniment of the *teponaztli* or old Mexican timbrels. For
some account of the ancient Peruvian music, see Garcilasso,
Comentarios reales, pt. i. lib. ii. cap. xxvi. An interesting
collection of Zuñi melodies, recorded upon phonographic cyl-
inders by Dr. Fewkes, of the Hemenway Archæological Expedition, may be found in the *Journal of American Ethnology
and Archæology*, vol. i. pp. 63–92.

Thus the ice was broken. It is needless to say that the young chieftain was well received, or that he was satisfied with what he saw. The invitation was given, and one of the Dominicans, the noble Luis de Barbastro, who was the most fluent of the four in the Quiché language, now made his way into the inaccessible fastnesses of Tuzulutlan, escorted by the young chief and the Indian traders. By the first of November, six months after the beginning of the enterprise, Father Luis had converted the cacique and several clan-chiefs, a rude church had been built, and human sacrifices prohibited by vote of the tribal-council.[1] Then Las Casas, with another monk, arrived upon the scene. There was much excitement among the tawny people of Tuzulutlan. The hideous priests of the war-god were wild with rage. They reminded the people, says Remesal, that the flesh of these white men, dressed with chile sauce, would make a dainty dish. Some secret incendiary burned the church, but as the cacique and so many clan-chiefs had been gained, there was no open rebellion. Before another year had elapsed the Indians had voluntarily destroyed their idols, renounced cannibalism, and promised

The first positions carried

[1] As already observed, there are many indications in the history of the conquest of Mexico and Central America that a considerable portion of the people were by no means unwilling to bid farewell to their cruel religions.

298

to desist from warfare unless actually invaded.
And now were to be seen the fruits of the mas-
terly diplomacy of Las Casas. Though the
cacique had thrice defeated the Spaniards, he
knew well how formidable they were. By ac-
knowledging the supremacy of Charles V. — a
sovereign as far off as the sky — and *The victory*
paying a merely nominal tribute, he *won*
had the word of Las Casas, which no Indian
ever doubted, that not a Spaniard, without the
express permission of the Dominicans, should
set foot upon his territory. This arrangement
was made, the peaceful victory was won, and
Las Casas returned to Guatemala, taking with
him the cacique, to visit Alvarado, who had
just returned from Spain.

This rough soldier, it will be remembered,
was the man who by his ill-judged brutality had
precipitated the catastrophe of the Spaniards in
the city of Mexico on the May festival of 1520.
In his hard heart there was, however, a gallant
spot. He knew a hero when he saw him, and
he well knew that, with all his military qualities,
he could never have done what Las Casas had
just done. So when the stern conqueror and
lord of Guatemala, coming forth to greet Las
Casas and the Indian king, took off his plumed
and jewelled cap, and bent his head in reverence,
it seems to me one of the beautiful moments in
history, one of the moments that comfort us

299

with the thought of what may yet be done with frail humanity when the spirit of Christ shall have come to be better understood. Of course Alvarado confirmed the agreement that no lay Spaniard should be allowed to enter Tuzulutlan; was he not glad enough thus to secure peace on this difficult and dangerous frontier?

Las Casas now, in 1539, went to Spain and had the agreement confirmed in a most solemn and peremptory order from Charles V. The order was obeyed. The " Land of War " was The "Land of True Peace " left unmolested and became thenceforth a land of peace.[1] Not only did it cease to trouble the Spaniards, but it became a potent centre for missionary work and a valuable means of diffusing Christian influences among other Indian communities. The work was permanent. Las Casas had come, he had seen, and he had conquered; and not a drop of human blood had been shed!

Meanwhile he had not been idle in other directions, and at length had gained the most powerful of allies. That reformation within the Papacy, which was one of the consequences of Luther's revolt, was beginning. Paul III. was a Pope of different type from either the wretched Borgia or the elegant and worldly Medici. In

[1] A part of this region has ever since borne the name Vera Paz, or " True Peace," and thus upon every map is this noblest of conquests recorded.

the summer of 1537, while Las Casas and his
monks were preparing their mission to the
" Land of War," the Pope issued a   Enslavement
brief forbidding the further enslave-   of Indians
forbidden by
ment of Indians, under penalty of ex-   the Pope
communication.   Henceforth any governor who
should give, or any settler who should receive,
a new *encomienda* of Indians, or who should
forcibly deprive them of their goods, was to be
refused the sacraments of the church.   Thus
the further spread of slavery was to be stopped.
Before leaving Guatemala for Spain, Las Casas
had the pleasure of translating this decree into
Spanish and sending it to all parts of the Indies.[1]
He was detained five years in Spain, as the
emperor needed his advice, and it was during
this period that he wrote his " Destruction of
the Indies " and other famous books.   In 1542
he won his grand and decisive triumph in the
promulgation of the New Laws by   The New
Charles V. The decisive clause was   Laws
as follows : " Item. We order and command
that henceforward for no cause whatever, whether
of war, rebellion, ransom, or in any other manner, can any Indian be made a slave."   This
clause was never repealed, and it stopped the
spread of slavery.   Other clauses went further,
and made such sweeping provisions for imme-

---

[1] A copy of the text of this papal brief is given in Remesal,
lib. iii. cap. xvii.

diate abolition that it proved to be impossible to enforce them.[1] The rebellion in Peru, which ended in bringing Gonzalo Pizarro's head to the block, was chiefly a rebellion against the New Laws, and as will be inferred from our account of Gasca's proceedings, it was suppressed chiefly by repealing those clauses that operated as a confiscation of property in slaves already existing. The matter was at last compromised by an arrangement that *encomiendas* should be in-
The final heritable during two lives, and should
compromise then escheat to the Crown. This reversion to the Crown meant the emancipation

[1] "It is well known that the liberation of the Indians from personal servitude was a measure, not only of humanity and justice, but also of policy, on the part of the Spanish government, to weaken the growing power of the conquerors and early colonists. The troubles in Peru give a good example of the state of affairs." Bandelier, in *Peabody Museum Reports*, vol. ii. p. 445. There is some reason for believing that at the time of Gasca's arrival in Peru, Gonzalo Pizarro was intending to throw off his allegiance to Spain entirely and make himself king, in which he would doubtless have been upheld by the settlers had not Gasca been able to bring the news of the modification in the New Laws. See the letter from Carvajal to Pizarro, dated March 17, 1547 : "Y esto suplico á vuestra Señoria, que se hierre por mi cabeça ; porque para la corona de Rey, con que, en tan breves dias, emos de coronar á vuestra Señoria, avra muy gran concurso de gente. Y para entonces, yo quiero tener cargo de aderecerlas, y tenerlas como conviene." Fernandez, *Historia del Peru*, pt. i. lib. ii. cap. xlix.

Leyes y ordenanças nueuaméte hechas
por su Magestad/pa la gouernacion de las Indias y buen trata
miento y conseruacion de los Indios: que se han de guardar en el
consejo y audiéctas reales q̃ en ellas residen: y por todos los otros
gouernadores/iuezes y personas particulares dellas.

☙ Con priuilegio imperial.

TITLE–PAGE OF NEW LAWS OF THE INDIES, 1542

of the slaves. Meanwhile such provisions were made, and by degrees more and more stringently enforced, as to protect the lives of the Indians and keep them together in their own communities, so that the dreadful *encomienda* reverted to the milder form of the *repartimiento*. Absolute slavery was transformed into villenage. In this ameliorated form the system continued. As generations passed from the scene, the Spanish Crown was persuaded to extend the inheritance of the *encomienda* to a third and a fourth life, but without surrendering the reversion. Moreover, there were always some reversions falling in for want of heirs, so that there was gradual emancipation from the first. In this way Indian slavery was tethered and restricted until, after the middle of the eighteenth century, under the enlightened administration of Count Florida Blanca, it was annulled.

Though it took so long to reap the full result of the heroic labours of Las Casas, the triumph was none the less his triumph. It was he that, in despite of all harrowing rebuffs and disappointments, brought Pope and Emperor to his side in the unconquerable determination that the enslavement of Indians *Immense re-sults of his labours* must be stopped. He arrested the evil, and though he did not live to see it eradicated, he gave such a direction to things that their further course was upward and not downward. Before he died there was in every part of Spanish America a staff of crown officers charged with the duty of protecting the interests of the Crown in the reversion of the *encomiendas*.[1] Then it was no longer possible with impunity to repeat the horrors of Hispaniola and of Nicaragua. It was Las Casas that saved the greater part of Spanish America from such a fate.[2]

[1] The contemporary testimony of one of the greatest and noblest of Spanish historians to the improvement already wrought in Peru through the work of Las Casas is worth citing : "In the audiences there are learned men of great piety, who punish those Spaniards that oppress the Indians in any way ; so that now there is no one who can ill treat them, and, in the greater part of these kingdoms, they are as much masters of their own estates and persons as are the Spaniards themselves. Each village is moderately assessed with the amount to be paid as tribute. I remember that, when I was in the province of Xauxa a few years ago, the Indians said to me with much satisfaction : ' This is a happy time, like the days of Tupac Inca Yupanqui ; ' a king of ancient times, whose memory they hold in great veneration." Cieza de Leon, ed. Markham, vol. i. p. 13.

[2] The words of Sir Arthur Helps are strictly just and true : "His was one of those few lives that are beyond biography, and require a history to be written in order to illustrate them. His career affords perhaps a solitary instance of a man who, being neither a conqueror, a discoverer, nor an inventor, has by the pure force of benevolence become so notable a figure that large portions of history cannot be written, or at least cannot be understood, without the narrative of his deeds and efforts being made one of the principal threads upon

LAS CASAS

The remaining years of this noble life, full as they are of interest, must be passed over briefly. After refusing the bishopric of Cuzco, Las Casas was persuaded to accept the humbler position of Bishop of Chiapa near Guatemala. He never could be prevailed upon to accept a reward or present of any sort, but he took the see of Chiapa, as a soldier would undertake to storm a redoubt. He knew there was hard work in store for him there in enforcing the New Laws. When he arrived upon the scene in 1544, it was much as if Garrison in 1860 had secured from the United States government a decree of emancipation, and then had gone to Charleston with authority to enforce it. The new bishop was greeted with howls of rage. In any other than a Spanish community it might have gone hard with him, but the fiercest Spaniard would always be pretty sure to stop short of laying violent hands upon a prince of the church.[1] The dignity, the com-

Las Casas made Bishop of Chiapa

which the history is strung." *Spanish Conquest*, vol. iv. p. 350.

[1] " For such is the reverence they bear to the church here, and so holy a conceit they have of all ecclesiastics, that the greatest Don in Spain will tremble to offer the meanest of them any outrage or affront." Letter of August 15, 1623, referring to the death of Thomas Washington, page to Prince Charles on his visit with Buckingham to Spain, discovered by Mr. Henry FitzGilbert Waters, in the British Museum. See *The Visitor*, Salem, Mass., February 11, 1891.

manding tact, of Las Casas was moreover such that a terrible mob at Ciudad Real ended in the rioters throwing themselves in tears at his feet, kissing the hem of his robe, and begging his forgiveness.[1] After three years Las Casas resigned his bishopric and returned to Spain. It was a time when the New Laws were imperilled, and he felt that his steadying hand was needed at the Spanish court, while he had now in the New World so many Dominicans devoted to the good work that he could afford to leave it to the care of these faithful lieutenants.[2] During the vicissitudes of his long struggle he had crossed the Atlantic not less than fourteen times; he His final re-   had once, it appears, sailed down the turn to Spain   Pacific to Peru; he had four times travelled far into Germany to get the emperor's ear at some critical moment. Now his journeyings were to cease. After leaving America in 1547 he returned no more, but lived for the remaining nineteen years of his life at the Dominican college of San Gregorio at Valladolid.

In 1550 he took part in a great controversy with Juan de Sepulveda, one of the most celebrated scholars of that time. Sepulveda wrote

[1] See the thrilling accounts in Remesal, lib. vii. cap. viii.-x. ; Helps, iv. 303-312.

[2] I would by no means be understood as wanting in appreciation of the glorious work of Motolinia and other noble Franciscans, but our subject has its limitations.

CBreuissima rela
cion de la destruycion de las Indias: colegida por el Obispo dõ
fray Bartolome de las Casas /o
Casaus de la orden de Sãcto Do
mingo.

Año. 1552.

TITLE–PAGE OF BOOK BY LAS CASAS, 1552

a book in which he maintained the right of the Pope and the king of Spain to make war upon the heathen people of the New World and bring them forcibly into the fold of Christ. This was contrary to the doctrine which Las Casas had set forth fifteen years before in the Latin treatise above mentioned. He felt that it was dangerous, and determined to answer Sepulveda. After the fashion of those days, Charles V. convoked at Valladolid a council of learned theologians, and the cause was argued before them at great length by Las Casas and Sepulveda. The doughty champions assailed each other with texts from the Bible and Aquinas, scholastic logic and patristic history, and every other weapon known in the mediæval armory. For a man of such fervour as Las Casas it was a delicate situation. In maintaining his ground that persuasion is the only lawful method for making men Christians, extreme nicety of statement was required, for the least slip might bring him within the purview of the Inquisition. Men were burning at the stake for heresy while this discussion was going on, and the controversy more than once came terribly near home. But as Sepulveda said afterwards, with unfeigned admiration of his antagonist, he was " the most crafty and vigilant of mortals, and so ready with his tongue that in comparison with him Homer's Ulysses was a

His controversy with Sepulveda

thick-witted stutterer."[1] When it came to a judgment the council did not dare to occupy the position of Las Casas, and so they gave a hesitating judgment in favour of Sepulveda; but the emperor, doubtless with a pleasant smile for Master Bartholomew, proceeded forthwith to suppress Sepulveda's book, and sent stringent orders to America to have any copies of it found there seized and burned.

In 1555 Charles V. retired to the monastery of Yuste, and his son Philip II. became king Las Casas and of Spain. Philip's plans, as all know, Philip II. were so vast and so impossible that he wrecked himself and Spain with them. At the outset he was short of money, and there were advisers at hand to remind him that the colonists in America would jump at the chance of buying in the reversion of their *encomiendas* at a handsome price in hard cash. This would at once put a very large sum of money into Philip's hands, and it would put the Indians back into absolute slavery, as in the old days in Hispaniola. The temptation was great, and against such a frightful disaster Las Casas, now

[1] "Longum esset præstigias, artes et machinamenta commemorare, quibus me deprimere, et veritatem atque justitiam obscurare conatus est artifex ille versutissimus, et idem vigilantissimus et loquacissimus, cui Ulysses Homericus collatus iners erat et balbus." Sepulveda, *Opera*, Madrid, 1780, tom. iii. p. 241.

Bartolomè de Las Casas

in his eighty-second year, came forth to contend. Fortunately the power of the church, reinforced by political considerations already mentioned, was firmly enlisted on his side, and he prevailed. This was the last of his triumphs, and it is worth remembering that pretty much the only praiseworthy thing Philip II. ever did was done under his influence.

In his eighty-seventh year, in the peaceful seclusion of the college at Valladolid, Las Casas brought to a close the great "History of the Indies," which he seems to have begun in the monastery at San Domingo *The History of the Indies.* more than thirty years before. A remark of Remesal's makes it probable that the book was begun, perhaps in so far as the sketching of its general outline was concerned, as early as 1527, but its knowledge of contemporary writers and events proves that it was for the most part written between 1552 and 1561. In a formal note dated November, 1559, Las Casas consigned the book in trust to the college of San Gregorio, expressing his wish that it should not be made public before the end of that century. Partly from the inertia attendant upon all human things, partly because of the plainness with which it told such terrible truths, the book was allowed to lie in manuscript for more than three hundred years. During the present century such writers as Irving, Helps, and a few

others, read it to good purpose in the manuscript, and at length in 1875 it was published.
In a far truer sense than any other book, it may
be called the corner-stone of the history of the
American continent. It stops at 1522, when
Las Casas became a Dominican monk. One
wishes that it might have been continued to
1547, when he took his last leave of the New
World. But there are limits even to what the
longest and strongest life can do. After finishing his work upon this book, and in his ninetieth year, Las Casas wrote a valuable treatise
on the affairs of Peru. His last act was to go
to Madrid and secure a royal decree promoting
in certain ways the welfare of the natives of
Guatemala. Having accomplished this, he died
Death of Las
Casas at Madrid, after a few days' illness, at
the age of ninety-two. In all this
long and arduous life — except for a moment,
perhaps, on the crushing news of the destruction of his colony upon the Pearl Coast — we
find no record of work interrupted by sickness,
and to the very last his sight was not dim nor
his natural force abated.

In contemplating such a life as that of Las
Casas, all words of eulogy seem weak and frivo-
lous. The historian can only bow in reverent
awe before a figure which is in some respects
the most beautiful and sublime in the annals of

Christianity since the Apostolic age. When now and then in the course of the centuries God's providence brings such a life into this world, the memory of it must be cherished by mankind as one of its most precious and sacred possessions. For the thoughts, the words, the deeds of such a man, there is no death. The sphere of their influence goes on widening forever. They bud, they blossom, they bear fruit, from age to age.

311

XII

THE WORK OF TWO CENTURIES

THE wreck of the admiral's flagship on
the Christmas of 1492 determined the
site of the first European colony in the
New World, and perhaps it is not too much to
say that by this accident the fortunes of Columbus were from that day forth linked to the island of Hispaniola. There the Spanish colonial
Hispaniola   society assumed its earliest type.
the centre of
Spanish colo- From that island we have seen the
nization   lines of discovery and conquest radiating westward with Velasquez and Cortes, and
southward with Balboa and the Pizarros. To
Hispaniola we returned in order to trace the
beginnings of Indian slavery and the marvellous
career of Las Casas. From Hispaniola we must
now again take our start, but to return no more.
We have to follow the lines of discovery northward with Ponce de Leon and Pineda, and far
beyond them, until we have obtained a sketch
of the development of the knowledge of the
huge continental mass of North America. This
development was the Work of Two Centuries,
and during that period much other work of

cardinal importance was going on in the world, which had resulted before its close in the transfer of maritime supremacy and the lead in colonial enterprise from Spain and Portugal to France and England. In completing our geographical story, therefore, we shall return no more to Hispaniola, but shall be led farther and farther away from that earliest centre, A change of under the guidance of various leaders scene with various aims, until the epilogue will take us into the frozen zone which was visited in our prologue, and once more we shall see a stout Scandinavian captain land upon the shores of North America, coming this time, however, from the Siberian coast with Russian ships, to sever the last link that in men's minds continued to connect the New World with the continent of Asia. In covering so much ground in a single chapter, we must be content with a mere sketch of the outlines; for that will be most conducive to clearness and will best harmonize with the general plan upon which this work has been from the outset conceived.

As we have already seen, it is in a high degree probable that the peninsula of Florida was circumnavigated, and a portion of the Atlantic coast to the northward visited, in the First voyage spring and summer of 1498, by an of Vespucius expedition in which Pinzon and Solis were the commanders, with Vespucius and Ledesma assisting as pilots. Reasons have also been given why that voyage was not followed up and came to be well-nigh forgotten, as was also the case, though to a less extent, with the voyages of John Cabot and the Cortereals. The Indian Ocean, with its spices, being the region toward which men's eager eyes were turned, the wild coasts of North America were hastily glanced at and abandoned, very much as your dog sniffs at an unpromising bone, and turns away. As already observed, the only probable effect of a voyage around Florida at that moment would be to throw more or less discredit upon Marco Polo.

Stories from eastern Asia had not, however, lost their charm for adventurers. In Mandeville's multifarious ragout there is mention of a Fountain of Youth at a place called Polombe. The author cribbed it from a spurious letter purporting to come from Prester John, which made its way through Europe in the latter part

The Fountain of Youth of the twelfth century. Those that drink of this fountain, says the old rogue, seem always young, as he knows because he has tried it himself![1] Now this Fons Juven-

---

[1] "At the heued of þis ilk forest es þe citee of Polombe; and besyde þat citee es a mountayne, wharoff þe citee takeȝ þe name, for men calleȝ þe mountayne Polombe. And at þe fote of þis mountayne es a well, noble and faire; and þe wa-

314

tutis had its remote origin in folk-lore, and there is nothing strange in the Spaniards hearing things said by the Indians that reminded them of it. From something thus said by the Indians they got the idea that upon an island called Bimini, northward from Hispaniola, this famous fountain was situated; [1] and in 1512 the brave Juan Ponce de Leon, who had come out with Columbus in his second voyage, obtained King Ferdinand's permission to go and conquer Bimini. He sailed with three caravels from Porto Rico in March, 1513, and on the

ter þeroff has a swete sauour and reflaire, as it ware of diuerse maner of spicery. And ilke houre of þe day þe water chaungeʒ diuersely his sauour and his smell. And wha so drinkes fastand thryes of þat well, he sall be hale of what maner of malady þat he hase. And forþi þat wonneʒ nere þat well drynkeʒ þeroff ofter, and þerfore þai hafe neuermore sekeness, bot euermore þai seme yung. I, John Maundeuill, sawe þis well and drank þeroff thrys and all my felawes, and euermore sen þat tyme I fele me þe better and þe haler and supposeʒ for to do till þe tyme þat Godd of his grace will make me to passe oute of þis dedly lyf. Sum men calleʒ þat well *Fons iuuentutis,* þat es for to say, þe well of yowthehede ; for þai þat drinkeʒ þeroff semeʒ all way yung. And þai say þis well commeʒ fra Paradys terrestre, for it es so vertuous. Thurghe oute all þis cuntree þer growes þe best gynger þat es ower whare ; and marchaundes commeʒ þider fra ferre cuntreeʒ for to bye it." Roxburghe Club's *Buke of Mandeuill,* p. 84.

[1] Peter Martyr, dec. ii. lib. x. ; cf. Oviedo, pt. i. lib. xix. cap. xv.

27th of that month, being Easter Sunday, which in Spanish is called Pascua Florida, he came within sight of the coast ever since known as that of Florida. On the 2d of April Ponce de Leon landed a little north of the site of St. Au-

The Land of Easter

gustine, and then turned back and followed the coast of the peninsula around to its west side in latitude 27° 30′. Further exploration was prevented at that time by the breaking out of war with the Caribs. It was not until 1521 that Ponce de Leon was able to take a colony to the Land of Easter. His party was attacked with great fury by the Indians, and instead of finding his fountain of youth he received a wound in the thigh from a flint arrow, which caused him to abandon the enterprise and retreat to Cuba, where he died after prolonged suffering.

Proof was already at hand that Florida was not an island, for in 1519 Alvarez de Pineda had followed that coast as far as the site of Tampico in Mexico, where he found Cortes and his men in the course of their preliminary wanderings before founding Vera Cruz. Pineda

Pineda's discovery of the Mississippi, 1519

then turned back, and after a while entered the mouth of the Mississippi, which he called Rio de Santo Espiritu. He seems to have been the first European to sail upon this great river. How far he ascended it is not clear, but he spent six weeks upon its waters and its banks, trading with the Indians, who seemed friendly and doubtless laboured under the usual first impression as to the supernatural character of the white men. Pineda said that he saw one considerable Indian town and no less than forty hamlets, and that the Indians wore gold ornaments.[1]

This voyage increased the interest in exploration to the northward, and another cause now began to operate in the same direction. When the remnant of Magellan's expedition returned to Spain in 1522, after its three years' voyage, it first began to be dimly realized in Europe that there was an immense ocean between Mundus Novus and Asia. It now became an object to find ways of getting past or through this barrier of land which we now call America, in order to make the voyage to Asia. In 1525 Garcia de Loaysa was sent by the Spanish government to the Strait of Magellan, and arrived there. Early in 1526 one of Loaysa's ships was caught by a storm in the Atlantic, near the strait, and driven southward as far as Cape Horn, but this fact did not at- Cape Horn tract general attention. The voyage of Magel-

[1] See Navarrete, *Coleccion*, tom. iii. pp. 147–153 ; Herrera, dec. ii. lib. x. cap. xviii.; Peter Martyr, dec. v. cap. i. In his visit to Tampico, Pineda was preceded by Diego de Camargo, who sailed thither in 1518. See Las Casas, *Hist. de las Indias*, tom. iv. p. 466.

lan did not end the controversy between Spain and Portugal as to the ownership of the Moluccas, for their longitude was variously reckoned. Did they lie west or east of the meridian antipodal to Pope Alexander's dividing line on the Atlantic? With the best of intentions, the problem of longitude was in those days very difficult, and a discrepancy of a thousand miles or more between the Spanish and Portuguese reckonings was likely enough to occur, even had there been no bias on the part of the reckoners. As it was, there was no hope of agreement between the two powers, except through some political compromise. In 1524 the question was submitted to what is known as the Congress of Badajos, an assembly of cosmographers, pilots, and lawyers, including such famous names as Ferdinand Columbus and Sebastian Cabot, with Estevan Gomez, Sebastian Elcano, Diego Ribeiro, and others. "They were empowered to send for persons and papers, and did in reality have before them pilots, papal bulls, treaties, royal grants and patents, log books, maps, charts, globes, itineraries, astronomical tables, the fathers of the church, ancient geographies and modern geographers, navigators with their compasses, quadrants, astrolabes, etc. For two months they fenced, ciphered, debated, argued, protested, discussed, grumbled, quarrelled, and almost

318

fought, yet they could agree upon nothing."[1]
The congress broke up without any definite
result, and Spain retained her hold upon the
Spiceries. The Philippine archipelago, which
equally with the Moluccas lies on the Portuguese side of the dividing line, remains in Spanish hands to this day. But in 1529 Charles V.
ceded his claim upon the Moluccas to Portugal
for 350,000 gold ducats. His original intention was merely to grant a long lease, but by
some oversight no precise period was mentioned,
and the lease was suffered to become perpetual.
In 1548 the emperor was urged by his legal
advisers to recall the lease, but would not;
whereat " some marvelled and others grieved,
but all held their peace."[2]

Now since the Portuguese used their own
route across the Indian Ocean to the Spiceries,
many years elapsed before much attention was
paid to the southern extremity of South America. The next person to see Cape Horn was
Sir Francis Drake in 1578, and the first person to sail around it was the Dutch navigator

[1] Stevens, *Historical and Geographical Notes*, p. 42.
" Estuvieron muchos dias mirando globos, cartas y relaciones,
y alegando cada qual de su derecho, y porfiando terribilissi-
mamente." Gomara, *Historia general de las Indias*, Antwerp, 1554, fol. 131 verso.
[2] Guillemard's *Magellan*, p. 16.

Schouten van Horn, after whom it was named. This was not until 1616.

It was the excessive length of the voyage from Europe to Asia by this southwestern route that prevented activity in this direction. Sailors began trying to find shorter routes. As it was now proved that there was a continuous coast-line all the way from the Strait of Magellan to the St. John's River in Florida, one immediate effect of Magellan's voyage was to turn people's attention to the northward in the hope of finding a northwest passage from Europe to Asia. A most pathetic and thrilling story is that of the persistent search for the Northwest Passage, kept up for 330 years, and gradually pushed farther and farther up among Arctic ice-floes, until at length in 1854 the passage was made from Bering Strait to Davis Strait by Sir Robert McClure. For more than a century after Magellan did navigators anxiously scan the North American coast and sail into the mouths of great rivers, hoping to find them straits or channels leading into the western ocean; for it began to be plain that this coast was not Asia, but a barrier in the way thither, and until long inland expeditions had been made, how was anybody to know anything about the mass of the northern continent, or that it was so many times wider than Central America?

Search for a Northwest Passage, 1524–1854

320

The first of these navigators was Lucas Vasquez d'Ayllon, who came up in 1524 from Hispaniola and tried the James River and Chesapeake Bay. Not finding a northwest passage, but liking the country, he obtained a grant of it from Charles V., and in 1526 began to build a town called San Miguel, about where the English founded Jamestown eighty-one years afterward. Negro slaves were employed by the Spaniards in this work, and this would seem to be the first instance of slave-labour on the part of negroes within the territory since covered by the United States. Ayllon had 600 people with him, both men and women, besides 100 horses; and Antonio Montesino accompanied him as missionary preacher. If this enterprise had succeeded, the future course of American history might have been strangely modified. But Ayllon died of a fever, and under the combined effects of hunger and sickness, internecine quarrels, negro insurrection, and attacks from the Indians, the little colony soon succumbed; and of the survivors the greater part were shipwrecked on the way back to Hispaniola. Antonio Montesino was sent in 1528 to Venezuela, where he disappears from history. When or where he died we do not know, save that in the register of the Dominican monastery of San Estevan, in Salamanca, against the honoured name of Antonio Mon-

Spanish colony on James River, 1526

tesino there is written in some unknown hand this marginal note, *Obiit martyr in Indiis*, " died a martyr in the Indies," which must probably mean that he was somewhere slain by poor stupid red men unable to recognize their best friends.

While Ayllon was losing his own life and those of his people on the bank of the James River, another navigator was searching for a new route for the ships of Charles V. to the Moluc-

Voyage of Gomez, 1525

cas. In the course of the year 1525 Estevan Gomez, the pilot who had so basely deserted Magellan, coasted from Labrador to Florida, taking notice of Cape Cod, Narragansett Bay, and the mouths of the Connecticut, Hudson, and Delaware rivers. The comment of Peter Martyr upon this voyage of Gomez is very significant, as illustrating the small favour with which such voyages as those of the Cabots and the first of Vespucius had been regarded. " Stephanus Gomez, . . . neither finding the straight, nor Gaitaia [Cathay] which he promised, returned backe within tenn monethes after his departure. I always thought and presupposed this good man's imaginations were vayn and friuolous. Yet wanted he no suffrages and voyces in his fauour and defence. Notwithstanding he found pleasant and profitable countries, agreeable with our parallels and degrees of the pole. . . . *But what need haue we of these things which are common with all the people of Europe?* To the South, to the South for the great and exceeding riches of the Equinoctiall : they that seek riches must not go vnto the cold and frosen North."[1]

Gomez seems to have been preceded on these coasts by more than one navigator sailing in the service of France. We have already observed Norman and Breton sailors taking their share in the fisheries upon the banks of Newfoundland from the beginning of the century.[2] Francis I. of France manifested but slight reverence for Pope Alexander VI. and his bulls. According to Bernal Diaz he sent word to his great rival Charles V., asking him by what right he and the king of Portugal undertook to monopolize the earth. Had our first father Adam made them his sole heirs ? If so it would be no more than proper for them to produce a copy of the will ; and meanwhile he should feel at

---

[1] Martyr, dec. viii. cap. x. ; Herrera, dec. iii. lib. viii. cap. viii. ; Gomara, cap. xl. ; Oviedo, cap. x. In Diego Ribeiro's map, made in 1529, the regions about Virginia are called "land of Ayllon," and the regions from New Jersey to Rhode Island are called "land of Estevan Gomez." The name given by Gomez to what was afterwards called Hudson's River was Rio de San Antonio. See De Costa, *Sailing Directions of Henry Hudson*, Albany, 1869, p. 44.

[2] For Léry's attempt to found a colony at Cape Breton in 1518, see Sixte Le Tac, *Histoire chronologique de la Nouvelle France*, pp. 40, 58.

THE DISCOVERY OF AMERICA

liberty to seize upon all he could get. Among the corsairs active at that time in the French marine was one known to the Spaniards as Juan Florin or Florentin. His name was Giovanni da Verrazano, and he seems to have been born about 1480 at Florence, where his family had attained distinction. In 1523 he captured the treasure on its way from Cortes, in Mexico, to the Emperor Charles V. ; and early in the next year he crossed the Atlantic with one ship and about fifty men. The first land sighted was probably near Cape Fear, in North Carolina. From that point Verrazano skirted the coast northward as far as latitude 50°, and seems to have discovered the Hudson River, and to have landed upon Rhode Island and at some point not far from the mouth of the Piscataqua. Little or nothing is known of Verrazano after this voyage.[1] It has been said that he was caught by the Spaniards in 1527 and hanged for piracy, and there is another story that he was roasted and eaten by

Voyage of Verrazano, 1524

[1] It has been doubted whether Verrazano ever made any such voyage. See Murphy, *The Voyage of Verrazano*, New York, 1875. Mr. Murphy's conclusions have not been generally sustained. For further discussions see Brevoort, *Verrazano the Navigator*, New York, 1874 ; Asher's *Henry Hudson*, London, 1860, pp. 197–228 ; Kohl's *Discovery of Maine*, chap. viii. ; De Costa, *Verrazano the Explorer*, New York, 1881, with a full bibliographical note ; Winsor, *Narr. and Crit. Hist.*, iv. 1–30.

the Indians in that year, but all this is quite doubtful.

The staggering blows inflicted upon Francis I. by Charles V. in the Italian campaign of 1525 prevented any further activity in following up the voyage of Verrazano. Ten years later came Jacques Cartier, who explored the lower portion of the river St. Lawrence, and found an Iroquois town, named Hochelaga, on an eminence which he called Montreal. Before Champlain's arrival, seventy years later, the Iroquois had been driven from this region. In 1540–43 an unsuccessful attempt was made by the Sieur de Roberval, aided by Cartier, to establish a French colony in Canada. Connected with this expedition was the voyage of the pilot Jehan Allefonsce, of Saintonge, in which he seems to have visited the coast between Cape Cod and Cape Ann.[1] Little more was done by the French in this direction until the time of Champlain.

Cartier and Roberval, 1534–43

The maps made about this time reflect the strong desire for a northwest passage to Cathay in the extreme slimness which they assign to a part of the North American mainland. In 1529 Hieronimo da Verrazano made a map in which

[1] For a discussion of this voyage, see De Costa, *Northmen in Maine*, pp. 80–122 ; and his chapter in Winsor, *Narr. and Crit. Hist.*, vol. iv. chap. ii. ; see also Weise, *Discoveries of America*, New York, 1884, chap. xi.

he undertook to represent his brother's discoveries;[1] and upon this map we find Florida
The "Sea of   connected with the Verrazano region
Verrazano"   by a slender isthmus. The imaginary
sea washing the western shore of this isthmus
was commonly known as the Sea of Verrazano.
Possibly the notion may have arisen from a
misinterpretation of some small neck of land
with a bay or sound beyond it somewhere upon
the Atlantic coast explored in the voyage of
1524. But, in whatever misconception it may
have had its origin, the Sea of Verrazano continued to be reproduced on maps for many
years, until inland exploration expelled it. Two
interesting illustrations, toward the middle of
the sixteenth century, show respectively the wet
and the dry theories of the relation of the North
American coast to Asia. The first of these
maps, made at Venice in 1536, by Baptista
Agnese, cuts off the hypothetical unvisited
coasts to the south of Peru[2] and to the west
and north of Mexico with a dotted line, but
gives the equally hypothetical coast of the Verrazano sea as if its existence were quite undoubted. According to this map the voyage to

[1] For a reduced copy of the map, see Winsor, *Narr. and
Crit. Hist.*, iv. 26. The original is in the college of the
Propaganda at Rome.

[2] The coast from the Strait of Magellan northward to Peru
was first explored by Alonso de Camargo in 1539–40.

SEBASTIAN MÜNSTER'

Hibernia

FRANCISCA

C. Britonum

Corterar

Exteriores

Hispania

Oceanus occidentalis

Medera

Fortunatæ inf.

VBA

HISPANIOLA

Selana

Antillæ

Inf. Hesperidum

AFRICAE
pars

amica

Dominica

S. Iacobi

PARIAS abundat
auro et margaritis

Sinus
Atlanticus

IS

Canibali

ea quam uocant Brasilij
& Americam

Regio Gigantum

7. insulæ Mar-
gueritaru

Fretum Magaliani

OF AMERICA, 1540

Cathay by the Verrazano route would be at least as simple as the voyage to Peru by way of Panama. A very different view is given upon the "Carta Marina" by Jacopo Gastaldi, published in the Ptolemy of 1548. Here Florida and Mexico appear as parts of Asia, and the general conception is not unlike that of the globe of Orontius Finæus; but the Verrazano sea appears to the north of Florida. Here, therefore, it does not afford a ready means of access to China, but to some northern ocean washing the shores of an "Upper India," concerning which it may be suspected that the map-maker's ideas were not of the clearest.

From this chart of Gastaldi's the position of the Verrazano sea naturally leads us to the map by Sebastian Münster, published in the Ptolemy of 1540. Though thus published eight years earlier than Gastaldi, this map represents in some respects a later development toward the more correct views heralded by Mercator.[1] There is an approach toward the conception of the western hemisphere as a distinct and integral whole, though the Pacific is still very narrow and Zipangri (Japan) still comes very near to Mexico, as in the Stobnicza map of 1512. The reader will also observe the New World with its Catigara, the significant mark of a Ptolemaic pedigree, although now quite torn asunder

---

[1] See above, vol. ii. p. 386.

from Asia. Pizarro and his pilots would, I suspect, have laughed somewhat rudely at the promontory on which this Catigara is placed, —

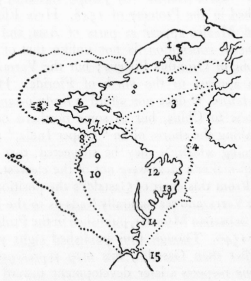

Sketch of Agnese's map, Venice, 1536.[1]

an imaginary fragment of Asia that happened to stay on this side when the tear came. As to the

[1] KEY: "1. Terra de bacalaos. 2. (*dotted line*) El viage de France. 3. (*dotted line*) El viage de Peru. 4. (*dotted line*) El viago a maluche. 5. Temistetan. 6. Iucatan. 7. Nombre de dios. 8. Panama. 9. La provintia del peru. 10. La provintia de chinagua. 11. S. paulo. 12. Mundus novus. 13. Brazil. 14. Rio de la plata. 15. El Streto de ferdinando de Magallanas." Winsor, *Narr. and Crit. Hist.*, iv. 40.

328

Verrazano sea, when we compare it upon this
map and that of Agnese, as well as upon Mi-

Gastaldi's Carta Marina, 1548.[1]

chael Lok's map more than forty years later,

[1] KEY : " 1. Norvegia. 2. Laponia. 3. Gronlandia. 4.
Tierra del Labrador. 5. Tierra del Bacalaos. 6. La Florida.
7. Nueva Hispania. 8. Mexico. 9. India Superior. 10. La
China. 11. Ganges. 12. Samatra. 13. Java. 14. Panama.
15. Mar del Sur. 16. El Brasil. 17. El Peru. 18. Strecho de
Fernande Magalhaes. 19. Tierra del Fuego." Winsor, *Narr.
and Crit. Hist.*, iv. 43. Observe that Gastaldi retains the
mediæval notion of Greenland as connected with Norway.

we can understand how it was that even as late as the seventeenth century such a navigator as Henry Hudson should try to get through his river into the Pacific.

The only means of correcting these inadequate and fluctuating views were to be found in expeditions into the interior of the continent, and here the beginnings were slow and painful. The first Spaniard to avail himself of Pineda's discoveries was Panfilo de Narvaez, the man who Expedition of had been sent to Mexico to arrest and Narvaez supersede Cortes, and had so ingloriously failed in that attempt. Pineda's mention of gold ornaments on the Mississippi Indians was enough to set Narvaez in motion. If there was so much glory and plunder in one direction, why not in another? He obtained permission to conquer and govern all the northern coast of the Gulf of Mexico, and started from Cuba in March, 1528, with four ships, carrying 400 men and eighty horses. Landing at Apalache Bay, he made a bootless excursion into the country, and on his return to the seashore was unable to find his ships, which were sailing to and fro on the watch for him. After travelling westward on foot for a month, Narvaez and his men, with desperate exertions, built five frail boats and pursued their journey by water. After six weeks of coasting they came to the mouth of a river so great that it freshened the sea so that they could drink the sea-water. At the mouth of this river, the Mississippi, two of the boats, one of them containing Narvaez himself, were capsized, and all their company lost. The other three boats were thrown ashore, probably somewhere in eastern Texas, and such of their crews as escaped starvation were murdered by the natives. Four men, however, the treasurer Cabeza de Vaca, with two Spanish comrades, Dorantes and Castillo, and a negro called Estevánico, or "Little Steve," had a wonderful course of adventures. They were captured by different parties of Indians and carried about in various directions in the wilderness of western Louisiana and eastern Texas. Cabeza de Vaca achieved some success as a trader, bartering shells and wampum from the coast for "flint flakes, red clay, hides and skins, and other products of the regions inland."[1] A reputation early acquired as a medicine-man or sorcerer proved helpful to him, and may very likely have preserved his life. After strange vicissitudes and terrible sufferings the

Adventures of Cabeza de Vaca

[1] The journey of Cabeza de Vaca and his comrades is ably described and their route traced by Mr. Bandelier, *Contributions to the History of the Southwestern Portion of the United States,* Cambridge, 1890 (Papers of the Archæological Institute of America — American Series. V. Hemenway Southwestern Archæological Expedition).

four comrades were thrown together again at some point west of the Sabine River in Texas. Circumstances happened to give them all a reputation for skilful sorcery, and by degrees they made use of this singular power to induce the parties of Indians with them to move in certain directions rather than others. With a vague hope of finding the seashore they kept in the main a westerly course, and presently their fame grew to such a height that Indians came to them in throngs bringing gifts. Proceeding in this way they presently crossed the Rio Pecos near its junction with the Rio Grande ; then ascending the latter river they made their way across Chihuahua and Sonora to the Gulf of California, and then turning southward at length in May, 1536, reached Culiacan, then an extreme frontier of the Spaniards, after this wonderful pilgrimage of nearly 2000 miles.

The reports of this journey aroused much interest among the Spaniards in Mexico. Not less than four attempts at exploration upon the Pacific coasts had been made by Cortes, but not much had been accomplished beyond the discovery of Lower California. Now there were reasons that made the idea of an inland expedition to the northward seem attractive. Legend of the There was a tradition afloat in Europe, that on the occasion of the conquest of the Spanish peninsula by the Arabs in the

332

¶La relacion que dio Aluar nu-
ñez cabeça de vaca delo acaescido enlas Indias
enla armada donde yua por gouernador pã
philo de narbaez desde el año de veynte
y siete hasta el año d treynta y seys
que boluio a Seuilla con tres
de su compañia.:.

TITLE–PAGE OF CABEZA DE VACA'S RELACION, 1542

eighth century, a certain bishop of Lisbon with a goodly company of followers took refuge upon an island or group of islands far out on the Sea of Darkness, and founded seven cities there. With the fabulous Antilia, which was commonly regarded as the island of the Seven Cities, we have already made acquaintance. Its name, slightly modified into "Antilles," came to be applied to the West Indies. Its seven cities were curiously transferred into the very heart of the American continent. Among the Nahuatl tribes there was a legend of Chicomoztoc, or the Seven Caves from which at some period in the past their ancestors issued. As soon as the Spaniards got hold of this legend they contrived to mix up these Seven Caves with their Seven Cities. They were supposed to be somewhere to the northward, and when Cabeza de Vaca and his comrades had disclosed the existence of such a vast territory north of Mexico, it was resolved to search for the Seven Cities in that direction. The work was entrusted to Fray Marcos of Nizza, or Nice, as we now call it since it has been " reunited " — that is the Fray Marcos orthodox French way of expressing it — to France. He was a Franciscan monk of great ability, who had accompanied Pizarro on the first march to Caxamarca to meet Atahualpa. He had afterward gone to Quito and thence seems to have accompanied Alvarado on his return to Guatemala. He had lately found his way to Mexico, and was selected by the great viceroy Antonio de Mendoza to go and find the Seven Cities.[1] He was attended on the journey by the negro Estevánico and a few Pima Indians who had been educated at Mexico; and their reception by the natives along the route was extremely hospitable. At Matape, an Indian village in Sonora, they heard definite news of a country situated thirty days' march to the northward, where there were seven large cities, " with houses of stone and lime, . . .

The Seven Cities of Cibola

the smallest ones of two stories and a flat roof, and others of three and four stories, and that of the lord with five, all placed together in order; and on the door-sills and lintels of the principal houses many figures of turquoise stones . . . and [it was said] that the people of these cities are very well clothed," etc.[2] The name of the first of these cities was said to be Cibola. And from that time forth this became a common name for the group, and we hear much of the Seven Cities of Cibola.

[1] Like so many other travellers and explorers Fray Marcos has been charged with falsehood; but his case has been to a considerable extent cleared up in Bandelier's excellent monograph already cited, *Contributions to the History of the Southwestern Portion of the United States.*

[2] Bandelier, *op. cit.* p. 130.

These were the seven pueblos of Zuñi, in New Mexico, of which six were still inhabited at the end of the sixteenth century. The name Cibola was properly applied to the group, as it referred to the whole extent of territory occupied by the Zuñis. The surviving pueblo which we know to-day as Zuñi will probably serve as an excellent sample of the pueblo towns visited by the Spaniards in their first wanderings in North America. As Fray Marcos drew near to it he heard much of the power and glory of Cibola, and began to feel that his most romantic anticipations were about to be verified; but now came his first misfortune on this journey, and it was a sharp one. Hitherto the white man and the black man had been treated with the reverence due to supernatural beings, or to persons who at least were mighty wizards. But at Kiakima, the first of the Zuñi pueblos, the negro's "medicine" was not accepted. Estevánico travelled some miles in advance of Fray Marcos. When he arrived at the first of the cities of Cibola, flaunting the turquoises and the handsome Indian girls, with whom he had been presented in the course of the journey, — much to the disgust of the Franciscan friar, — the elders and chiefs of the pueblo would not grant him admittance. He was lodged in a small house outside the enclosure, and was cautiously catechised. When he an-

335

nounced himself as the envoy and forerunner of a white man, sent by a mighty prince beyond the sky to instruct them in heavenly things, the Zuñi elders were struck with a sense of incongruity. How could black represent white, or be the envoy and forerunner of white? To the metaphysics of the middle status of barbarism the question wore a very uncanny look, and to the common sense of the middle status of barbarism the self-complacent Estevánico appeared to be simply a spy from some chieftain or tribe that wanted to conquer the Zuñis. A Cortes might easily have dealt with such a situation, but most men would consider it very uncomfortable, and so did poor silly " Little Steve." While the elders were debating whether they should do reverence to him as a wizard, or butcher him as a spy, he stole out of his lodging and sought safety in flight; and this act, being promptly detected, robbed him of all dignity and sealed his fate. A hue and cry went after him, and an arrow soon found its way to his heart. The news of this catastrophe checked the advance of Fray Marcos. His Indian comrades were discouraged, and the most he could do was to keep them with him while he climbed a hill whence he could get a Pisgah sight of the glories of Cibola. After he had accomplished this, the party returned with all possible haste to Culiacan, and

Murder of Estevánico and retreat of Fray Marcos

A Street in Zuñi

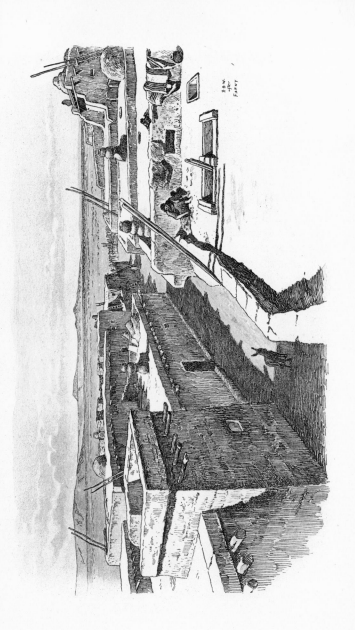

H.S.W.
after
Farey

arrived there in August, 1539, after an absence of five months.

As an instance of the tenacious vitality of tradition, and its substantial accuracy in dealing with a very simple and striking fact, it is interesting to find that to this day the Zuñis remember the fate of Estevánico. In one of the folk-tales taken down by Mr. Cush- *Zuñi recollection of the affair* ing from the lips of Zuñi priests, it is said that "previous to the first coming of the *Mexicans* (the Zuñi Indian calls all the Spanish-speaking people Mexicans), a *black Mexican* made his appearance at the Zuñi village of Kiakima. He was very greedy, voracious, and bold, and the people killed him for it. After his death the Mexicans [*i. e.* Spaniards] made their appearance in numbers for the first time, and made war upon the Zuñis, conquering them in the end." [1]

[1] Bandelier, *op. cit.* p. 154. I think I never spent a pleasanter afternoon than once at Manchester-by-the-sea, with Mr. Cushing and three Zuñi priests who had come thither for the summer to assist him in his work. These Indians of the middle status told me their delightful yarns in exchange for Norse and Russian folk-tales which I told them, and Mr. Cushing served as a lively and dramatic interpreter. These Zuñis were very handsome men, abounding in kindliness and droll humour, while their refined grace of manner impressed me as hardly inferior to that of Japanese gentlemen. The combination of this civilized demeanour with the primeval naïveté of their thoughts was in a high degree piquant and interesting.

It was indeed only the next year that the Spaniards made their appearance, accompanied by their terrible horses. Six months after the return of Fray Marcos to Culiacan, an army of Expedition of 300 Spaniards and 800 Mexican In-Coronado dians, under Francisco de Coronado, started for Cibola. They visited the Zuñi and Moqui pueblos, discovered the grand cañon of the Colorado, and marched northward as far as a village called Quivira, concerning the site of which there is some diversity of opinion. The farthest point reached by Coronado may have been somewhere near the boundary between the states of Kansas and Nebraska, or perhaps farther west at some point on the south fork of the Platte River.[1] He passed quite beyond the semi-civilized region of the pueblos, and was disgusted at finding Quivira only a rude village of thatched wigwams instead of the fine city for which he had been looking. The supply of maize and bison-meat prevented the famine which so commonly overwhelmed such long expeditions, and Coronado took excellent care of his men. Many subordinate explorations were undertaken by detached parties, and a vast extent of country was visited. At length, in the

[1] A detailed account of Coronado's expedition is given in the chapter on "Early Explorations of New Mexico," by H. W. Haynes, in Winsor, *Narr. and Crit. Hist.*, vol. ii. chap. vii.

spring of 1542, the army returned to Mexico, greatly vexed and chagrined at having discovered no gold nor any wealthy kingdom, and this disappointment found a vent in anathemas vented upon Fray Marcos, which have ever since been echoed by historians.

Not only in the far West, but also in the East, did the experience of Cabeza de Vaca serve to stimulate the desire to explore the interior of the continent. To Fernando de Soto, no less than to the viceroy Mendoza, it seemed as if in such a wide extent of territory there must Expedition be kingdoms worth plundering. We of Soto have already met with Soto serving under Pizarro in Peru. In 1537 he was appointed governor of Cuba, and was authorized to conquer and occupy the country embraced within the patent of Narvaez. He started from Havana in May, 1539, with nine vessels, containing 570 men and 223 horses. Landing about thirty miles west of the bay of Juan Ponce, he marched laboriously as far northward as the Savannah River, and then turned westward. The golden country for which he was seeking did not appear, but the Indians on the route were very hostile. Though Soto had roundly blamed Pizarro for his treatment of Atahualpa, his own conduct toward Indians seems to have been at once cruel and foolish. The Spaniards had to

339

fight their way across the country, and the tribes
of the Creek Confederacy were no mean antago-
nists. At a palisaded village called Mauvila, a
few miles above the junction of the Tombigbee
and Alabama rivers,[1] there was a desperate fight,
in the autumn of 1541, in which Soto lost 170
of his men, while from the Spanish estimate of
2500 as the loss of the Indians it would perhaps
be safe to strike off a cipher.[2] In December the
Spaniards reached the Yazoo, and spent the
winter in that neighbourhood. In the spring
they crossed the Mississippi at the lowest of the
Chickasaw bluffs, and ascended the western
bank of the great river as far, perhaps, as New
Madrid. Finding no signs of El Dorado in that
direction, they turned southward. On the 21st
of May, 1542, Soto died of a fever, and was
buried in the Mississippi. His men, commanded by Luis de Moscoso, built boats in
which they descended the river and coasted
westward along the shores of Texas. On the

[1] It was probably *Mauvila*, or *Maubila*, that gave the
name *Mobile* to the river formed by the junction of these two.
See Charlevoix, *Journal historique*, p. 452.

[2] The later experiences of American backwoodsmen in
fighting these formidable barbarians should make us distrust all
stories of battles attended with great disparity of loss. If Soto
killed 250 of them without losing more than 170 of his own
men, he came off remarkably well. Compare Roosevelt's
Winning of the West, vol. i. p. 83 ; vol. ii. p. 123.

10th of September, 1543, the survivors of the expedition, 311 in number, reached Tampico.[1]

The work of founding colonies in North America languished. In 1546–49 a party of Dominican friars, led by the noble Luis de Barbastro, who had been with Las Casas in Tuzulutlan, made an attempt to found a mis- Dominicans sionary settlement in Florida, but they in Florida were all massacred by the Indians. The work was then taken up by Guido de Labazares and Tristan de Luna, under the auspices of Luis de Velasco, the humane and enlightened viceroy of New Spain. Their little colony was barely rescued from destruction by Angelo de Villafañe in 1561, and in the autumn of that year Philip II. announced that there would be no further attempts to colonize that country. As no gold was to be found, the chief reason for occupying Florida was to keep the French from getting hold of it, and it was thought

[1] An excellent account of Soto's expedition by one of the survivors was translated into English in 1611, by Richard Hakluyt, and is now among the publications of the Hakluyt Society : *The Discovery and Conquest of Florida*, London, 1851. A brief relation by Luis de Biedma is appended to this book. Garcilasso de la Vega also wrote a narrative (*La Florida del Ynca*, Lisbon, 1605) based upon reports of survivors, but uncritically treated. See also Pickett's *History of Alabama*, pp. 25–41. In this connection the reader will find much that is instructive in Jones's *Antiquities of the Southern Indians*, New York, 1873.

341

there was no danger of the French coming for the present.

Curiously enough, however, just about this time the French did come to Florida. Two French attempts at colonization grew directly out of the wars of religion. The illustrious Coligny was one of the first men, if not the very first, to conceive the plan of founding a Protestant state in America. In 1555 a small expedition, under Nicholas de Villegagnon, was Huguenots in Brazil sent to the coast of Brazil. A landing was made on the site of Rio de Janeiro, huts were built, and earthworks thrown up. A large reinforcement of Huguenots, with several zealous ministers from Geneva, arrived on the scene in 1557. But fierce theological disputes combined with want of food to ruin the little community. Villegagnon returned to France to carry on his controversy with the clergy, and the next year the miserable survivors of the colony were slaughtered by the Portuguese.[1]

Coligny's next attempt was made upon the coast of Florida, under the lead of Jean Ribaut, a hardy Huguenot of Dieppe. On May day, 1562, Ribaut, with a small advance party,

[1] The story of the Huguenots in Brazil is fully told by Lescarbot, *Histoire de la Nouvelle France*, Paris, 1612, livre ii.

reached the St. John's River, whence they coasted northward as far as the spot to which they gave the name Port Royal, in what is now South Carolina. Here they built a small fortress, and thirty men were left in charge of it while Ribaut returned to France to bring out his colony. For a while the little garrison lived on the hospitality of the Indians, until the latter, who had at first revered them as children of the Sun, began to despise them as sturdy beggars. Then as hunger began to pinch them, they mutinied and slew their commander. The time wore on, and nothing was heard of Ribaut. At last, in sheer despair, they contrived to patch together a crazy brigantine and set sail for France. Their scanty stock of food gave out while they were in mid-ocean, and one of the party had been devoured by his comrades, when they were picked up by an English cruiser and carried off to London.

The return of Ribaut had been delayed by the breaking out of war between the Huguenots and the Guise party; but in 1563 the truce of Amboise made things quiet for a while, and in the following year a new expedition set out for Florida, under the leadership of Ribaut's friend René de Laudonnière, a pious and valiant knight and a kinsman of Coligny. This company was much larger and better equipped than the former, but there was

343

an essential vice in its composition. There were plenty of soldiers and gentlemen unused to labour, and a few clever mechanics and tradesmen, but no tillers of the soil. In France, indeed, the rural population remained wedded to the old faith, and there were no Protestant yeomen as in England. The new expedition landed at the St. John's River, and built a fort near its mouth, which, in honour of Charles IX., was called Fort Caroline. This work off their hands, they devoted themselves to injudicious intrigues with the Indian potentates of the neighbourhood, explored the country for gold, and sent home to France for more assistance. Then they began to be mutinous, and presently resorted to buccaneering, with what fatal consequences will presently be seen. A gang of malcontents stole two of the pinnaces, and set out for the coast of Cuba, where, after capturing a small Spanish vessel, they were obliged to go ashore for food, and were thereupon arrested. Carried before the authorities at Havana, they sought to make things right for themselves by giving full information of the settlement at Fort Caroline, and this ill-omened news was not slow in finding its way to the ears of the king of Spain. It came at an opportune moment for Philip II. He had just found a man after his own heart, Pedro Menendez de Avilès, an admirable soldier and matchless liar, brave as a

344

mastiff and savage as a wolf. This man had persuaded Philip to change his mind and let him go and try to found a colony in Florida, whereby the Indians might be converted to Christianity. Just as Menendez was getting ready to start, there came from Havana the news of the ill-fated Lau- donnière and his enterprise. These heretics were trespassers on the territory which Holy Church had assigned to the Spanish Crown, and, both as trespassers and as heretics, they must be summarily dealt with. Rumour had added that Ribaut was expected from France with a large armament, so that no time was to be lost. The force at Menendez's disposal was largely in- creased, and on the 29th of June, 1565, he set sail from Cadiz, with eleven ships and more than 1000 fighting men, hoping to forestall the arrival of the French commander. The mood in which Menendez started was calculated to make him an ugly customer. He was going on a *crusade*. The original crusades were under- taken for a worthy purpose, and helped to save the Cross from being subdued by the Crescent. But after a while, when heresy became rife, the Pope would proclaim a crusade against heretics, and a bloody affair this was apt to be, as the towns of southern France once had reason to know. We may fitly call Menendez the Last of the Crusaders.

Menendez, the Last of the Crusaders

Things had fared badly with the colony at Fort Caroline. Mutiny had been checked by the summary execution of a few ringleaders, but famine had set in, and they had come to blows with the Indians. Events succeeded each other curiously. On the 3d of August, in the depth of their distress, Elizabeth's doughty sea-king Sir John Hawkins touched at the mouth of the St. John's, gave them food and wine, and offered them a free passage to France in his own ships, and on Laudonnière's refusal left with them a ship with which to make the voyage for themselves if they should see fit. On the 28th of August Ribaut at last arrived with seven ships, bringing 300 men and ample supplies. On the 4th of September, toward midnight, appeared the Spanish fleet!

The squadron of Menendez had undergone great hardships, and several of the vessels had been wrecked. Five ships now arrived, but after exchanging defiances with the French, Menendez concluded not to risk a direct attack, and crept off down the coast until he came to the site of St. Augustine. Some 500 negroes had been brought on the fleet, and were at once set to work throwing up entrenchments. One of the French ships, hanging in the rear, had taken note of these proceedings, and hurried back to Fort Caroline with the information. It was then decided to leave

Beginnings of St. Augustine

346

Laudonnière with a small force to hold the fort, while Ribaut by a sudden naval attack should overwhelm the Spanish fleet and then pounce upon the troops at St. Augustine before their entrenchments were completed. This plan seemed to combine caution with boldness, but the treachery of wind and weather defeated it. On the 10th of September Ribaut set sail, and early next morning his whole fleet bore down upon the Spaniards. But before they could come to action there sprang up an equinoctial gale which drove the French vessels out to sea, and raged so fiercely for several days as to render it morally certain that, wherever they might be, they could not have effected a return to their fort. It was now the turn of Menendez to take the offensive. On the morning of the 17th, with the storm still raging, he started forth, with 500 men and a couple of Indian guides to force his way through the forest. For thrice twenty-four hours they waded through swamps and forded swollen brooks, struggling with tall grass and fighting with hatchets the tangled underbrush, — until just before dawn of the 20th, drenched with rain, covered from head to foot with mud, torn with briars, fainting with hunger Slaughter of and weariness, but more than ever the people in Fort Caroline maddened with bigotry and hate, this wolfish company swept down the slope before Fort Caroline. The surprise was complete,

and the defences, which might barely have suf-
ficed against an Indian assault, were of no avail
to keep out these more deadly foes. Resistance
was short and feeble. Laudonnière and a few
others escaped into the woods, whence, some
time afterward, they sought the shore, and were
picked up by a friendly ship and carried home
to France. Of those who staid in the fort, men,
women, and children, to the number of 142,
were slaughtered. A few were spared, though
Menendez afterward, in his letter to the king,
sought to excuse himself for such unwarranted
clemency.

Meanwhile the ships of Jean Ribaut were
hopelessly buffeting the waves. One after another they were all wrecked somewhere below
Matanzas Inlet, a dozen miles south of St. Augustine. Most of the crews and troops were
saved, and, collecting in two bodies, began to
work their way back toward Fort Caroline. On
the 28th of September the first body, some 200
in number, had halted at Matanzas
Inlet, which they had no means of
crossing, when they encountered Menendez, who with about 70 men was on the
lookout for them. The two parties were on
opposite sides of this arm of the sea, and the
Spaniard so disposed his force among the bushes
that the enemy could not estimate their real
number. A boat was then sent out, and three

First massacre
at Matanzas
Inlet

348

or four French officers were decoyed across the river under promise of safety. They now learned that their fort was destroyed, and their wives and comrades murdered. At the same time they were requested, in courteous terms, to lay down their arms and entrust themselves to the clemency of Menendez. Hard as it seemed, starvation stared them in the face as the only alternative, and so after some discussion it was deemed most prudent to surrender. The arms were first sent across the river, and then the prisoners were brought over, ten at a time, each party being escorted by twenty Spaniards. As each party of ten arrived, they were led behind a sand-hill some distance from the bank, and their hands were tied behind their backs. A great part of the day was consumed in these proceedings, and at sunset, when the whole company of Huguenots had thus been delivered defenceless into the hands of their enemy, they were all murdered in cold blood. Not one was left alive to tell the tale.

A day or two later Ribaut himself, with 350 men, his entire remaining force, arrived at the inlet, and found Menendez duly ambushed to receive him. Once more the odious scene was acted out. The Frenchmen were judiciously informed of what had been done, but were treated with much courtesy, regaled with bread and wine, and coaxed to surrender. This time

349

there was a difference of opinion. Some 200 swore they would rather be devoured by the In-

Second massacre at Matanzas Inlet

dians than trust to the clemency of such a Spaniard ; and they contrived to slip away into the forest. The remaining 150, with Ribaut himself, were ferried across in small detachments, disarmed and bound, as had been done to their comrades, and when all had been collected together, all but five were put to death. That is to say, five were spared, but besides these, one sailor, who was not quite killed, contrived to crawl away, and after many adventures returned to France, to tell the harrowing tale. From this sailor, and from one of the five who were spared, we get the French account of the affair. The Spanish account we have from Menendez himself, who makes his official report to the king as coolly as a farmer would write about killing pigs or chickens. The two accounts substantially agree, except as regards the promise of safety by which the Frenchmen were induced to surrender. Menendez represents himself as resorting to a pious fraud in using an equivocal form of words, but the Frenchman declares that he promised most explicitly to spare them, and even swore it upon the cross. I am inclined to think that the two statements may be reconciled, in view of the acknowledged skill of Menendez and all his kith and kin as adroit dissemblers. After

350

all said and done, it was a foul affair, and the name Matanzas, which means "slaughterings," came naturally enough to attach itself to that inlet, and remains to this day a memento of that momentary fury of a New World crusade.

It used to be said in the days of Philip II. that wherever in any country there turned up a really first-class job of murder, you might be sure the king of Spain had something to do with it. The St. Bartholomew affair, for example, was a case in point. The Philip II. job done by Menendez, though small in scale, was certainly a thorough one, for it ended the Huguenot colony in Florida. Of the remnant of Ribaut's force which did not surrender, some disappeared among the Indians. Some were captured by Menendez, and the lives of these he spared, inasmuch as from the glut of slaughter some of his own men recoiled and called him cruel. From his master, however, Menendez received hearty approval for his ferocity, relieved by a slight hint of disapprobation for his scant and tardy humanity. "Tell him," said Philip, "that as to those he has killed, he has done well, and as to those he has saved, they shall be sent to the galleys."

This massacre of Frenchmen by Spaniards was perpetrated in a season of peace between the two governments. It was clearly an insult to France, inasmuch as the Huguenot expeditions had been undertaken with the royal commission. But the court of Catherine de' Medici was not likely to call Philip II. to account for anything he might take it into his head to do. Redress was not far off, but it came in a most unexpected way and at the hands of a private gentleman.

Dominique de Gourgues was a Gascon of noble birth, who had won high distinction in the Italian wars. It is not clear whether he was Dominique Catholic or Protestant, but he bore de Gourgues a grudge against the Spaniards, by whom he had once been taken prisoner and made to work in the galleys. He made up his mind to avenge the fate of his fellow-countrymen; it should be an eye for an eye and a tooth for a tooth. So he sold his family estate and borrowed money besides, and fitted up three small ships and enlisted about 200 men. In August, 1567, he sailed to the Guinea coast, armed with a royal commission to kidnap negroes. After an autumn and winter of random cruising he crossed the ocean, and it was when approaching Cuba that he first revealed to his followers his purpose. Little persuasion was required. With eager enthusiasm they turned their prows toward the Land of Easter, and soon came to anchor a few miles to the north of the Spanish fort. The Indians were overjoyed at their arrival. At first they had admired Menendez for his craft and the thoroughness with which he disposed of his enemies. But they had since found ample cause to regret their change of neighbours. On the arrival of Gourgues they flocked to his standard in such numbers that he undertook at once to surprise and overwhelm the Spanish garrison of 400 men. The march was conducted with secrecy and despatch. The Spaniards, not dreaming that there could be such a thing as a Frenchman within three thousand miles of Florida, had grown careless about their watch, and were completely surprised. At midday, just as they had finished their dinner, the French and Indians came swarming upon them from all points of the compass. A wild panic ensued, the works were carried and the defenders slaughtered. Of the whole Spanish force not a man escaped the sword, save some fifteen or twenty whom Gourgues reserved for a more ignominious fate, and to point a moral to this ferocious tale. At the capture of Fort Caroline, it is said that Menendez hanged several of his prisoners to trees near by, and nailed above them a board with the inscription, — " Not as to Frenchmen, but as to Lutherans." Gourgues now led his *Quid pro quo* fifteen or twenty surviving captives to these same trees, and after reading them a severe lecture hanged them all, and nailed above them the inscription, — " Not as to Spaniards, but as to liars and murderers." The fort was then totally demolished, so that not a beam or a stone was left in place. And so, having done his work in a thorough and business-like way, the redoubtable avenger of blood set sail for France.

In the matter of repartee it cannot be denied that Gourgues was successful. The retort would have had still more point if Menendez had been one of the hanged. But — unfortunately for the requirements of poetic justice — the principal liar and murderer was then in Spain, whence he returned a couple of years later, to rebuild his fort and go on converting the Indians.

These sanguinary events were doubtless of real historic importance. Unpromising as was the beginning of the Florida colony, it was no more so than the earliest attempts to settle Canada and Louisiana. In the brief glimpses that we get of Ribaut we can discern the outlines of a steadfast character that would have been likely to persevere until a solid result had been accomplished. So Menendez seems to have thought when he wrote to the king that by killing this man he believed himself to have dealt a heavier blow to France than if he had beaten an army. No doubt the affair of Matanzas removed what might have become an additional and serious obstacle in the way of the English, when France

Historic importance of the affair

354

and England came to struggle for the mastery over North America.[1]

As for Spain herself, owing to causes presently to be mentioned, she had about reached the limit of her work in the discovery and conquest of America. For the brief remainder of our story we have to deal chiefly with Frenchmen on land and with Englishmen on sea. The work of demonstrating the character of the continental mass of North America and its internal configuration was mostly done by Frenchmen. The expeditions of Soto and Coronado had made a goodly beginning, but as they were not followed up they did not yield so much increase of geographical knowledge as one might suppose. Two interesting maps made in England early in the last quarter of the sixteenth century represent respectively the wet and dry styles of

Knowledge of North American geography about 1580

---

[1] The story of the Huguenots in Florida is superbly told by Francis Parkman, in his *Pioneers of France in the New World*, Boston, 1865. The chief primary sources are Ribaut's *Whole and True Discovery of Terra Florida*, englished and reprinted by Hakluyt in 1582 ; Basanier, *L'histoire notable de la Floride*, Paris, 1586 ; Challeux, *Discours de l'histoire de la Floride*, Dieppe, 1566 ; *La reprinse de la Floride par le Cappitaine Gourgues*, printed in the collection of Ternaux-Compans ; the Spanish chaplain Mendoza's narrative, contained in the same collection ; and the MS. letters of Menendez to Philip II., preserved in the archives of Seville and first made public by Mr. Parkman.

interpreting the facts as they looked to carto-
graphers at that time. The map dedicated to
Sir Philip Sidney by Michael Lok, and published in Hakluyt's " Divers Voyages " in 1582,[1]
retains the " Sea of Verrazano," but gives enough
continent to include the journeys of Soto and
Coronado. In one respect it is interesting as
showing just about the extent of North America
that was known in 1582, ninety years after the
first crossing of the Atlantic by Columbus.
The reader will observe that the imaginary
islands of Brazil and St. Brandan have not disappeared, but are shifted in position, while the
Frislanda of the Zeno narrative appears to the
south of Greenland. A conspicuous feature is
the large island of Norombega (equivalent to
New England with Acadia), separated from the
mainland by what is apparently the Hudson
River figured as a strait communicating with the
St. Lawrence.[2]

Beyond the limits of the known land, and in
the regions which therefore might be either sea
or land for aught that Michael Lok could tell,
his map places a hypothetical ocean. On the
map presented to Queen Elizabeth in 1580 by

[1] The copy here given is photographed from the reduced
copy in Winsor, *Narr. and Crit. Hist.*, iv. 44.

[2] It was very commonly believed at that time that the
river discovered by Verrazano and afterward to be named for
Hudson was such a strait.

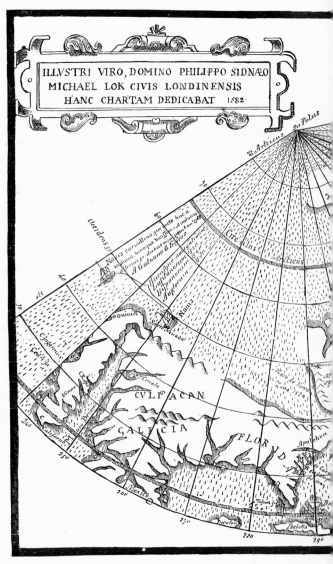

MICHAEL

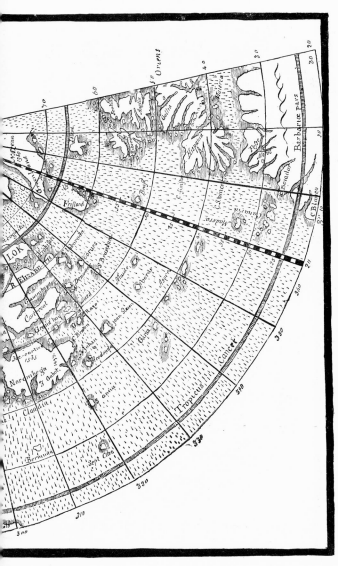

MAP, 1582.

Dr. John Dee, and now preserved in the British Museum, it is just the other way.[1] Beyond the limits reached by Coronado and Soto and Cartier, this map indicates a vast stretch of unvisited continent, and in its general outline it seems to come nearer to an adequate conception of the dimensions of North America than any of its predecessors.[2] It is noticeable, too, that although this is a "dry" map there is no indication of a connection between America and Asia. The western hemisphere was emerging in men's minds as a distinct and integral whole. Though people generally were not as yet enlightened to this extent,[3] there were many navigators and geographers who were.

[1] The sketch here given is taken from Winsor (iv. 98) after Dr. Kohl's copy in his Washington Collection.

[2] The legends on Dee's map are as follows : —

1. Estotiland.	14. C. de S. Roman.
2. Drogeo.	15. C. de Sta Hellena.
3. Belisle.	16. La Bermuda.
4. C. de Raso.	17. La Emperada.
5. C. de Bryton.	18. Terra Florida.
6. S. Brandan.	19. Rio de Spirito Santo.
7. Norombega.	20. Rio de Palmas.
8. R. de Gamas.	21. Mexico.
9. R. de San Antonio.	22. S. Thoma.
10. C. de Arenas.	23. C. California.
11. C. de St. Iago.	24. Ys de Cedri.
12. C. de S. John.	25. Y del reparo.
13. C. de terra falgar.	

[3] Thomas Morton, of Merrymount, in his *New English Canaan*, Amsterdam, 1637, writes of New England, " what

The most striking difference between Dr. Dee's map and that of Louis Joliet, to which we shall presently invite the reader's attention, is in the knowledge respecting the St. Lawrence and Mississippi rivers. Dee fails to give the information obtained by Soto's expedition. He interprets the St. Lawrence correctly as a river and not a strait, as many were still inclined to regard it. But this interpretation was purely hypothetical, and included no suspicion of the existence of the Great Lakes, for in 1580 no one had as yet gone above the site of Montreal. The exploration of the St. Lawrence and Mississippi valleys, with the determination of their relations to each other, was the most important inland work that was done in the course of American discovery. It was done by a succession of great Frenchmen, among whose names those of Champlain and La Salle are the most illustrious; and it was a result of the general system upon which French colonization in America, so different from English colonization, was conducted.

Work of the great French explorers

It was not until the wars of religion in France had been brought to an end by Henry IV. that the French succeeded in planting a colony in America. About that time they had begun to

part of this mane continent may be thought to border upon the Country of the Tartars, it is yet unknowne."

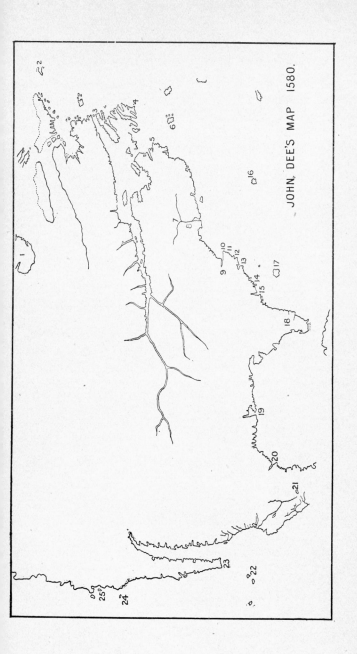

JOHN DEE'S MAP 1580.

feel an interest in the fur-trade, the existence of which had been disclosed through transactions with Indians on the coast, and sundry attempts were made at founding a permanent colony. This was at length effected through the persistent energy and self-sacrificing devotion of Samuel de Champlain, who made a settlement at Quebec in 1608 and became the founder of Canada. Champlain was one of the most remarkable Frenchmen of his day, — a beautiful character, devout and high-minded, brave and tender. Like Columbus and Magellan, like Livingstone in our own time, he had the scientific temperament. He was a good naturalist, and has left us the best descriptions we have of the Indians as they appeared before they had been affected by contact with white men. Champlain explored our northeastern coast quite carefully, and gave to many places the names by which they are still known.[1] He was the first white man to sail on the beautiful lake which now bears his name, and he pushed his explorations so far inland as to discover lakes Ontario and Huron.

It was the peculiar features of French policy in colonization that led to this long stride into the interior of the continent. Those features were developed during the lifetime of Cham-

[1] As, for example, Mount Desert, which retains a vestige of its old French pronunciation in accenting the final syllable.

plain and largely under the influence of his romantic personality. The quaint alliance of

Features of French colonization

missionary and merchant, the black-robed Jesuit and the dealer in peltries; the attempt to reproduce in this uncongenial soil the institutions of a feudalism already doomed in the Old World; the policy of fraternization with the Indians and participation in their everlasting quarrels; the policy of far-reaching exploration and the occupation of vast areas of territory by means of well-chosen military posts; all these features, which give to early Canadian history such fascinating interest,[1] were by no means accidental. They were parts of a deliberate system originating chiefly with Champlain, and representing the romantic notions of empire that were a natural outgrowth of the state of French society in the days of Henry IV. For Champlain to succeed at all, it

[1] It is full of romantic incident, and abounds in instructive material for the philosophical student of history. It has been fortunate in finding such a narrator as Mr. Francis Parkman, who is not only one of the most picturesque historians since the days of Herodotus, but likewise an investigator of the highest order for thoroughness and accuracy. The presence of a sound political philosophy, moreover, is felt in all his works. The reader who wishes to pursue the subject of French exploration in North America should begin with Mr. Parkman's *Pioneers of France, Jesuits in North America,* and *La Salle.* A great mass of bibliographical information may be found in Winsor, *Narr. and Crit. Hist.,* vol. iv. chaps. iii.–vi.

became necessary for him to accept the alliance of the Jesuits, although his own sympathies were with the national party in France rather than with the Spanish and ultramontane policy of the followers of Loyola. As another condition of success he deemed it necessary to secure the friendship of the Algonquin tribes in the valley of the St. Law- Causes which drew the French into the interior rence, and with this end in view he aided them in defeating the Mohawks near Ticonderoga in July, 1609. The result was that permanent alliance of the Five Nations, first with the Dutch settlers in the valley of the Hudson and afterward with the English, which is one of the great cardinal facts of American history down to 1763. The deadly hostility of the strongest Indian power upon the continent was a feature of the situation with which the French had to reckon from the very start, and the consequences were for them in many ways disastrous.[1] But what here concerns us is chiefly the effect of these circumstances in drawing the French at once into the interior of the continent. The hostile Iroquois could and sometimes did effectually cut off the fur-trade between the northwestern

[1] For example, it was the Iroquois who in 1689 defeated the scheme of Louis XIV. for capturing New York and securing to the French the valley of the Hudson. The success of that scheme might have changed the whole current of American history and prevented the formation of our Federal Union.

forests and the lower St. Lawrence ; so that for commercial reasons it was necessary for the French to occupy positions flanking the Long House, and this military necessity soon carried their operations forward as far as Lake Huron. As religion and commerce went hand in hand, it was there that those heroic Jesuits, Brébeuf and Lalemant, did their noble work and suffered their frightful martyrdom ; and it was in the destruction of this Huron mission that the Iroquois dealt their first staggering blow against the French power in America.

Somewhat later, when it became apparent that at sundry centres between the seashore and the Alleghany Mountains a formidable English power was growing up, French schemes involving military control of the interior of the continent assumed still larger dimensions, and a far-reaching work of exploration was undertaken Robert de by that man of iron, if ever there was La Salle one, Robert Cavelier de La Salle. As Champlain had laid the foundations of Canada and led the way to the Great Lakes, so La Salle completed the discovery of the Mississippi and carried the empire of France in theory from the crest of the Alleghanies to that of the unvisited Rocky Mountains. In the long interval since 1542 the work of Soto and Coronado had almost lapsed into oblivion. Of the few who remembered their names there were fewer who could have told you where they went or what they did, so that the work of the French explorers from Canada had all the characteristics of novelty. In 1639 Jean Nicollet reached the Wisconsin River, and heard of a great water beyond, which he supposed must be the Pacific Ocean, but which was really the Mississippi River. In the following years Jesuit missionaries penetrated as far as Lake Superior, and settlements were made at Sault Sainte Marie and Michilimackinac. In 1669 La Salle made his first western journey, hoping somewhere or somehow to find a key to the solution of the problem of a northwest passage. In the course of this expedition he discovered the Ohio River and perhaps also the Illinois. La Salle's feudal domain of Saint Sulpice, near Montreal, bears to this day the name of La Chine (China), which is said to have been applied to it in derision of this fruitless attempt to find the Pacific and the way to Cathay.[1] By this time the French had heard much about the Mississippi, but so far from recognizing its identity with the Rio de Espiritu Santo of the Spaniards, they were inclined to regard it as flowing into the Pacific, or into the " Vermilion Sea," as they called the narrow gulf between Mexico and Old California. In Marquette 1673 this view was practically refuted and Joliet by the priest Marquette and the fur-trader

[1] Parkman's *La Salle*, p. 21.

363

Joliet, who reached the Mississippi by way of the Wisconsin, and sailed down the great river as far as the mouth of the Arkansas.

La Salle now undertook to explore the Mississippi to its mouth, and prepare for the establishment of such military posts as would effectually confirm the authority of Louis XIV. throughout the heart of the continent, and permanently check the northward advance of New Spain and the westward progress of the English colonies. La Salle was a man of cold and haughty demeanour, and had made many enemies by the uncompromising way in which he pushed his schemes. There was a widespread fear that their success might result in a gigantic commercial monopoly. For these and other reasons he drew upon himself the enmity of both fur-traders and Jesuits; and, as so often happens with men of vast projects, he had but little ready money. But he found a powerful friend in the viceroy Count Frontenac, and like that picturesque and masterful personage he had rare skill in managing Indians. At length, in 1679, after countless vexations, a vessel was built and launched on the Niagara River, a small party of thirty or forty men were gathered together, and La Salle, having just recovered from a treacherous dose of poison, embarked on his great enterprise. His departure was clouded by the news that his impatient creditors had laid hands upon his Canadian estates, but, nothing daunted, he pushed on through the lakes Erie and Huron, and after many disasters reached the southern extremity of Lake Michigan. The vessel was now sent back with half the party to Niagara, carrying furs to appease the creditors and purchase additional supplies for the remainder of the journey, while La Salle with his diminished company pushed on to the Illinois, where a fort was built and appropriately named Fort Crèvecœur. It was indeed at a heart-breaking moment that Fort Crève-cœur it was finished, for so much time had elapsed since the departure of their little ship that all had come to despair of her return. No word ever came from her. Either she foundered on the way, or perhaps her crew may have deserted and scuttled her, carrying off her goods to trade with on their own account.

After a winter of misery, in March, 1680, La Salle started to walk to Montreal. Leaving Fort Crèvecœur and its little garrison under the command of the brave Henri de Tonty, a lieutenant who could always A thousand miles in the wilderness be trusted, he set out, with four Frenchmen and one Mohegan guide; and these six men fought their way eastward through the wilderness, now floundering through melting snow, now bivouacking in clothes stiff with frost, now stopping to make a bark canoe, now

365

leaping across streams on floating ice-cakes, like the runaway slave-girl in "Uncle Tom's Cabin;" in such plight did they make their way across Michigan and Ontario to the little log-fortress at Niagara Falls. All but La Salle had given out on reaching Lake Erie, and the five sick men were ferried across by him in a canoe. Thus because of the sustaining power of wide-ranging thoughts and a lofty purpose, the gentleman reared in luxury and trained at college surpassed in endurance the Indian and the hunters inured to the forest. He had need of all this sustaining power, for at Niagara he learned that a ship from France, freighted for him with a cargo worth 20,000 livres, had been wrecked and totally lost in the St. Lawrence. Nothing daunted by this blow he took three fresh men, and completed his march of a thousand miles to Montreal.

There he collected supplies and reinforcements and had returned as far as Fort Frontenac, at the lower end of Lake Ontario, when further woeful tidings greeted him. A message from the fort so well named "Heartbreak" arrived in July. The garrison had mutinied and pulled that blockhouse to pieces, and made their way back through Michigan. Recruiting their ranks with other worthless freebooters, they had plundered the station at Niagara, and their canoes were now cruising on Lake Ontario in the hope of crowning their work with the murder of La Salle. These wretches, however, fell into their own pit. The indomitable commander's canoes were soon swarming on the lake, and he was not long in overtaking and capturing the mutineers, whom he sent in chains to the viceroy. La Salle now kept on his way to the Illinois River, intending to rebuild his fort and hoping to rescue Tonty with the few faithful followers who had survived the mutiny. That little party had found shelter among the Illinois Indians; but during the summer of 1680 the great village of the Illinois was sacked by the Iroquois, and the hard-pressed Frenchmen retreated up the western shore of Lake Michigan as far as Green Bay. When La Salle reached the Illinois he found nothing but the horrible vestiges of fiery torments and cannibal feasts. Without delay he set to work to secure the friendship and alliance of the western tribes, on the basis of their common enmity to the Iroquois. After thus spending the winter to good purpose, he set out again for Canada, in May, 1681, to arrange his affairs and obtain fresh resources. At the outlet of Lake Michigan he fell in with his friend Tonty, and together they paddled their canoes a thousand miles, and so came to Fort Frontenac.

The enemies of the great explorer had grown

merry over his apparent discomfiture, but his stubborn courage at length vanquished the adverse fates, and on the next venture things went smoothly. In the autumn he started with a fleet of canoes, passed up the lakes from Ontario to the head of Michigan, crossed the narrow portage from the Chicago River to the Illinois, and thence coming out upon the Mississippi glided down to its mouth. On the 9th of April, 1682, the fleurs-de-lis were duly planted, and all the country drained by the great river and its tributaries, a country vaster than La Salle imagined, was declared to be the property of the king of France, and named for him Louisiana.

Descent of the Mississippi, 1682

Returning up the Mississippi after this triumph, La Salle established a small fortified post on the Illinois River, which he called St. Louis. Leaving Tonty in command there, he lost no time in returning to France for means to complete his far-reaching scheme. A colony was to be founded at or near the mouth of the Mississippi, and a line of military posts was to connect it with Canada. La Salle was well received by the king, and a fine expedition was fitted out, but everything was ruined by the incompetence or ill fortune of the naval commander, Beaujeu. The intention was to sail directly to the mouth of the Mississippi, but the pilots missed it and passed beyond; some of the ships were wrecked on the coast of Texas; the captain, beset by foul weather and pirates, disappeared with the rest, and was seen no more; and two years of misery followed. At last, in March, 1687, La Salle started on foot in search of the Mississippi, hoping to ascend it and find succour at Tonty's fort; but he had scarcely set out with this forlorn hope when two or three mutinous wretches skulked in ambush and shot him dead.

La Salle's last expedition, 1687

These explorations of Joliet, Marquette, and La Salle opened up the centre of the continent, and in the map dedicated by Joliet to Count Frontenac, in 1673,[1] we see a marked advance beyond Dr. Dee's map of 1580. The known part of the continent of North America represented has come to be very large, but Joliet has no suspicion of the huge dimensions of the portion west of the Mississippi, and his style of theorizing is oceanic in so far as he fills up

---

[1] The sketch here given is reduced from the sketch in Winsor, iv. 208, after the coloured facsimile accompanying Gravier's *Étude sur une carte inconnue*, Paris, 1879. There is another coloured facsimile in the *Magazine of American History*, vol. ix. p. 273, in connection with the excellent bibliographical articles by Mr. Appleton Griffin, of the Boston Public Library, on the discovery of the Mississippi, pp. 190–199, 273–280. This is the earliest map of the

the unknown spaces with water rather than land. A freezing ocean usurps the place of northwestern British America, and Hudson Bay appears as an open gulf in this ocean. From this great inland sea, forever memorable for Henry Hudson's wild and tragic fate, and from the shores of Lake Superior, rival lines of fur-trade were presently to carry the know-

Hennepin in the Minne-sota country

ledge and influence of the white men still farther into the unknown West. About the time that La Salle was starting from Fort Crèvecœur for Montreal,

Mississippi valley that is based upon real knowledge. The legends are as follows : —

1. Mer Glaciale.
2. Les sauvages habitent cette isle.
3. Baye d'Hudson.
4. Labrador.
5. Le fleuve de St. Laurent.
6. Tadoussac.
7. Le Saguenay.
8. Quebec.
9. Montroyal.
10. Acadie.
11. Baston [i. e. Boston].
12. Nouvelle Suède.
13. La Virginie.
14. La Floride.
15. Cap de la Floride.
16. Fort de Frontenac.
17. Lac Frontenac ou Ontario.
18. Lac Erie.
19. Lac Huron.
20. Le Sault Ste Marie.
21. Lac Supérieur.
22. Lac des Illinois ou Missihiganin.

23. Riviere Miskonsing.
24. Riviere de Buade.
25. Paoutet, Maha, Atontauka, Il-linois, Peouaria, 300 cabanes, 180 canots de bois de 50 pieds de long.
26. Minongio, Pani, Ouchagé, Kansa, Missouri.
27. Riviere de la Divine ou l'Outre-laize.
28. Riv. Ouabouskigou [i. e. Ohio].
29. Akansea sauvages.
30. Riviere Basire.
31. Tapensa sauvages.
32. Le Sein de Mexique.
33. Le Mexique.
34. La Nouvelle Granade.
35. Mer Vermeille, ou est la Cali-fournie, par ou on peut aller au Perou, au Japon, et à la Chine.

370

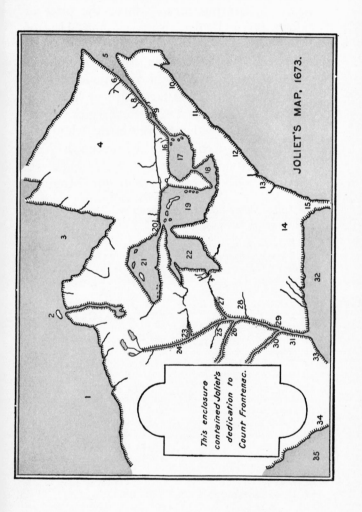

JOLIET'S MAP, 1673.

This enclosure contained Joliet's dedication to Count Frontenac.

the Recollet friar, Louis de Hennepin, with two companions, set out from the same point with La Salle's directions to explore the Illinois River to its mouth. The little party were captured by Sioux Indians and carried off into the Minnesota country as far as the Falls of St. Anthony and beyond. Hennepin's pocket compass was regarded by these redskins as potent medicine, so that he was adopted by an old chief and held in high esteem. After many romantic adventures he found his way back to Montreal, and indeed to Paris, where in 1683 he published a narrative of his experiences.[1] What he had done and suffered entitle him to a fair meed of fame, but in 1697, after La Salle had been ten years dead, and after the silly friar had passed into the service of England, he published another account in which he declared that before his capture by the Sioux he had descended the Mississippi River to its mouth and returned to the spot where he was captured.[2] The impudent lie was very easily exposed, and Father Hennepin's good fame was ruined. His genuine

[1] Hennepin, *Description de la ↩ouisiane, nouvellement découverte,* Paris, 1683.

[2] Hennepin, *Nouvelle découverte d'un très grand pays situé dans l'Amérique, entre le Nouveau Mexique et la Mer Glaciale,* Utrecht, 1697 [dedicated to King William III.]. It has the earliest known engraved plate showing Niagara Falls, and a fine map containing results of explorations north of Lake Superior.

adventures, however, in which the descriptions can be verified, are none the less interesting to the historian; and from that time forth the French began to become familiar with the Lake Superior country, and to extend their alliances among the northwestern Indians.

About the same time a rival claim to the profits of the fur-trade was set up by the English. It was the time when Charles II. was so lavish with his grants of American territories and their produce, without much heeding what or where they were, or to whom they belonged. In 1670 he granted to his cousin Prince Rupert and several other noblemen " the sole trade and commerce of all those seas, straits, bays, rivers, lakes, creeks, and sounds lying within the entrance of Hudson's Straits, with all the lands, countries, and territories upon the coasts and confines " of the same. This was the beginning of the Hudson Bay Company, and from that day until lately the vast and vaguely defined country which has been the scene of its operations has been known as " Rupert's Land." From that day to this it has been a huge " preserve for fur-bearing animals and for Indians who might hunt and trap them," a natural home for beavers, " otters, martens, musk-rats, and all the other species of amphibious creatures, with countless herds of buffaloes, moose, bears, deer, foxes, and wolves." In the

The Hudson Bay Company

time of which we are treating, these beasts had freely multiplied, "the aborigines killing only enough of them for their clothing and subsistence till the greed of traffic threatened their complete extirpation."[1] Upon the shores of Hudson Bay the agents of the company set up fortified trading stations and dealt with the tribes in the interior. These proceedings aroused the jealous wrath of the French, and furnished occasions for scrimmages in the wilderness and diplomatic wrangling at Westminster and Versailles. More than once in those overbearing days of Louis XIV. the English forts were knocked to pieces by war parties from Canada; but after the treaty of Utrecht this sort of thing became less common.

In the great war which that treaty of Utrecht ended, a brave young lieutenant, named Pierre Gaultier de Varennes, was wounded and left for dead on the field of Malplaquet, but recovered and lived to play a part in American history. He was a native of Three Rivers in Canada, and returned thither after the war, assuming for some reason the name of La Vérendrye, by which he has since been known. About 1728 La Vérendrye, being in command of a fort to the north of Lake Superior, was led by Indian reports to believe that the western

La Vérendrye

[1] See the admirable description of Rupert's Land by Dr. George Ellis, in Winsor, *Narr. and Crit. Hist.*, viii. 12.

ocean could be reached by journeys in canoes and on foot from that point. He was empowered to make the experiment at his own expense and risk, and was promised a monopoly of the fur-trade in the countries he should discover. This arrangement set all the traders against him, and the problem assumed very much the same form as that with which La Salle had struggled. Nine years were consumed in preliminary work, in the course of which a wide territory was explored and a chain of forts erected from the Lake of the Woods to the mouth of the river Saskatchewan. From this region La Vérendrye made his way to the Mandan villages on the Missouri; and thence his two sons, taking up the work while he was temporarily disabled, succeeded in reaching the Bighorn range of the Rocky Mountains on New Year's day, 1743. At this point, marvelling at the interminable extent of the continent and believing that they must at last be near the Pacific, though they were scarcely within a thousand miles of it, they felt obliged to turn back. Another expedition was contemplated, but by this time so many jealousies had been aroused that the remaining energies of the family La Vérendrye were frittered away. The Hudson Bay Company incited the Indians of the Saskatchewan region to hostilities against the

French discovery of the Rocky Mountains, 1743

French ; and it was not long before all their romantic schemes were swallowed up in the English conquest of Canada.[1]

The crossing of the continent was not completed until the beginning of the nineteenth century. After President Jefferson's purchase of the Louisiana territory from France had carried the western frontier of the United States up to the crests of the Rocky Mountains, the question as to what power belonged the Oregon territory beyond remained undecided. Discovery of the Columbia River, 1792 It is not necessary to encumber our narrative with a statement of this complicated question.[2] It is enough to observe that in 1792 Captain Robert Gray, in the ship Columbia, of Boston, in the course of a voyage around the world, ascended for some distance the magnificent river to which he gave the name of his vessel. It was only fourteen years since that part of the North American coast had been mapped out by the famous Captain Cook, but neither he nor Vancouver, who was on that coast in the same year with Gray, discovered the Co-

[1] In writing this paragraph I am under obligations to Mr. Parkman's paper on "The Discovery of the Rocky Mountains," *Atlantic Monthly*, June, 1888.

[2] For a statement of it, see Hubert Bancroft's *Northwest Coast*, vol. i. ; Barrows's *Oregon ;* Vancouver's *Voyage of Discovery*, London, 1798 ; Winsor, *Narr. and Crit. Hist.*, vii. 555–562.

lumbia River. Gray was unquestionably the first white man to enter it and to recognize it as an immense river and not a mere arm of the sea; and upon the strength of this discovery the United States laid claim to the area drained by the Columbia. To support this claim by the further exploration of the valley, and possibly also to determine by inspection of the country what bearings, if any, the purchase of Louisiana might have upon the question, Captains Meriwether Lewis and William Clark[1] were sent out, with thirty-two men, upon the same enterprise that had been attempted by La Vérendrye and his sons. Lewis and Clark, like the Frenchmen, took their final start from one of the Mandan villages. From April 7 till August 11, 1806, they worked up the Missouri River and its Jefferson fork in boats and canoes, and then made their way through the mountains to the headwaters of the Columbia, down which they sailed to its mouth, and came out upon the Pacific on the 7th of November, after a journey of nearly 4000 miles from the confluence of the Mississippi with the Missouri. The progress across the continent, begun by Champlain, was thus completed, two hundred years later, by Lewis and Clark.

First crossing of the continent, 1806

[1] He was brother to George Rogers Clark, conqueror of the Northwest Territory.

The final proof of the separation of North America from Asia by Vitus Bering was an incident in the general history of arctic exploration. When the new continent from Patagonia to Labrador came to be recognized as a barrier in the way to the Indies, the search for a northwest passage necessarily became restricted to the arctic regions, and attempts were also made to find a northeast passage around Siberia into the Pacific. This work was begun by the English and Dutch, at about the time when Spanish activity in discovery and colonization was coming to a standstill. There is much meaning in the simultaneous expeditions of Drake and Frobisher, just at the time of Queen Elizabeth's alliance with the revolted Netherlands. In the reign of Elizabeth's grandfather England had for a moment laid a hand upon North America; she now went far toward encompassing it, and in the voyage of Drake, as in that of Cabot, a note of prophecy was sounded. In the years 1577–80 Drake passed the Strait of Magellan, followed the coast northward as far as some point in northern California or southern Oregon, and took formal possession of that region, calling it New Albion. Thence he crossed the Pacific directly to the Moluccas, a much shorter transit than that of Magellan, and thence returned to England by way of the Cape of Good

Search for a northwest passage

Drake and Frobisher

Hope. This was the second circumnavigation of the earth. Its effect upon the geographical knowledge of North America was to sustain the continental theory indicated upon Dr. Dee's map of 1580.[1] About the same time, in 1576–78, Sir Martin Frobisher in three voyages entered the strait which bears his name and that which is called after Hudson, in search of a passage to Cathay.[2]

The second attempt in these arctic waters was made by that scientific sailor, John Davis, who in 1585–87 penetrated as far as latitude 72° 12′ and discovered the Cumberland Islands.[3] Attention was at the same time paid to the ocean between Greenland and Norway, both by the Muscovy Company in London, of which Dr. Dee was now one of the official advisers, and by Dutch navigators, under the impulse and guidance of the eminent Flemish merchant, Balthasar Moucheron. In 1594–96 William Barentz discovered Spitzbergen and

Davis and Barentz (margin note)

[1] See Drake's *World Encompassed*, ed. Vaux, London, 1854 (Hakluyt Soc.). There is a story that a Greek sailor, Apostolos Valerianos, who had served in the Spanish marine under the name of Juan de la Fuca, came after Drake in 1592, and discovered the strait which bears that name. See Peschel, *Geschichte der Erdkunde*, bd. i. p. 273.

[2] See Frobisher's *Three Voyages*, ed. Collinson, London, 1867 (Hakluyt Soc.).

[3] See Davis's *Voyages and Work on Navigation*, ed. A. H. Markham, London, 1880 (Hakluyt Soc.).

thoroughly explored Nova Zembla, but found little promise of a route to Cathay in that direction.[1] Then came Henry Hudson, grandson of one of the founders of the Muscovy Company. In 1607 and 1608 he made two voyages in the service of that company. In the first he tried to penetrate between Greenland and Spitzbergen and strike boldly across the North Pole; in the second he tried to pass between Spitzbergen and Nova Zembla. His third voyage was made in 1609, in that famous little eighty-ton craft the Half-Moon, and in the service of the Dutch East India Company. He had with him some letters which his friend Captain John Smith had sent him from Virginia, in which allusion was made to the great river which, as we now know, had already been visited by Verrazano and Gomez, and probably also by sporadic French traders, who may have ascended it as far as the mouth of the Mohawk in quest of peltries.[2] It seemed to Smith, from what he

Henry Hudson

[1] See Motley's *United Netherlands*, vol. iii. pp. 552–576; Gerrit de Veer, *Three Voyages to the Northeast*, ed. Koolemans Beynen, London, 1876 (Hakluyt Soc.).

[2] See Weise's *Discoveries of America*, New York, 1884, chap. xi. Mr. Weise suggests that the name *Terre de Norumbega* may be a corruption of *Terre d' Anormée Berge, i. e.* "Land of the Grand Scarp," from the escarpment of palisaded cliffs which is the most striking feature as one passes by the upper part of Manhattan Island. See the name Anorumbega on Mercator's map, 1541, above, vol. ii. p. 386. Thevet

had heard, that this water might be a strait leading into a western ocean. When Hudson
reached Nova Zembla, he found the sea as full
of ice as before, and thereupon, in excess of his
instructions, he faced about and stood across the
Atlantic, in the hope of finding his northwest
passage at about the fortieth parallel. His exploration of the river which has since borne his
name served to turn the attention of Dutch
merchants to the fur-trade, and thus led to the
settlement of New Netherland, while at the
same time it proved that no passage to Cathay
was to be found in that direction. In the following year Hudson had returned to the English service, and in a further search for the
passage he found his way into that vast inland
sea which is at once " his tomb and his monument." In midsummer of 1611 he was turned
adrift in an open boat by his mutinous crew
and abandoned on that gloomy waste of waters.[1]

(1556) says that *Norombègue* is a name given to the Grand
River by the French. Laudonnière (1564) has it *Norum-
berge*. The more common opinion is that the Norumbega
River was the Penobscot, and that the name is a presumed
Indian word *Aranbega*, but this is doubtful. In the loose
nomenclature of the time the name Norumbega may have been
applied now to the Penobscot and now to the Hudson, as it
was sometimes to the whole country between them.

[1] See Asher's *Henry Hudson the Navigator*, London,
1860 (Hakluyt Soc.) ; Read's *Historical Inquiry concerning
Henry Hudson*, Albany, 1866 ; De Costa, *Sailing Direc-*

The result of this memorable career, embraced as it was within four short years, was to dispel illusory hopes in many directions, and limit the search to the only really available route — the one which Hudson would probably have tried next — by way of the strait discovered by Davis. This route was resumed in 1615 by William Baffin, who left his name upon a long stretch of sea beyond that explored by Davis, and reached the 78th parallel, discovering Jones and Lancaster sounds, as well as the sound which commemorates the name of the merchant prince, Sir Thomas Smith, first governor of the East India Company.[1] Nothing more was accomplished in this direction until Sir John Ross, in 1818, opened the modern era of arctic exploration.[2]

One consequence of these voyages was to

tions of Henry Hudson, Albany, 1869. Portuguese sailors seem to have entered the bay called after Hudson as early as 1558–69 ; see Asher, p. cxliv.

[1] See Markham's Voyages of William Baffin, London, 1881 (Hakluyt Soc.). For a brief account of Sir Thomas Smith (or Smythe) see Fox-Bourne, English Merchants, vol. i. pp. 315–317 ; there is a portrait of him in Winsor, Narr. and Crit. Hist., vol. iii. p. 94.

[2] Just as this final chapter goes to press I have received the sheets of Winsor's Christopher Columbus, a few days in advance of publication. On page 651 he cites the unsuccessful voyages of Luke Fox and Thomas James in Hudson's Bay in 1631 as checking further efforts in this direction.

abolish the notion of a connection between Greenland and Europe, and to establish the outlines of the northeastern coast of North America, in such wise as to suggest, in the minds of the few northern scholars who knew anything about the Vinland traditions, the correct association of the idea of Vinland with the idea of America. As I have already observed, there was nothing to suggest any such association of ideas until the period of the four great navigators, Frobisher, Davis, Hudson, and Baffin; at that period we begin to catch glimpses of it, dimly and dubiously in 1570 with Stephanius, briefly but distinctly in 1610 with Arngrim Jonsson;[1] and at last in 1705 a general interest in the subject was awakened by Torfæus.

Effect upon the conception of Vinland

While Frobisher and his successors were groping for a northwest passage to Cathay, the Russians were steadily advancing by overland conquests toward that land of promise. Between 1560 and 1580 the Cossack Irmak crossed the Ural Mountains and conquered Siberia as far as the Obi River. Thence, urged on by the quest for gold and peltries, and the need for subduing unruly neighbours, the Russian arms pressed eastward, until in 1706 the peninsula of Kamtchatka was added to their domains. At that

Russian conquest of Siberia

[1] See above, vol. ii. p. 71.

period the northern Pacific and the wild coasts on either side of it were still a region of mystery. On the American side nothing was known north of Drake's " New Albion," on the Asiatic side nothing north of Japan. Some still believed that the two continents were joined together; others held that they were separated by a strait, for how else could there be a northwest passage?[1] Peter the Great wished to settle such questions and ascertain the metes and bounds of his empire, and in 1724, shortly before his death, he appointed the Danish captain Vitus Bering[2] to the command of an expedition for exploring the eastern shores Vitus Bering of the Kamtchatka and Chukchi peninsulas, to see if any strait could be found there. In one respect this was an enterprise of unparalleled difficulty, for the starting point of the navigation was some 5000 miles distant from St. Peters-

[1] The wish was father to the thought, and the so-called Strait of Anian appears on many old maps, beginning with Mercator's chart of 1569. Some maps have also a gulf of Anian ; possibly from a misunderstanding of the Gulf of Annan (*i. e.* Tongking) mentioned in a passage interpolated into Marco Polo, book iii. chap. iv. See Lauridsen's *Vitus Bering*, p. 202. But this explanation is doubtful.

[2] Until lately the Danish name has appeared in English with a German and incorrect spelling, as *Behring*. The best book on this navigator is Lauridsen's *Vitus Bering*, Chicago, 1889, translated by Professor Julius Olson, of the University of Wisconsin.

burg, and more than half this distance was through a howling wilderness. Many were the obstacles that had to be surmounted before Bering could build and launch his stout little ship, the Gabriel, in the early summer of 1728. The point from which he started was not far from Cape Kamtchatka. He bore to the northward, keeping in sight of the coast, and on the 11th of August sighted on the starboard the island which he named St. Lawrence. On the 14th he left East Cape receding astern, and seemed to have open sea on both sides of him, Discovery of Bering Strait, 1728 for he did not descry the American coast about forty miles distant. After a day's sail into the Arctic Ocean, he turned and passed back through the strait without seeing the opposite coast. He believed, and rightly as it happened, that he had found an end to Asia, and completed the proof of the existence of a continuous sea-coast from the mouth of the Lena River to Kamtchatka. A gigantic enterprise was now set on foot. The Siberian coast was to be charted from Nova Zembla to the Lena; Japan was to be reached from the north; and the western shore of America was to be discovered and explored. As to the latter part, with which we are here concerned, a Russian officer, Gvosdjeff, sailed into Bering's Strait in 1732 and saw the American coast.[1] Before

[1] Lauridsen, *op. cit.* p. 130.

more extensive work could be done it was necessary to build the town of Petropavlovsk, in Kamtchatka, as a base of operations. From that point the two ships St. Peter and St. Paul, under Bering's command, set sail in the summer of 1741. At first they took a southeasterly course in order to find an imaginary " Gamaland," which was by a few theorizers supposed to lie in mid-Pacific, east of Japan. Thus they missed the Aleutian Islands. After reaching latitude 46°, not far from the 180th meridian, they gave up the search for this figment of fancy, and steering northeasterly at length reached the Alaska coast under the volcano St. Elias. On the more direct return voyage, which took them through the Aleutian archipelago, they encountered fierce storms, with the added horrors of famine and scurvy. When they came to the island known as Bering's, not more than a hundred miles from the Kamtchatka coast, they were cast ashore, and there the gallant Bering succumbed to scurvy and ague, and died in his sixtieth year. Such were the expeditions that completed the discovery of North America as a distinct and separate continent, and gave to Russia for a time an American territory as spacious as France and Germany together.

Bering's discovery of Alaska, 1741

The work of Vitus Bering may be regarded

as the natural conclusion of that long chapter in the history of discovery which began with Ponce de Leon's first visit to the Land of Easter. When Bering and Gvosdjeff saw the two sides of the strait that separates America from Asia, quite enough had been done to reveal the general outlines and to suggest the broadness of the former continent, although many years were still to elapse before anybody crossed it from ocean to ocean. The discovery of the whole length of the Mississippi, with its voluminous tributaries, indicating an extensive drainage area to the west of that river, the information gained in the course of trade by the Hudson Bay Company, the stretch of arctic coast explored by Baffin, and finally the discovery of Bering Strait, furnished points enough to give one a fairly correct idea of North America as a distinct and integral mass of land, even though there was still room for error, here and there, with regard to its dimensions. Our story impresses upon us quite forcibly the fact that the work of discovery has been a gradual and orderly development. Such must necessarily be the case. Facts newly presented to the mind must be assimilated to the preëxisting stock of knowledge, and in the process an extensive destruction of wrong or inadequate conceptions takes place ; and this sort of thing takes a great deal of time, especially

The discovery of America was a gradual development

386

since the new facts can be obtained only by long voyages in unknown seas, or tramps through the trackless wilderness, at great cost of life and treasure. The Discovery of America may be regarded in one sense as a unique event, but it must likewise be regarded as a long and multifarious process. The unique event was the crossing of the Sea of Darkness in 1492. It established a true and permanent contact between the eastern and western halves of our planet, and brought together the two streams of human life that had flowed in separate channels ever since the Glacial period. No ingenuity of argument can take from Columbus the glory of an achievement which has, and can have, no parallel in the whole career of mankind. It was a thing that could be done but once. On the other hand, when we regard the Discovery as a long and multifarious process, it is only by a decision more or less arbitrary that we can say when it began or when it ended. It emerged from a complex group of facts and theories, and was accomplished through a multitude of enterprises in all quarters of the globe. We cannot understand its beginnings without paying due heed to the speculations of Claudius Ptolemy at Alexandria in the second century of our era, and to the wanderings of Rubruquis in Tartary in the thirteenth ; nor can we describe its consummation without recalling to memory the motives and results of cruises in the Malay archipelago and journeys through the snows of Siberia. For our general purpose, however, it is enough to observe that a period of two hundred years just about carries us from Dias and Columbus to Joliet and La Salle, or from Ponce de Leon to Vitus Bering. The sixteenth and seventeenth centuries carried far toward completion the work of 1492.

In our brief survey of the work of discovery during those two centuries, one striking contrast forces itself upon our attention. We began this chapter in company with Spaniards; toward its close our comrades have been chiefly Frenchmen and Englishmen. In the days of Cortes and Magellan, the Spain of Charles V. was the foremost power in the world; in the days of La Salle the France of Louis XIV. was the foremost power. The last years of Louis XIV. saw Spain, far sunken from her old preëminence, furnishing the bone of contention between France and England in the first of the two great struggles which won for England the foremost place. As regards America, it may be observed that from 1492 until about 1570 the exploring and colonizing activity of Spain was immense, insomuch that upon the southern half of the New World it has left its stamp for-

Cessation of Spanish exploring and colonizing activity after about 1570

388

ever, so that to-day the Spanish is one of the few imperial languages. After 1570 this wonderful manifestation of Spanish energy practically ceased, and this is a fact of supreme importance in the history of North America. But for this abrupt cessation of Spanish energy the English settlements at Jamestown and Plymouth would have been in quite as dangerous a position as Ribaut's colony in Florida. It is worth while, therefore, to notice one or two eloquent items of chronology. In 1492 Spain was relieved of a task which had long absorbed all her vital energies, the work of freeing her soil from the dominion of the Moors. In 1570 she was entering upon another task which not only absorbed but well-nigh exhausted her energies, the attempt to suppress Protestantism in Europe and to subdue the revolted Netherlands. When she had once put her hand to this work, Spain had no surplus vitality left for extending her sway in America. She was scarcely able to maintain the ground she had already occupied ; she could not defend the West Indies against the buccaneers, and the end of the seventeenth century saw Hispaniola in the hands of France and Jamaica in the hands of England, and various lesser Antilles seized by the one or the other of these two powers.

It is furthermore worthy of notice that there was a clear causal connection between the task which Spain finished in 1492 and that upon which she entered a little before 1570. The transition from the crusade against the infidel to the crusade against the heretic was easy, and in her case almost inevitable. The effects of the

The long struggle between Spaniards and Moors

long Moorish war upon Spanish character and Spanish policy have often been pointed out. The Spaniard of the sixteenth century was what eight hundred years of terrible warfare, for home and for religion, had made him. During a period as long as that which in English history has now elapsed since the death of William the Conqueror, the Mussulman invaders held sway in some part of the Spanish peninsula; yet they never succeeded in entering into any sort of political union with the native inhabitants. From first to last they behaved as invaders and were treated as invaders, their career in this respect forming a curious and instructive parallel to that of the Turks in eastern Europe, though as a people the Arab-Moors were of far higher type than Turks. Entering Spain in 711, they soon conquered the whole peninsula. From this deluge about a century later the Christian kingdom of Leon began to emerge. By the middle of the eleventh century the Spaniards had regained half their country, and the Mahometans were placed upon the defensive. By the middle of the thirteenth, the Moorish dominion became

390

restricted to the kingdom of Granada; and finally we have seen Granada subdued in the same year in which Columbus discovered America. During all this period, from 711 to 1492, the years when warfare was not going on along the fluctuating frontier between Spaniard and Moor were few indeed. Among the Spaniards industrial life was almost destroyed. The way to obtain the necessaries of life was to make raids upon the Mussulmans, and the career of the bandit became glorified. In the central and southern provinces, on the other hand, the Moors developed a remarkable industrial civilization, surpassing anything to be seen in Christian Europe except in Constantinople down to the end of the twelfth century. As the frontier moved gradually southward, with the advance of the Christians, the industrious Mussulman population in large part became converted to Christianity, and went on cultivating *Its effect in* the arts of life. These converts, who *throwing discredit upon* were known as Moriscoes, were al- *labour* ways despised and ill-treated by the Spaniards. Such a state of things continued to throw discredit upon labour. Spinning and weaving and tilling the soil were regarded as fit occupations for unclean Moriscoes. It was the prerogative of a Christian Spaniard to appropriate the fruits of other people's labour; and we have seen this feeling at work in many details of the Spanish

391

conquest in America. Not that it was at all peculiar to Spaniards. Devices for appropriating the fruits of other people's labour have in all countries been multifarious, from tomahawks to tariffs. But the circumstances of Spanish history were such as to cast upon labour a stigma especially strong by associating it with men of alien race and faith who were scarcely regarded as possessing any rights that Christians should feel bound to respect.

This prolonged warfare had other effects. It combined the features of a crusade with those of a fight for the recovery of one's patrimony. The general effect of the great Crusades, which brought different Christian peoples in contact with each other and opened their eyes to many excellent features in eastern civilization, was an education for Europe. From these liberalizing experiences the Spanish peninsula was in great measure cut off. It was absorbed in its own private crusade, and there was altogether too much of it. While other nations occasionally turned their attention to wars of religion, Spain had no attention left for anything else. It was one long agony through five and twenty gen-

Its effect in strengthening religious bigotry

erations, until the intruder was ousted. Thus, although Visigothic institutions smacked of sturdy freedom as much as those of any other Germanic people, nevertheless this unceasing militancy trained

392

the Spaniards for despotism. For the same reason the church acquired more overweening power than anywhere else in Europe. To the mediæval Spaniard orthodoxy was practically synonymous with patriotism, while heresy like manual industry was a mark of the hated race. Unity in faith came to be regarded as an object to secure which no sacrifices whatever could be deemed too great. When, therefore, the Protestant Reformation came in the sixteenth century, its ideas and its methods were less intelligible to Spaniards than to any other European people. By nature this land of mediæval ideas was thus marked out as the chief antagonist of the Reformation ; and when it was attempted to extend to the Netherlands the odious measures that were endured in Spain, the ensuing revolt called forth all the power that Philip II. could summon to suppress it. To overthrow the rebellious heretic seemed as sacred a duty as to expel the Moslem. A crusade against heresy, headed by Pope Innocent III. and Philip Augustus of France, had once been crowned with success, and one of the most gruesome chapters in human history had been written in blood at Beziers and Carcassonne. Such a crusade did Spain attempt against the Netherlands, until England, too, was drawn into the lists against her, and the crisis was reached in 1588, in the destruction of

Spain's crusade in the Netherlands

the Invincible Armada, a military overthrow scarcely paralleled until the wreck of Napoleon's army in Russia.

The defeat of the Armada was such a blow to Spain's prestige that France, England, and the Netherlands soon proceeded to their work of colonization in North America with little fear of hindrance. But while France and England paid much attention to America, the Dutch paid comparatively little, and for a reason that is closely linked with our general subject. The attention of the Dutch was chiefly concentrated upon the East Indies. After the Turks had cut off the Mediterranean routes, and Portugal had gained control of the Asiatic trade, the great Netherland towns began to have relatively fewer overland dealings with Venice and Genoa, and more and more maritime dealings with Lisbon. The change favoured the Dutch more than the Flemish provinces, by reason of the greater length of the Dutch coast-line. By dint of marvellous energy and skill the coast of Holland and Zealand became virtually one vast seaport, a distributing centre for the whole north of Europe, and during the sixteenth century the volume of Dutch merchant shipping was rapidly and steadily increased. Now it happened in 1578 that the king Sebastian of Portugal, who has furnished a theme for so many romantic

Effects of oceanic discovery in developing Dutch trade

legends, led an army into Morocco, and there was killed in battle. Philip II. forthwith declared the throne of Portugal vacant, and in 1580 seized the kingdom for himself. This act abruptly cut off the East India trade of the Dutch, and at the same time it made all the Portuguese colonies dependencies of Spain, and thus left the Dutch free to attack them wherever they saw fit. Borgia's meridian was thus at last wiped out. After 1588 the Dutch proceeded at once to invade the colonial world of Portugal. They soon *Conquest of the Portuguese Indies by the Dutch* established themselves in Java and Sumatra, and by 1607 they had gained complete possession of the Molucca Islands. This was the beginning of the empire which Holland possesses to-day in the East Indies, with a rich territory four times as large as France, a population of 30,000,000, and a lucrative trade. From this blow Portugal never recovered. She regained her independence in 1640, but has never since shown the buoyant vigour that made the days of Prince Henry the Navigator and of Albuquerque so remarkable.

The overthrow of the Invincible Armada thus marks the downfall of maritime power for both the rival nations of the Iberian peninsula. It would be wrong, however, to attribute such an enduring calamity to a single great naval defeat, or even to the exhausting effects of the unsuc-

cessful war against the Dutch. A healthy nation
quickly repairs the damage wrought by a mili-
Disastrous
results of
persecuting
heretics tary catastrophe, but Spain was not
in a healthy condition. The over-
mastering desire to put down heresy,
to expel the " accursed thing," possessed her.
The struggle with the Moors had brought this
semi-suicidal craving to a height which it never
reached with any other European nation. In
the present narrative we have had occasion to
observe that as soon as Ferdinand and Isabella
had finished the conquest of Granada, they tried
to add to the completeness of their triumph by
driving all Jews from their homes and seizing
their goods. In times past, the conquered
Moors had in great numbers embraced Christianity, but it was with difficulty that the Spaniards tolerated the presence of these Moriscoes
in their country.[1] In 1568, the Moriscoes,
goaded by ill treatment, rose in rebellion among

---

[1] On the rich and important subject of the Moors in Spain,
see Al Makkari, *History of the Mohammedan Dynasties in
Spain*, transl. by Gayangos, London, 1840, 2 vols. in quarto ;
Conde, *Dominacion de los Arabes en España*, Paris, 1840
(to be read with caution) ; Coppée, *Conquest of Spain by the
Arab-Moors*, Boston, 1881, 2 vols. ; Reinaud, *Invasions
des Sarrazins en France*, Paris, 1836 ; Chénier, *Recherches
historiques sur les Maures*, Paris, 1787, 3 vols. ; Circourt,
Histoire des Mores Mudejares et des Morisques, Paris, 1846,
3 vols. ; see, also, with reference to the Jews, Grætz, *Les
Juifs d' Espagne*, Paris, 1872.

the mountains of Granada, and it took three years of obstinate fighting to bring them to terms. Their defeat was so crushing that they ceased to be dangerous politically, but their orthodoxy was gravely suspected. In 1602 the Archbishop of Valencia proposed that all the Moriscoes in the kingdom, except children under seven years of age, should be driven into exile, that Spain might no longer be polluted by the merest suspicion of unbelief. The Archbishop of Toledo, primate of Spain, wished to banish the children also. It is said *Expulsion of* that Friar Bleda, the Dominican, *the Moriscoes* *from Spain,* urged that all Moriscoes, even to the *1609* new-born babe, should be massacred, since it was impossible to tell whether they were Christians at heart or not, and it might safely be left to God to select his own. The views of the primate prevailed, and in 1609, about a million people were turned out of doors and hustled off to Morocco. These proceedings involved an amount of murder that has been estimated as about equivalent to the massacre of St. Bartholomew. Of the unfortunate people who reached Africa, thousands perished of hunger, or were slain by robbers, or kidnapped into slavery.

These Moriscoes, thus driven from the land by ecclesiastical bigotry, joined with hatred of their race, were the most skilful labourers Spain possessed. By their expulsion the manufacture of silk and paper was destroyed, the cultivation of sugar, rice, and cotton came to an end, the wool-trade stopped short, and irrigation of the soil was discontinued. The disturbance of industry, and the consequent distress, were so far-reaching that in the course of the next seventy years the population of Madrid was decreased by one half, and that of Seville by three quarters ; whole villages were deserted, large portions of arable land went out of cultivation and brigandage gained a foothold which it has kept almost down to the present day. The economic ruin of Spain may be said to date from the expulsion of the Moriscoes. Yet no deed in history was ever done with clearer conscience or more unanimous self-approval on the part of the perpetrators than this. Even the high-minded and gentle-hearted Cervantes applauded it, while Davila character-ized it as the crowning glory of Spanish history. This approval was the outcome of a feeling so deeply ingrained in the Spanish mind that we sometimes see curious remnants of it to-day, even among Spaniards of much liberality and enlightenment. Thus the eminent historian Lafuente, writing in 1856, freely confessed that the destruction of Moorish industries was eco-nomically a disaster of the first magnitude ; but after all, he says, just think what an " immense

Terrible con-sequences

398

advantage " it was to establish " religious unity "
throughout the nation and get rid of differences
in opinion.[1] Just so : to insure that from the
Pyrenees to Gibraltar all people should appear
to think exactly alike about questions confessedly
unfathomable by human intelligence, — this
seemed to the Spaniards an end of such supreme
importance as to justify the destruction of a
hundred thousand lives and the overthrow of
some of the chief industries of the kingdom.
It was a terrible delusion, but perhaps we are
not entitled to blame the Spaniards too severely
when we reflect that even among ourselves, in
spite of all the liberalizing influences to which
the English race has so long been subjected, the
lesson is only just beginning to be learned that
variety in religious beliefs is not an evil, but a
positive benefit to a civilized commu-   Uniformity in
nity, whereas uniformity in belief   religious be-
                                        liefs is not
should be dreaded as tending toward   desirable
Chinese narrowness and stagnation. This is the
true lesson of Protestantism, and it is through
this lesson, however imperfectly learned, that
Protestantism has done so much to save the
world from torpor and paralysis.

But it was not merely in the expulsion of the
Moriscoes that the Spanish policy of enforcing
uniformity was suicidal. Indeed, the disastrous

[1] Lafuente, *Historia de España*, Madrid, 1856, tom. xvii.
p. 340.

effects which we are wont to attribute to that striking catastrophe cannot really be explained without taking into account another and still more potent cause. The deadly Inquisition, working steadily and quietly year after year while fourteen generations lived and died, wrought an amount of disaster which it is diffi-

Dreadful work of the Inquisition

cult for the mind to grasp. Some eight or ten years ago an excavation happened to be made in the Plaza Cruz del Quemadero in Madrid, the scene of the most terrible part of Victor Hugo's "Torquemada." Just below the surface the workmen came upon a thick stratum of black earth 150 feet long. On further digging it was found to consist chiefly of calcined human bones, with here and there a fragment of burnt clothing. Dark layers varying from three to nine inches in thickness were here and there interrupted by very thin strata of clay or sand.[1] A singular kind of geological problem was thus suggested : how many men and women must have died in excruciating torments in order to build up that infernal deposit ? During the fifteen years

[1] This deposit was examined by men of science and antiquarians, and the newspapers began publishing the details of their investigations, whereat the clergy grew uneasy, and persuaded the government to have the whole stratum dug away and removed as quickly as possible, so as to avoid further scandal. See *The Nation*, New York, 1883, vol. xxxvi. p. 470.

when Torquemada was inquisitor-general, from 1483 to 1498, about 10,000 persons were burned alive. The rate was probably not much diminished during the sixteenth century, and the practice was kept up until late in the eighteenth ; the last burning of a heretic was in 1781. From the outset the germs of Protestantism were steadily and completely extirpated. We sometimes hear it said that persecution cannot kill a good cause, but that " the blood of the martyrs is the seed of the church." This is apt to be true because it is seldom that sufficient unanimity of public opinion is enlisted in support of persecution to make it thorough. It was not true in Spain. The Inquisition there did suppress free thought most effectively. It was a machine for winnowing out and destroying all such individuals as surpassed the average in quickness of wit, earnestness of purpose, and strength of character, in so far as to entertain opinions of their own and boldly declare them. The more closely people approached an elevated standard of intelligence and moral courage, the more likely was the machine to reach them. It

It was a device for insuring the survival of the unfittest

worked with such fiendish efficiency that it was next to impossible for such people to escape it ; they were strangled and burned by tens of thousands, and as the inevitable result, the average character of the Spanish people was lowered.[1] The brightest and boldest were cut off in their early prime, while duller and weaker ones were spared to propagate the race; until the Spaniard of the eighteenth century was a much less intelligent and less enterprising person than the Spaniard of the sixteenth. Such damage is not easily repaired; the competition among nations is so constant and so keen, that when a people have once clearly lost their hold upon the foremost position they are not likely to regain it.

Under this blighting rule of the Inquisition the general atmosphere of thought in Spain remained mediæval. Ideas and methods which other nations were devising, to meet the new exigencies of modern life, were denied admission to that unfortunate country. In manufactures, in commerce, in the control of the

The Spanish policy of crushing out individualism resulted in universal stagnation

[1] In this connection the reader should carefully study the admirable book lately published by our great historian of mediæval institutions, Henry Charles Lea, *Chapters from the Religious History of Spain*, Philadelphia, 1890. I have been especially struck with the chapter on the "Censorship of the Press," where the subject is treated with a prodigious wealth of learning. We are apt to sigh over popular ignorance even in these days of elaborate educational appliances and untrammelled freedom of discussion. Under the rule of the Spanish Inquisition all the zeal and energy which we now devote to developing and stimulating popular intelligence was devoted to stunting and repressing it.

various sources of wealth, Spain was soon left behind by nations in which the popular intelligence was more flexibly wielded, and from which the minds hospitable toward new ideas had not been so carefully weeded out. It was not in religious matters only, but in all the affairs of life, that the dull and rigid conservatism was shown. Amid the general stagnation and lack of enterprise, and with the universal discredit of labour, the stream of gold and silver poured into Spain from the New World did more harm than good, inasmuch as its chief effect was to diminish the purchasing power of the precious metals. Economically, perhaps, the whole situation might be summed up by saying that Spanish expenditure was not productive but unproductive, and not simply unproductive but destructive. It was devoted to checking the activities of the human mind, to doing precisely the reverse of what we are trying to do in these days with books and newspapers, schools and lectures, copyrights and patents.

It is profoundly significant that the people who have acquired by far the greater part of the maritime empire to which Spain once aspired, and who have supplanted her in the best part of the territories to which she once felt entitled in virtue of Borgia's bulls, should be the people who have differed most widely from the

Spaniards in their attitude toward novelties of doctrine and independence of thought. The policy of England, in giving full play to individualism, has developed a type of national character unsurpassed for buoyancy. No class of people in England ever acquired such control of the whole society as the clergy acquired in Spain. In the worst days of English history attempts have been made to crush individuality of thought and to put a stop to the free discussion of religious and political questions. But such attempts have been feeble and sporadic; no such policy has ever prevailed. The history of religious persecution in England affords a most suggestive illustration. The burning of heretics began in 1401, and the last instance occurred in 1611. During that time the total number of executions for heresy was about 400. Of these about 300 occurred in the brief spasm of 1555–57 under Mary Tudor, daughter of a Spanish princess, and wife of the worst of Spain's persecuting monarchs. The total of 100 victims scattered through the rest of that period of two centuries makes a startling contrast to what was going on in other countries. As no type of character has thus been sedulously winnowed out by violent methods, neither has any set of people ever been expelled from England, like the Moriscoes from Spain or the Huguenots from France. On the

It has been the policy of England to give full scope to individualism

contrary, ever since the days of the Plantagenets it has been a maxim of English law that whosoever among the hunted and oppressed of other realms should set his foot on the soil of Britain became forthwith free and entitled to all the protection that England's stout arm could afford. On that hospitable soil all types of character, all varieties of temperament, all shades of belief, have flourished side by side, and have interacted upon one another until there has been evolved a race of men in the highest degree original and enterprising, plastic and cosmopolitan. It is chiefly this circumstance, combined with their successful preservation of self-government, that has won for men of English speech their imperial position in the modern world. When we contrast the elastic buoyancy of spirit in Shakespeare's England with the gloom and heaviness that were then creeping over Spain, we find nothing strange in the fact that the most populous and powerful nations of the New World speak English and not Spanish. It was the people of Great Britain that, with flexible and self-reliant intelligence, came to be foremost in devising methods adapted to the growth of an industrial civilization, leaving the Middle Ages far behind. Wherever, in any of the regions open to colonization, this race has come into competition with

That policy has been the chief cause of the success of English people in founding new nations

other European races, it has either vanquished or absorbed them, always proving its superior capacity. Sometimes the contest has assumed the form of strife between a civilization based upon wholesome private enterprise and a civilization based upon government patronage. Such was the form of the seventy years' conflict that came to a final decision upon the Heights of Abraham, and not the least interesting circumstance connected with the discovery of this broad continent is the fact that the struggle for the possession of it has revealed the superior vitality of institutions and methods that first came to maturity in England and now seem destined to shape the future of the world.

APPENDIX A

THE Latin is the original text, for an account of which see above, vol. ii. p. 27, note 2. The Italian is from the version in the *Vita dell' Ammiraglio*, concerning which M. Harrisse says that it is "très-inexact et interpolée." I have here italicised the portions of either text which do not occur in the other, so that the reader may judge for himself how far such a charge is justified.

A Cristoforo Colombo Paolo fisico salute. Io veggo il nobile e gran desiderio tuo di voler passar là, dove nascono le spezerie, onde per risposta d' una tua lettera ti mando la copia d' un' altra lettera, che alquanti giorni fa io scrissi ad un mio amico, domestico del serenissimo re di Portogallo, avanti le guerre di Castiglia, in risposta d' un' altra, che per commissione di Sua Altezza egli mi scrisse sopra detto caso : e ti mando un' altra carta navigatoria,

407

simile a quella ch' io mandai a lui, per la qual resteranno soddisfatte le tue dimande. La c o p i a di quella mia lettera è questa.

Copia misa christofaro colonbo per paulum fisicum cum una carta navigacionis.

Ferdinando martini canonico vlixiponensi paulus phisicus salutem. a tua valitudine de gracia et familiaritate cum rege vestro genero[siss]imo [et] magnificentissimo principe iocundum mihi fuit intelligere. cum tecum allias locutus sum de breuiori via ad loca aromatum per maritimam navigacionem quam sit ea quam facitis per guineam, querit nunc S[erenissimus] rex a me quandam declaracionem ymo potius ad occulum ostensionem vt *etiam mediocriter doti* illam viam caperent et intelligerent. Ego autem quamvis cognoscam posse hoc ostendi per formam spericam ut est mundus tamen deter-

A Fernando Martinez canonico di Lisbona Paolo fisico salute. Molto mi piacque intendere la domestichezza che tu hai col tuo sereniss. e magnificentiss. re, e quantunque volte io abbia ragionato del *brevissimo* cammino che è di qua all' *Indie*, dove nascono le spezierie, per la via del mare, il quale io tengo più breve di quel che voi fate per Guinea, tu mi dici che Sua Altezza vorrebbe ora da me alcuna dichiarazione, o dimostrazione, acciocchè si intenda e si possa prendere detto cammino. Laonde, come ch' io sappia di poter ciò mostrarle con la sfera in mano, e farle veder come sta il mondo; nondimeno

408

minaui, pro faciliori intelligencia ac etiam pro faciliori opera, ostendere, viam illam per quam carte navigacionis fiunt illud declarare. Mito ergo sue Maiestati cartam manibus meis factam in qua designantur

litora vestra et insule ex quibus incipiatis iter facere verius occasum senper

et loca ad que debeatis peruenire et quantum a polo vel a linea equinotiali debeatis declinare et per quantum spacium siue per quot miliaria debeatis peruenire ad loca fertilissima omnium aromatum et gemarum, et non miremini si voco occidentales partes vbi sunt aromata cum communiter dicantur orientales,

quia nauigantibus ad occi-

ho deliberato per più facilità e per maggiore intelligenza dimostrar detto cammino per una carta simile a quelle c h e s i fanno per navigare, e così la mando a Sua Maestà, fatta e disegnata di mia mano : nella quale è dipinto *tutto il fine del ponente, pigliando da Irlanda all' austro insino al fin di Guinea,* con *tutte* le isole *che in tutto questo cammino giacciono* ; per fronte alle quali dritto per ponente *g i a c e dipinto il principio dell' Indie* con le isole e luoghi dove potete andare, e quanto dal polo *artico* vi potete discostare per l a linea equinoziale, e per quanto spazio, c i o è in quante leghe potete giungere a quei luoghi fertilissimi d' ogni sorte di spezeria, e di gemme e pietre preziose. E non abbiate a maraviglia, se io chiamo Ponente il paese ove nasce la spezeria, la qual comunemente dicesi che nasce in Levanti ; perciocchè

dentem senper ille partes inueniuntur *per subterraneas nauigaciones.* Si enim per terram et per superiora itinera, ad orientem senper reperrientur[1] l i n e e ergo recte in longitudine carte signate ostendunt distanciam ab orientem[2] versus occidens, que autem transuerse sunt, ostendunt spacia a meridie versus septentrionem. notaui autem in carta diuersa loca ad que peruenire potestis pro maiori noticia nauigancium siue ventis vel casu aliquo alibi quam existimarent venirent; *partin[8] autem vt ostendant incolis ipsos habere noticiam aliquam patrie illius, quod debebit esse iocundum satis.*

non considant[4] autem in insulis nisi mercatores as-

coloro, che navigheranno al ponente, sempre troveranno detti luoghi in ponente; e quelli, che anderanno per terra al levante, sempre troveranno d e t t i luoghi in levante. Le linee dritte, che giacciono al lungo in detta carta, dimostrano la distanza che è dal ponente al levante; le altre, che sono per obliquo, dimostrano la distanza che è dalla tramontana al mezzogiorno. Ancora io dipinsi in detta carta molti luoghi nelle parte *dell' India* dove si potrebbe andare, avvenendo alcun caso di fortuna o di venti contrari, o qualunque altro caso, che non si aspettasse, che dovesse avvenire.

E appresso, p e r darvi piena informazione di tutit quei luoghi, i quali desiderate molto conoscere, sappiate, che in tutte quelle isole non abitano nè praticano altri che mercatanti; av-

---

erit.[1] ibi enim tanta copia navigancium est cum mercimoniis vt in toto reliquo orbe non sint sicuti in vno portu nobilisimo vocato zaiton. aserunt enim centum naues p i p e r i s magne in eo portu singulis annis deferri, sine aliis nauibus portantibus allia aromata. patria illa est populatisima *ditisima* multitudine prouinciarum et regnorum et ciuitatum sine numero, sub vno principe qui dicitur magnus Kan quod nomen significat in latino rex regum, cuius s e d e s et residencia est vt plurimum in provincia Katay. antiqui sui desi-d e r a b a n t consorcium christianorum iam sunt .200. annis,[2] miscerunt [3] ad papam et postulabant plurimos dotos in fide vt illuminarentur ; sed qui missi sunt, inpediti in itinere redierunt. etiam

vertendovi quivi e s s e r e così gran quantità di navi e di marinari con mercatanzie, come in ogni altra parte del mondo, specialmente in un porto nobilissimo, chiamato Zaiton, dove caricano e discari-c a n o ogni anno cento navi grosse di pepe, oltre alle molte altre navi, che caricano a l t r e spezerie. Questo paese è popolatissimo, e sono molte provincie e molti regni e città senza numero sotto il dominio di un principe chiamato il gran Cane, il qual nome vuol dire re de' re, la residenza del quale la maggior parte del tempo è nella provincia del Cataio. I suoi antecessori desiderarono molto aver pratica e amicizia con cristiani, e già dugento anni mandarono ambasciatori al sommo pontefice, supplicandolo che gli mandasse

---

1 Perhaps meant for *asseritur*, "it is related." Columbus may have forgotten to finish the word. Or perhaps Toscanelli may have inadvertently used the active *asserit*, " he relates," meaning Marco Polo.

2 Read *anni*.   3 Read *miserunt*.

tempore Eugenii v e n i t
vnus ad eugenium qui de
beniuolentia magna erga
christianos afirmabat et
ego

secum longo sermone lo-
cutus sum de multis, de
magnitudine edificiorum
regalium et de magnitu-
dine fluuium [1] in latitudine
et longitudine mirabili et
de multitudine ciuitatum
in ripis fluuium,[1] vt in vno
flumine .200. circiter ciu-
itates sint constitute, et
pontes marmorei magne
latitudinis et longitudinis
vndique colonpnis ornati.

hec patria digna est vt per
latinos queratur, non so-
lum quia lucra ingencia ex
ea capi posunt auri argenti

molti savij e dottori, che
gl' insegnassero la nostra
fede, ma per gl' impedi-
menti ch' ebbero detti ambasciatori, tornarono in-
dietro senza arrivare a
Roma. E ancora a papa
Eugenio IV. venne uno
ambasciatore, il quale gli
raccontò la grande ami-
cizia che quei principi e i
loro popoli hanno coi cristiani; e io parlai lunga-
mente con lui di molte
cose, e delle grandezze
d e l l e fabriche regalè, e
della grossezza de' fiumi
in larghezza e in lung-
hezza, ed ei mi d i s s e
molte cose maravigliose
della moltitudine d e l l e
città e luoghi che son fon-
dati nelle rive loro; e che
solamente in un fiume si
trovava dugento città edi-
ficate con ponte di pietre
di marmo, molto larghi e
lunghi, adornati di molte
colonne. Questo paese è
degno tanto, quanto ogni
altro, che si abbia trovato;
e non solamente vi si può

---

[1] Read *fluminum*.

gemarum omnis generis et aromatum que nunquam ad nos deferuntur, verum propter doctos viros philosofos et astrologos peritos et quibus ingeniis et artibus ita potens et magnifica prouincia gubernentur[1] ac etiam bella conducant.

hec pro aliquantula satisfactione ad suam peticionem, quantum breuitas temporis dedit et occupaciones mee conscepscerunt,[2] paratus in futurum regie maiestati quantum volet latius satisfacere. data florencie 25 iunii 1474.

A ciuitate vlixiponis per occidentem in directo sunt .26. spacia in carta sig-

trovar grandissimo guadagno, e molte cose ricche; ma ancora oro, e argento, e pietre preziose, e di ogni sorte di spezieria in grande quantità, della quale mai non si porta in queste nostre parti. Ed è il vero, che molti uomini dotti, filosofi, e astrologi, e altri grandi savij in tutte le arti, e di grande ingegno governano quella gran provincia, e ordinano le battaglie. ‖ E questo[3] sia per sodisfazione delle vostre richieste, quanto la brevità del tempo, e le mie occupazioni mi h a n n o concesso. E così io resto prontissimo a soddisfare e servir sua altezza, compiutamente in tutto quello che mi comanderà. Da Fiorenza, ai 25 giugno dell' anno 1474. ‖ Dalla città di Lisbona per dritto verso ponente sono in detta carta ventisei spazj, cias-

[1] Read *gubernetur*. [2] Read *concesserunt*.
[3] In the Italian arrangement this passage is transposed to the end of the letter, and the passage " Dalla città di Lisbona," etc. (which in the Latin arrangement forms a postscript) follows immediately after " battaglie."

nata quorum quodlibet habet miliaria .250. vsque ad nobilisim[am] et maximam ciuitatem quinsay. circuit enim centum miliaria et habet pontes decem et nomen eius sonat cita del cielo ciuitas celi et multa miranda de ea narrantur, de multitudine artificium et de reditibus.

        hoc spacium est fere tercia pars tocius spere, que ciuitas est in prouincia mangi, siue vicina prouincie Katay in qua residencia terre regia est. Sed ab insula antilia vobis

nota ad insulam nobilisimam cippangu sunt decem spacia. est enim

illa insula fertilissima aur[o] margaritis et gemmis, et auro solido cooperiunt tenpla et domos regias, *itaque per ygnota*

cun de' quali contien dugento e cinquanta miglia, fino alla nobilissima e gran città di Quisai, la quale gira cento miglia *che sono trentacinque leghe ;* ove sono dieci ponti di pietra di marmore. Il nome di questa città significa Città del Cielo, della qual si narrano cose maravigliose intorno alla grandezza degli ingegni, e fabriche, e rendite. Questo spazio è quasi la terza parte della sfera. Giace questa città nella prouincia di Mango, vicina alla provincia del Cataio, nella quale sta la maggior parte del tempo il re. E dall' isola di Antilia, *che voi chiamate di Sette Città*, della quale avete notizia, fino alla nobilissima isola di Cipango sono dieci spazj, *che fanno due mila e cinquecento miglia, cioè dugento e venticinque leghe ;* la quale Isola è fertilissima di oro, di perle, e di pietre preziose. E sappiate, che con piastre d' oro fino coprono i tempj e le case

itinera non magna maris spacia transeundum.

multa fortasse essent aperitus [1] declaranda, sed d i l i g e n s considerator per hec poterit ex se ipso reliqua prospicere. vale dilectisime.

regali. *Di modo che, per non esser conosciuto il cammino, tutte queste cose si ritrovano nascoste e coperte; e ad essa si può andar sicuramente. Molte altre cose si potrebbono dire; ma, come io vi ho già detto a bocca, e voi siete prudente e di buon giudicio, mi rendo certo che non vi resta cosa alcuna da intendere: e però non sarò più lungo.*

[1] Read *apertius.*

THE Latin text of this letter is preserved in the handwriting of Columbus upon the fly-leaf of one of his books in the Colombina at Seville. See above, vol. i. p. 356, note 3. I here subjoin a specimen of the handwriting of Columbus, from a MS. in the Colombina, reproduced in Harrisse's *Notes on Columbus.*

THE BULL *Inter Cetera.*

EXEMPLAR BVLLAE SEV
DONATIONIS, AVTORITATE
CVIVS, EPISCOPVS ROMANVS
Alexander eius nominis fextus, con-
cefsit et donauit Caftellæ regibus
et fuis fuccefforibus, regiones
et Infulas noui orbis in
Oceano occidentali His-
panorum nauigationi-
bus repertas.·.

LEXANDER EPISCOPVS, feruus feruo-
rum Dei, Charifsimo in Chrifto filio Ferdinando Regi, et Charifsimæ in Chrifto
filiæ Elizabeth Reginæ Caftellæ, Legionis,
Aragonum, Siciliæ, et Granatæ, illuftribus, falutem et
Apoftolicam benedictionem.

Inter cætera Diuinæ maieftati beneplacita opera
et cordis noftri defiderabilia, illud profecto potifimum
exiftit vt fides catholica et Chriftiana religio noftris
præfertim temporibus exaltetur ac vbilibet amplietur
ac dilatetur, animarumque falus procuretur, ac barbaricæ
nationes deprimantur et ad fidem ipfam reducantur.
Vnde cum ad hanc facram Petri fedem Diuina fauente
clementia (meritis licet imparibus) euocati fuerimus,

416

APPENDIX B

❡ THE COPPIE OF THE BULL
OR DONATION, BY TH[E] AU-
TORITIE WHEREOF, POPE
Alexander the fyxte of that name,
gaue and graunted to the kynges of
Caſtyle and theyr ſucceſſours the
Regions and Ilandes founde in
the Weſte Ocean ſea by
the nauigations of the
Spanyardes

Lexander byſhoppe, the ſeruaunte of the ſer-
uantes of God : To owre moſte deare beloued ſonne in Chriſt Kynge Ferdinande,
And to owre deare beloued doughter in
Chryſte Elyzabeth Queene of Caſtyle, Legion, Aragon,
Sicilie, and Granata, moſt noble Princes, Gretynge
and Apoſtolical benediction.

monge other woorkes acceptable to the diuine
ſtie and accordynge to owre hartes deſyre, this
einely is the chiefe, that the Catholyke fayth and
hriſtian religion, ſpecially in this owre tyme may in
all places bee exalted, amplified, and enlarged, wherby
the health of ſoules may be procured, and the Barbarous nations ſubdued and brought to the fayth. And
therefore wheras by the fauoure of gods clemencie
(although not with equall deſertes) we are cauled to

4I7

cognofcentes vos tanquam veros catholicos reges et
principes : quales femper fuiffe nouimus, et a vobis
præclare gefta, toti pene orbi notifsima demonftrant,
nedum id exoptare, fed omni conatu, ftudio et diligentia, nullis laboribus, nullis impenfis, nullifque par-
cendo periculis, etiam proprium fanguinem effundendo
efficere, ac omnem animum veftrum, omnefque conatus
ad hoc iam dudum dedicafse, quemadmodum recupe-
ratio regni Granatæ a tyrannide Saracenorum hodier-
nis temporibus per vos, cum tanta Diuini nominis
gloria facta teftatur. Digne ducimur non immerito,
et debemus illa vobis etiam fponte, ac fauorabiliter
concedere, per quæ huiufmodi fanctum ac laudabile
ab immortali deo acceptum propofitum, in dies feruen-
tiori animo ad ipfius dei honorem et Imperij Chri-
ftiani propagationem, profequi valeatis. Sane accepi-
mus quod vos qui dudum animum propofueratis aliquas
infulas et terras firmas remotas et incognitas, ac per
alios hactenus non repertas, quærere et inuenire, vt
illarum incolas et habitatores ad colendum Redemp-
torem noftrum et fidem catholicam profitendum re-
duceretis, hactenus in expugnatione et recuperatione
ipfius regni Granatæ plurimum occupati, huiufmodi
fanctum et laudabile propofitum veftrum ad optatum
finem perducere nequiuiftis : Sed tamen ficut Do[...]
placuit, regno predicto recuperato, volentes defideri[...]
veftrum adimplere, dilectum filium Chriftophorum C[...]
lonum virum vtique dignum et plurimum commendatum
ac tanto negotio aptum, cum nauigijs et hominibus ad
fimilia inftructis, non fine maximis laboribus, ac periculis, et expenfis deftinaftis vt terras firmas et Infulas
remotas et incognitas, huiufmodi per mare vbi hactenus

this holy feate of Peter, and vnderftandynge you to bee
trewe Catholyke Princes as we haue euer knowen you,
and as youre noble and woorthy factes haue declared
in maner to the hole worlde in that with all your
ftudie, diligence, and induftrye, you haue fpared no
trauayles, charges, or perels, aduenturynge euen the
fhedynge of your owne bludde, with applyinge yowre
hole myndes and endeuours here vnto, as your noble
expeditions achyued in recoueryng the kyngdome of
Granata from the tyrannie of the Sarracens in thefe
our dayes, doo playnely declare your factes with fo
great glorye of the diuine name. For the whiche as
we thinke you woorthy, fo owght we of owre owne free
wyl fauorably to graunt all thynges whereby you maye
dayely with more feruent myndes to the honoure of god
and enlargynge the Chriftian empire, profecute your
deuoute and laudable purpofe moft acceptable to the
immortall God. We are credably informed that wheras
of late you were determyned to feeke and fynde certeyne
Ilandes and firme landes farre remote and vnknowen
(and not heretofore found by any other) to th[e]in-
tent to bringe th[e]inhabitauntes of the fame to honoure owre redemer and to profeffe the catholyke fayth,
you haue hetherto byn much occupied in th[e]expug-
nation and recouerie of the kyngedome of Granata,
by reafon whereof yowe coulde not brynge yowre fayde
laudable purpofe to th[e]ende defyred. Neuertheleffe
as it hath pleafed almyghty god, the forefayde kynge-
einge recouered, wylling t[o]accomplyfhe your
fyre, you haue, not without great laboure,
and charges, appoynted owre welbeloued
fonn. iftopher Colonus (a man certes wel com-
mended as mofte worthy and apte for fo great a matter) well furnyfhed with men and fhippes and other
neceffaries, to feeke (by the fea where hetherto no
manne hath fayled) fuche firme landes and Ilandes

nauigatum non fuerat, diligenter inquireret. Qui tandem (Diuino auxilio facta extrema diligentia in mari Oceano nauigantes) certas infulas remotifsimas et etiam terras firmas, quæ per alios hactenus repertæ non fuerant, inuenerunt. In quibus plurimæ gentes pacifice vi-uentes, et (vt afferitur) nudi incedentes, nec carnibus vefcentes, inhabitant: Et vt præfati nuncij veftri pof-sunt opinari, gentes ipfæ in Infulis et terris prædictis habitantes credunt vnum deum creatorem in Cœlis efse, ac ad fidem catholicam amplexandum et bonis moribus imbuendum fatis apti videntur: Spefque habetur, quod fi erudirentur, nomen Saluatoris Domini noftri Iefu Chrifti in terris et infulis prædicts facile induceretur. Ac præfatus Chriftophorus in vna ex principalibus Infulis prædictis, iam vnam turrim fatis munitam, in qua certos Chriftianos qui fecum inerant, in cuftodiam et vt alias Infulas ac terras firmas remotas et incognitas inquirerent pofuit, conftrui et ædificari fecit. In quibus quidem Infulis et terris iam repertis, aurum, aromata, et aliæ quamplurimæ res præciofæ diuerfi generis et diuerfæ qualitatis reperiuntur. Vnde omnibus diligenter, et præfertim fidei catholicæ exal-tatione et dilatatione (prout decet Catholicos Reges et Principes) confideratis, more progenitorum veftrorum claræ memoriæ Regum, terras firmas et infulas præ-dictas, illarumque incolas et habitatores, vobis diuina fauente clementia fubiicere et ad fidem Catholicam reducere propofuiftis.

Nos itaque huiufmodi veftrum fanctum et laudabile propofitum plurimum in Domino commendantes, ac cupientes vt illud ad debitum finem perducatur, et ipfum nomen Saluatoris noftri in partibus illis induca-

farre remote and hitherto vnknowen. Who (by gods helpe) makynge diligente fearche in the Ocean fea, haue founde certeyne remote Ilandes and firme landes whiche were not heretofore founde by any other. In the which (as is fayde) many nations inhabite lyuinge peaceably and goinge naked, not accuftomed to eate flefhe. And as farre as yowre meffengers can coniecture, the nations inhabitynge the forefayde landes and Ilandes, beleue that there is one god creatoure in heauen : and feeme apte to be brought to th[e]imbrafinge of the catholyke faythe and to be imbued with good maners : by reafon whereof, we may hope that if they well be inftructed, they may eafely bee induced to receaue the name of owre fauiour Iefu Chrift. We are further aduertifed that the forenamed Chriftopher hathe nowe builded and erected a fortreffe with good munition in one of the forefayde principall Ilandes in the which he hath placed a garrifon of certeine of the Chriftian men that wente thyther with him : afwell to th[e]intent to defende the fame, as alfo to fearche other Ilandes and firme landes farre remote and yet vnknowen. We alfo vnderftande, that in thefe landes and Ilandes lately founde, is great plentie of golde and fpices, with dyuers and many other precious thynges of fundry kyndes and qualities. Therefore al thinges diligently confidered (efpecially th[e]amplifyinge and enlargyng of the catholike fayth, as it behoueth catholike Princes folowyng th[e]exemples of yowre noble progenitours of famous memorie) wheras yowe are determyned by the fauour of almightie god to fubdue and brynge to the catholyke fayth th[e]inhabitauntes of the forefayde landes and Ilandes.

Wee greatly commendynge this yowre godly and laudable purpofe in owr lorde, and defirous to haue the fame brought to a dewe ende, and the name of owre fauioure to be knowen in thofe partes, doo

tur, hortamur vos quamplurimum in Domino, et per
facri lauacri fufceptionem, qua mandatis Apoftolicis
obligati eftis, et per vifcera mifericordiæ Domini noftri
Iefu Chrifti attente requirimus, vt cum expeditionem
huiufmodi omnino profequi et affumere prona mente
orthodoxæ fidei zelo intendatis, populos in huiufmodi
Infulis et terris degentes, ad Chriftianam religionem
fufcipiendam inducere velitis et debeatis, nec pericula
nec labores vllo vnquam tempore vos deterreant, firma
fpe fiduciaque conceptis quod Deus omnipotens conatus veftros fœliciter profequetur. Et vt tanti negotij
prouintiam Apoftolicæ gratiæ largitate donati, liberius
et audacius affumatis, motu proprio non ad veftram vel
alterius pro vobis fuper hoc nobis oblatæ petitionis
inftantiam, fed de noftra mera liberalitate, et ex certa
fcientia, ac de Apoftolicæ poteftatis plenitudine, omnes
Infulas et terras firmas inuentas et inueniendas, detectas et detegendas verfus Occidentem et Meridiem,
fabricando et conftruendo vnam lineam a polo Arctico,
fcilicet Septemtrione, ad polum Antarcticum, fcilicet
Meridiem fiue terræ firmæ et infulæ inuentæ et inueniendæ fint verfus Indiam aut verfus aliam quamcunque partem quæ linea diftet a qualibet Infularum
quæ vulgariter nuncupantur de los Azores et Cabo
Verde centum leucis verfus Occidentem et Meridiem.

Itaque omnes Infulæ et terræ firmæ repertæ et re-
periendæ, detectæ et detegendæ a præfata linea verfis
Occidentem et Meridiem, quæ per alium Regem aut
Principem Chriftianum non fuerint actualiter poffeffæ
vfque ad diem natiuitatis Domini noftri Iefu Chrifti

exhorte yowe in owre Lorde and by the receauynge
of yowre holy baptifme wherby yowe are bounde to
Apoftolicall obedience, and erneftely require yowe by
the bowels of mercy of owre Lorde Iefu Chrift, that
when yowe intende for the zeale of the Catholyke
faythe to profecute the fayde expedition to reduce the
people of the forefayde landes and Ilandes to the
Chriftian religion, yowe fhall fpare no labours at any
tyme, or bee deterred with any perels, conceauynge
firme hope and confidence that the omnipotent godde
wyll gyue good fucceffe to yowre godly attemptes.
And that beinge autoryfed by the priuilege of the
Apoftolycall grace, yowe may the more freely and
bouldly take vpon yowe th[e]enterpryfe of fo greate a
matter, we of owre owne motion, and not eyther at
yowre requeft or at the inftant peticion of any other
perfon, but of owre owne mere liberalitie and certeyne
fcience, and by the fulneffe of Apoftolycall power, doo
gyue, graunt, and affigne to yowe, yowre heyres and
fucceffours, al the firme landes and Ilandes found or
to be found, difcouered or to be difcouered toward the
Weft and South, drawyng a line from the pole Artike
to the pole Antartike (that is) from the north to the
Southe : Conteynynge in this donation, what fo euer
firme landes or Ilandes are founde or to bee founde
towarde *India*, or towarde any other parte what fo
euer it bee, beinge diftant from, or without the fore-
fayd iyne drawen a hundreth leaques towarde the
Wefte and South from any of the Ilandes which are
commonly cauled *De los Azores* and *Cabo Verde*.

All the Ilandes therfore and firme landes, founde
and to be founde, difcouered and to be difcouered
from the fayde lyne towarde the Weft and South, fuch
as haue not actually bin heretofore poffeffed by any
other Chriftian kynge or prynce vntyll the daye of the
natiuitie of owre Lorde Iefu Chryfte lafte pafte, from

proxime præteritum, a quo incipit annus præfens
Milleſſimus Quadringenteſſimus Nonageſſimus tercius,
quando fuerunt per nuncios et capitaneos veſtros inuentæ aliquæ prædiƈtarum Inſularum, auctoritate omni-
potentis Dei nobis in beato Petro concefſa, ac vicariatus
Iefu Chriſti qua fungimur in terris, cum omnibus illarum
dominijs, ciuitatibus, caſtris, locis, et villis, iuribufque
et iurifdiƈtionibus ac pertinentijs vniuerſis, vobis here-
dibufque et fuccefſoribus veſtris (Caſtellæ et Legionis
regibus) in perpetuum tenore præfentium donamus
concedimus, et aſſignamus: Vofque et hæredes ac
fuccefſores præfatos illarum Dominos, cum plena,
libera, et omnimoda poteſtate, autoritate, et iurif-
diƈtione, facimus, conſtituimus, et deputamus. De-
cernentes nihilo minus per huiufmodi donationem,
concefſionem, et aſſignationem noſtram, nullo Chriſti-
ano Principi qui aƈtualiter præfatas Inſulas et terras
firmas poſſederit vſque ad prædiƈtum diem natiuitatis
Domini noſtri Iefu Chriſti ius quæsitum, fublatum in-
telligi pofſe aut auferri debere.

Et infuper mandamus vobis in virtutæ ſanƈtæ obedi-
entiæ (vt ſicut pollicemini et non dubitamus pro veſtra
maxima deuotione et regia magnanimitate vos efſe
faƈturos) ad terras firmas et Inſulas prædiƈtas, viros
probos et Deum timentes, doƈtos, peritos, et expertos,
ad inſtruendum incolas et habitatores præfatos in fide
Catholica et bonis moribus imbuendum, deſtinare debeatis, omnem debitam diligentiam in præmifſis adhi-
bentes.

Ac quibufcumque perſonis, cuiufcunque dignitatis,
etiam imperialis et regalis ſtatus, gradus, ordinis vel
conditionis, fub excommunicationis latæ ſententiæ
pœna quam eo ipfo ſi contra fecerint incurrant, dif-

424

the which begynneth this prefent yeare beinge the
yeare of owre Lorde. M. CCCC. lxxxxiii. when fo euer
any fuch fhalbe founde by your meffingers and capy-
taines, Wee by the autoritie of almyghtie God graunted
vnto vs in faynt Peter, and by the office which we beare
on the earth in the fteede of Iefu Chrifte, doo for euer
by the tenoure of thefe prefentes, gyue, graunte, affigne,
vnto yowe, yowre heyres, and fucceffoures (the kynges
of Caftyle and Legion) all thofe landes and Ilandes,
with theyr dominions, territories, cities, caftels, towres,
places, and vyllages, with all the ryght, and iurifdic-
tions therunto perteynynge: conftitutynge, affignynge,
and deputynge, yowe, yowre heyres, and fucceffours
the lordes thereof, with full and free poure, autoritie,
and iurifdiction. Decreeinge neuertheleffe by this
owre donation, graunt, and affignation, that from no
Chriftian Prince whiche actually hath poffeffed the
forefayde Ilandes and firme landes vnto the day of
the natiuitie of owre lorde beforefayde theyr ryght
obteyned to bee vnderftoode hereby to be taken away,
or that it owght to be taken away.

Furthermore wee commaunde yowe in the vertue
of holy obedience (as yowe haue promyfed, and as wee
doubte not you wyll doo vppon mere deuotion and
princely magnanimitie) to fende to the fayde firme
landes and Ilandes, honefte, vertuous, and lerned men,
fuche as feare God, and are able to inftructe th[e] in-
habitauntes in the Catholyke fayth and good maners, applyinge all theyr poffible diligence in the pre-
miffes.

We furthermore ftreightly inhibite all maner of
perfons, of what ftate, degree, order, or condition fo
euer they bee, although of Imperiall and regall dignitie, vnder the peyne of the fentence of excommunica-
tion whiche they fhall incurre yf they doo to the contrary, that they in no cafe prefume without fpeciall

trictius inhibemus ne ad Infulas et terras firmas inuentas et inueniendas, detectas et detegendas verfus
Occidentem et Meridiem, fabricando et conftruendo
lineam a polo Arctico ad polum Antarcticum, fiue
terræ firmæ et Infulæ inuentæ et inueniendæ fint verfus Indiam aut verfus aliam quamcunque partem quæ
linea diftet a qualibet Infularum quæ vulgariter nuncupantur de los Azores et Cabo Verde centum leucis
verfus Occidentem et Meridiem vt præfertur, pro mer-
cibus habendis vel quauis alia caufa accedere præfu-
mat abfque veftra ac hæredum et fuccefsorum veftrorum prædictorum licentia fpeciali : Non obftantibus
conftitutionibus et ordinationibus Apoftolicis, cæte-
rifque contrariis quibufcunque, in illo a quo imperia et
dominationes et bona cuncta procedunt : Confidentes
quod dirigente Domino actus veftros, fi huiufmodi
fanctum ac laudabile propofitum profequamini, breui
tempore cum fœlicitate et gloria totius populi Chrif-
tiani, veftri labores et conatus exitum fœlicifsimum
confequentur. Verum quia difficile foret præfentes
literas ad fingula quæque loca in quibus expediens
fuerit deferri, volumus ac motu et fcientia fimilibus
decernimus, quod illarum tranffumptis manu publici
notarij inderogati fubfcriptis, et figillo alicuius per-
fonæ in ecclefiaftica dignitate conftitutæ, feu curiæ
ecclefiafticæ munitis, ea prorfus fides in iudicio et
extra ac alias vbilibet adhibeatur, quæ præfentibus
adhiberetur fi efsent exhibitæ vel oftenfæ.

Nulli ergo omnino hominum liceat hanc paginam
noftræ commendationis, hortationis, requifitionis, donationis, concefsionis, afsignationis, conftitutionis, de-
putationis, decreti, mandati, inhibitionis, et voluntatis,
infringere vel ei aufu temerario contraire. Si quis autem hoc attentare præfumpferit, indignationem omni-

426

lycence of yowe, yowre heyres, and fucceffours, to
trauayle for marchaundies or for any other caufe, to
the fayde landes or Ilandes, founde or to bee found,
difcouered, or to bee difcouered, toward the weft and
fouth, drawing a line from the pole Artyke to the pole
Antartike, whether the firme lands and Ilandes found
and to be found, be fituate toward *India* or towarde
any other parte beinge diftant from the lyne drawen
a hundreth leagues towarde the weft from any of the
Ilandes commonly cauled *De los Azores* and *Cabo
Verde :* Notwithftandynge conftitutions, decrees, and
Apoftolycall ordinaunces what fo euer they are to the
contrary : In him from whom Empyres, dominions,
and all good thynges doo procede: Truftynge that almyghtie god directynge yowre enterprifes, yf yowe fol-
lowe yowre godly and laudable attemptes, yowre la-
boures and trauayles herein, fhall in fhorte tyme
obteyne a happy ende with felicitie and glorie of all
Chriftian people. But forafmuch as it fhulde bee a
thynge of great difficultie for thefe letters to bee caryed
to all fuche places as fhuld bee expedient, we wyll,
and of lyke motion and knowleage doo decree that
whyther fo euer the fame fhalbe fent, or wher fo euer
they fhalbe receaued with the fubfcription of a common
notarie therunto requyred, with the feale of any perfon
conftitute in ecclefiafticall dignitie, or fuche as are
autoryfed by the ecclefiafticall courte, the fame fayth
and credite to bee gyuen thereunto in iudgement or
els where, as fhulde bee exhibyted to thefe prefentes.

It fhall therefore bee lawefull for no man to in-
fringe or rafhely to contrarie this letter of owre commendation, exhortacion, requefte, donation, graunt,
affignation, conftitution, deputation, decree, com-
maundement, inhibition, and determination. And yf
any fhall prefume to attempte the fame, he owght to

APPENDIX B

potentis Dei, ac beatorum Petri et Pauli Apoſtolorum
eius, ſe nouerit incurſurum.∴

Datum Romæ apud ſanctum Petrum : Anno incar-
nationis Dominicæ. 1493. quarto nonas Maij : Pon-
tificatus noſtri anno primo.∴

knowe that he ſhall thereby incurre the indignation of almyghtie God and his holye Apoſtles Peter and Paule. (∴) (:) (⋯)

❡ Gyuen at Rome at ſaynt Peters : In the yeare of th[e] incarnation of owre Lord M.CCCC.LXXXXIII. The fourth day of the nones of Maye, the fyrſte yeare of owre ſeate. ( ) ( ) ( )

APPENDIX C

1. *Those who went out in the Santa Maria, and returned in the Niña :* —

Christopher Columbus, captain-general.

Juan de La Cosa, of Santoña, master, and owner of
the vessel.

Sancho Ruiz, pilot.

Maestre Alonso, of Moguer, physician.

Maestre Diego, boatswain (*contramaestre*).

Rodrigo Sanchez, of Segovia, inspector (*veedor*).

Terreros, steward (*maestresala*).

Rodrigo de Jerez, of Ayamonte.

Ruiz Garcia, of Santoña.

Rodrigo de Escobar.

Francisco de Huelva, of Huelva.

Rui Fernandez, of Huelva.

Pedro de Bilbao, of Larrabezua.

Pedro de Villa, of Santoña.

Diego de Salcedo, servant of Columbus.

Pedro de Acevedo, cabin boy.

Luis de Torres, converted Jew, interpreter.

2. *Those who went and returned in the Pinta :* —

Martin Alonso Pinzon, of Palos, captain.

Francisco Martin Pinzon, of Palos, master.

Cristóbal Garcia Xalmiento, pilot.

Juan de Jerez, of Palos, mariner.
Bartolomé Garcia, of Palos, boatswain.
Juan Perez Vizcaino, of Palos, caulker.
Rodrigo de Triana, of Lepe.
Juan Rodríguez Bermejo, of Molinos.
Juan de Sevilla.
Garcia Hernández, of Palos, steward (*despensero*).
Garcia Alonso, of Palos.
Gomez Rascon, of Palos, ⎱ owners of the vessel.
Cristóbal Quintero, of Palos, ⎰
Juan Quintero, of Palos.
Diego Bermudez, of Palos.
Juan Bermudez, of Palos.
Francisco Garcia Gallego, of Moguer.
Francisco Garcia Vallejo, of Moguer.
Pedro de Arcos, of Palos.

3. *Those who went and returned in the Niña :* —

Vicente Yañez Pinzon, of Palos, captain.
Juan Niño, of Moguer, master.
Pero Alonso Niño, of Moguer, pilot.
Bartolomé Roldan, of Palos, pilot.
Francisco Niño, of Moguer.
Gutierre Perez, of Palos.
Juan Ortiz, of Palos.
Alonso Gutierrez Querido, of Palos.

4. *Those who were left in Hispaniola, and perished,*
   most of them murdered by the natives : —

Pedro Gutierrez, keeper of the king's drawing room.
Rodrigo de Escobedo, of Segovia, notary.

431

APPENDIX C

Diego de Arana, of Cordova, high constable (*alguazil mayor*).

Alonso Velez de Mendoza, of Seville.

Alvar Perez Osorio, of Castrojeriz.

Antonio de Jaen, of Jaen.

The bachelor Bernardino de Tapia, of Ledesma.

Cristóbal del Alamo, of Niebla.

Castillo, silversmith and assayer, of Seville.

Diego Garcia, of Jerez.

Diego de Tordoya, of Cabeza de Buey, in Estremadura.

Diego de Capilla, of Almaden.

Diego de Torpa.

Diego de Mables, of Mables.

Diego de Mendoza, of Guadalajara.

Diego de Montalban, of Jaen.

Domingo de Bermeo.

Francisco Fernandez.

Francisco de Godoy, of Seville.

Francisco de Aranda, of Aranda.

Francisco de Henao, of Avila.

Francisco Ximénez, of Seville.

Gabriel Baraona, of Belmonte.

Gonzalo Fernandez de Segovia, of Leon.

Gonzalo Fernandez de Segovia, of Segovia.

Guillermo Ires [qy. William Irish, or William Harris?], of Galney [*i. e.* Galway], Ireland.

Fernando de Porcuna.

Jorge Gonzalez, of Trigueros.

Maestre Juan, surgeon.

Juan de Urniga.

Juan Morcillo, of Villanueva de la Serena.

432

Juan de Cueva, of Castuera.

Juan Patiño, of La Serena.

Juan del Barco, of Barco de Ávila.

Juan de Villar, of Villar.

Juan de Mendoza.

Martin de Logrosa, of Logrosa.

Pedro Corbacho, of Cáceres.

Pedro de Talavera.

Pedro de Foronda.

Sebastian de Mayorga, of Majorca.

Tristan de San Jorge.

Tallarte de Lages [qy. Arthur Laws, or Larkins ?], of England.

This list is taken from Captain Cesáreo Fernández Duro's learned monograph, *Colon y Pinzon. Informe relativo á los pormenores de descubrimiento del Nuevo Mundo*, Madrid, 1883.

Juan de La Cosa is usually spoken of as having accompanied Columbus on his second voyage but not on his first. An ordinance of the sovereigns, however, dated February 28, 1494, and preserved among the Simancas MSS., thus addresses La Cosa : " Fuistes por maestre de una nao vuestra á las mares del océano, donde en aquel viaje fueron descubiertas las tierras é islas de la parte de las Indias, é vos perdistes la dicha nao," *anglicè*, " You went as master of a ship of your own to the ocean seas where in that voyage were discovered the lands and islands of the Indies, and you lost the said ship." Navarrete, *Biblioteca maritima española*, tom. ii. p. 209. Mr. Winsor (*Christopher Columbus*, p. 184) seems to think that this La Cosa was a different person from the great pilot and cosmographer, who was a native of Santoña and resident of Puerto de Santa Maria; but Captain Duro (p. 292) makes him the same person. Cf. Harrisse, *Christophe Colomb*, i. 406

APPENDIX D

(After the corrected lists in Guillemard's *Magellan*.)

1. *The eighteen who returned to Seville in the Victoria.*

Juan Sebastian Elcano, captain-general.

Miguel de Rodas, boatswain (*contramaestre*) of the Victoria.

Francisco Albo, of Axio, boatswain of the Trinidad.

Juan de Acurio, of Bermeo, boatswain of the Concepcion.

Martin de Judicibus, of Genoa, superintendent of the Concepcion.

Hernando de Bustamante, of Alcántara, barber of the Concepcion.

Juan de Zuvileta, of Baracaldo, page of the Victoria.

Miguel Sanchez, of Rodas, skilled seaman (*marinero*) of the Victoria.

Nicholas the Greek, of Naples, *marinero* of the Victoria.

Diego Gallego, of Bayonne, *marinero* of the Victoria.

Juan Rodriguez, of Seville, *marinero* of the Trinidad.

435

Antonio Rodriguez, of Huelva, *marinero* of the Trinidad.

Francisco Rodriguez, of Seville (a Portuguese), *marinero* of the Concepcion.

Juan de Arratia, of Bilbao, common sailor (*grumete*) of the Victoria.

Vasco Gomez Gallego (a Portuguese), *grumete* of the Trinidad.

Juan de Santandres, of Cueto, *grumete* of the Trinidad.

Martin de Isaurraga, of Bermeo, *grumete* of the Concepcion.

The Chevalier Antonio Pigafetta, of Vicenza, passenger.

2. *The thirteen who were arrested at the Cape Verde islands.*

Pedro de Indarchi, of Teneriffe, master of the Santiago.

Richard, from Normandy, carpenter of the Santiago.

Simon de Burgos (a Portuguese), servant of Mendoza, the traitor captain of the Victoria.

Juan Martin, of Aguilar de Campo, servant of the same Mendoza.

Roldan de Argote, of Bruges, bombardier of the Concepcion.

Martin Mendez, of Seville, accountant of the Victoria.

Juan Ortiz de Gopega, of Bilbao, steward of the San Antonio.

Pedro Gasco, of Bordeaux, *marinero* of the Santiago.

Alfonso Domingo, *marinero* of the Santiago.

Ocacio Alonso, of Bollullos, *marinero* of the Santiago.

Gomez Hernandez, of Huelva, *marinero* of the Concepcion.

Felipe de Rodas, of Rodas, *marinero* of the Victoria.

Pedro de Tolosa, from Guipuzcoa, *grumete* of the Victoria.

3. *The four survivors of the Trinidad, who returned to Spain long after their comrades.*

Gonzalo Gomez de Espinosa, constable (*alguazil*) of the fleet.

Juan Rodriguez, of Seville (called "the deaf"), *marinero* of the Concepcion.

Ginez de Mafra, of Xeres, *marinero*.

Leon Pancaldo, of Savona near Genoa, *marinero*.

INDEX

INDEX

ABBOTT, C. C., American archæologist, discoveries in Trenton gravel, i. 9 ; his collection in the Peabody Museum, 11 n.

Aborigines in America, evidences, i. 5–15 ; and the Indians, 17, 18 n.

Abreu, Antonio d', Portuguese commander, voyage to the Moluccas, ii. 418.

Abyssinia and Prester John, i. 330 n.

Acamapichtli, first Aztec chief-of-men, iii. 13.

Adam of Bremen, German ecclesiastical historian, his *Historia Ecclesiastica* and Vinland, i. 240–244 ; Columbus's knowledge of his work, ii. 60–62.

Adelung, J. C., German philologist, on Indian languages, i. 46.

Adirondacks, Algonquin Indians, i. 52.

Admiral's map. *See* Waldseemüller.

Adobe brick, as a criterion of barbarism, i. 36 ; use by pueblo Indians, 98–100.

Æschylus, Greek poet, on the Arimaspians, i. 331 n.

Aeszler, Jacob, aids in Waldseemüller's Ptolemy, ii. 371.

Africa, ancient theories on circumnavigability, i. 340–342 ; story of Phœnician circumnavigation, 342–345, 348 ; ancient voyages along coast, 345–348 ; Mela's map, 349; Portuguese voyages on western coast, 371–375 ; circum-

navigated, 381 ; origin of name, ii. 369 n.

Agamemnon and Leif Ericsson, i. 225.

Agassiz, Louis, Swiss naturalist, on origins, i. 70 n.

Agathokles, Sicilian general, burns his ships, iii. 39 n.

Agnese, Baptista, Venetian cartographer, New World on his map, ii. 381 ; Verrazano's Sea on his map, iii. 326.

Agriculture, and horticulture, i. 57 ; Peruvian, iii. 113–116, 122, 169.

Aguado, Juan, royal agent to Hayti, ii. 174, 307 ; credentials, 308 n.

Ahuizotl, Aztec chief-of-men, iii. 16.

Ailly, Pierre d', *Imago Mundi*, ii. 46 ; at Saint Dié, 361.

Alaminos, Antonio de, Spanish pilot, in Córdova's expedition, iii. 31.

Albigenses on the Donation of Constantine, ii. 144 n.

Albuquerque, Alfonso de, Portuguese viceroy in the Indies, ii. 417, 418.

Alcántara, Martinez de, half brother of Pizarro, goes to Peru, iii. 212 ; killed, 236.

Alexander VI., pope, donation to Spain, ii. 141 ; bull of demarcation, 142–148.

Alfonso V. of Portugal, asks advice of Toscanelli, ii. 25 ; war with Castile, 40 n., 56.

Alfonso XI. of Castile, sumptuary laws, ii. 13 n.

441

INDEX

Alfragan, Arabian astronomer, influence on Columbus, ii. 51 n.

Algonquins, Indian group, culture status, i. 35, 52, 57; location, 51; reduced by Iroquois, 56.

Allefonsce, Jehan, French navigator, voyage on North American coast, iii. 325.

Alliacus, Petrus. *See* Ailly.

Almagro, Diego, partnership for expedition to Peru, iii. 206; character, 206; in first expeditions, 207–209; dislike of Pizarro's brothers, 212; arrival in Peru, 220; slighted, 226; lays claim to Cuzco, 226, 229; goes to Chili, 227; defeats Manco, 229; returns from Chili and seizes Cuzco, 229; executed, 230; supporters kill Pizarro, 235.

Almagro the lad, proclaimed governor of Peru, iii. 236; defeat and execution, 237.

Almeida, Francisco de, Portuguese viceroy in India, ii. 417, 418.

Alp Arslan, sultan of the Turks, devastates Asia Minor, i. 313.

Alphabet, criterion of civilization, i. 38.

Alvarado, Pedro de, called Tonatiuh by the Aztecs, iii. 28 n.; in Grijalva's expedition, 34; grudge against Grijalva, 36; precipitates conflict with Aztecs, 78–81; in Peru, 225; and Las Casas, 299.

Amazon River, Pinzon's discovery, ii. 322; Orellana's voyage, iii. 233; origin of name, 234 n.

Amazonians, South American Indians, iii. 95.

America, antiquity of man in, i. 5–15; former connection with Old World, 17; people from Old World, 17, 24; value as a field of archæological study, 43–45, 67, 170; discovery from Greenland almost inevitable, 204; unrecorded pre-Columbian voyages, 291; barrenness of pre-Colum-

bian voyages, 292–296; great step toward discovery, 321; prophecies of discovery, ii. 36 n., 43, 44; discovery an evolution, 133, 398, iii. 386–388; relation of Columbus and Cabral to discovery, ii. 325; steps in the application of name to South America, 359; first use of name, 366; why not named after Columbus, 369; original application of name, 371–382, 389 n.; extension of name to all South America, 382; realization of a western hemisphere, 385, 413, 418, 450, iii. 327; extension of name to whole hemisphere, ii. 385; objections by supporters of Columbus's claim, 386; attempts to change name, 396 n.; progress of discovery, iii. 29; discovery as a unique event, 387. *See also* Geography, Indians, North America, South America, Vinland, Voyages.

American Folk-Lore Society, valuable work, i. 62 n.

Anáhuac, no empire, iii. 5 n.

Andagoya, Pascual de, voyage toward Peru, iii. 206.

Andaman Islands, Indian Ocean, status of inhabitants, i. 378 n.

Anderson, R. B. American writer, on Columbus, ii. 60, 66 n.

Andrade, Fernam de, Portuguese commander, reaches China, ii. 418.

Anian, mythical strait on old maps, iii. 383 n.

Animals, pleistocene, i. 15; domestic, as criterion of barbarism, 32; domestic, introduced to America by Europeans, 32, 253, ii. 151, 154; Indians fear unknown, i. 216, ii. 157, 161, iii. 40, 217 n.; no domestic, left in Vinland, i. 252–255; domestic, in Peru, iii. 113; influence of cattle on social development, 117–120; etymological influence of cattle, 120 n.

INDEX

Anonymous Conqueror, companion of Cortes, on population of Mexico City, iii. 59.

Anonymous Jesuit, on Peruvian funeral customs, iii. 151 n.

Antilia, fabulous island, on Toscanelli's map, ii. 50.

Antilles, first appearance of name, ii. 236.

Antipodes, Cosmas on, i. 307; Mela on, 353; and Ceylon, 354. *See also* New World.

Apaches, Athabaskan Indians, i. 47.

Arabs, character, i. 310, 312; struggle with Portuguese in Indian Ocean, ii. 416.

Arago, D. F., French physicist, on Greenland's climate, i. 183 n.

Araucanians, Chilian Indian, iii. 96; resistance to the Spanish, 232.

Archæology, importance of American, i. 43–45, 170. *See also* Aborigines, Indians.

Architecture, relation to culture, i. 35; social basis of Indian, 77; Iroquois "long houses," 78–80; differences in Indian, 93; Mandan Indian houses, 94–96; origin and type of pueblos, 99–102; existing puebla, 103–106; Maya, 153–158; of Mexico City, iii. 55; Peruvian, 102, 103–111, 167–169.

Ari Marsson, voyage to Vinland, i. 238.

Ari Thorgilsson (Fródhi), first Icelandic historian, works, i. 236; mentions Vinland, 237–239.

Arickarees, Indian group, i. 50.

Arimaspians, persistent Asian myth, i. 331 n.

Ariosto, Ludovico, Italian poet, on Donation of Constantine, ii. 145 n.

Aristotle, Greek philosopher, on earth's shape and western route to Indies, ii. 41.

Armada, Spanish, effect of destruction, iii. 394, 395.

Arnold, William, stone mill at Newport, i. 248.

Arrapahos, Algonquin Indians, i. 51.

Asia, seat of human race, i. 4; absorbs external interest of Europe, 300–303, 323; visited by Nestorian missionaries, 309; Marco Polo's contribution to knowledge of, 328; myths, 329–331; origin of name, ii. 367 n.–369 n. *See also* North America and countries by name.

Asia Minor, contrasts in condition, i. 313.

Astrolabe, necessary to systematic ocean navigation, i. 297; introduction, 362; Behaim improves, ii. 73.

Atahualpa, usurping Inca, iii. 129, 213; courts Spanish favour, 214; meets Pizarro, 216; and Montezuma, 217; taken prisoner, 218; ransom, 219; executed, 221–223; method of his usurpation, 241.

Athabaskans, Indian group, culture status, i. 47.

Atlantis and Sargasso Sea, ii. 108 n.

Australia, primitive conditions, i. 69.

Avezac, M. A. P. de, French geographer, on transformation of names, i. 270 n; on birth of Columbus, ii. 11 n.; on date of Toscanelli's letter, 39 n.; on Bartholomew Columbus and Dias, 81 n.

Avienus, Festus, Roman poet, on the Saragossa Sea, ii. 107 n.

Avila. *See* Gonzalez, Pedrarias.

Axayacatl, Aztec chief-of-men, iii. 14.

Ayala, Pedro de, Spanish envoy at London, on John Cabot, ii. 216, 219.

Ayllon, Lucas Vasquez d', Spanish navigator, search for northwest passage, iii. 321; attempted colony in Virginia, 321; death, 321.

443

INDEX

Aymaras, Peruvian Indians, iii. 125.

Azcaputzalco, Mexico, Tecpanecas pueblo, iii. 13 ; destroyed, 14.

Azores Islands, visited by Portuguese, i. 369 ; colonized, 374 ; Columbus at, ii. 124.

Aztecs, Mexican Indians, culture, i. 25, 36, 39–41, 118 n., 142 ; confederacy, 118–121 ; tribal organization, 121 ; communism, 122 ; organization of clan, 122, 123 ; duties of phratry, 123 ; tribal council, 124, iii. 81 ; tribal executives, i. 125–127, 130–133, iii. 72–74 ; head of confederacy, i. 127 ; collection of tribute, 133 ; compared with Iroquois confederacy, 135 ; priesthood, 136 ; human sacrifice, 136–138 ; no caste, 136 n. ; slavery, 139 ; kinship through male, 140 ; marriage, 141 ; private property, 142 ; criticism of Morgan's views concerning, 143–150 ; at Tollan, iii. 9 ; relation to Toltecs and Chichimecs, 9–11 ; found Mexico City, 11 ; folk-lore of god Quetzalcoatl and advent of Spaniards, 20, 29, 41, 42, 78 ; method of warfare, 45 n. ; culture compared with Peruvian, 172–176. *See also* Mexicans, Mexico City.

Aztlan, situation, iii. 8.

Azurara, Gomez Eannes de, Portuguese chronicler, on early slave trade, iii. 251, 252 n.

Baccalaos, early name for Newfoundland, ii. 237.

Bachofen, J. J., Swiss sociologist, *Das Mutterrecht*, i. 65.

Bacon, Francis (Lord), on Bartholomew Columbus in England, ii. 88 n.

Bacon, Roger, on westward route to Asia, i. 322, ii. 45 ; and the compass, i. 361 ; and *Imago Mundi*, ii. 52 n.–54 n.

Badajos Congress, iii. 318.

Baffin, William, British navigator, search for northwest passage, iii. 381.

Baffin's Bay, Northmen in, i. 198.

Bajazet, sultan of the Turks, slaughter of French prisoners, iii. 129 n.

Balboa, Vasco Nuñez de, discovers Pacific Ocean, ii. 415, iii. 188 ; escapes from creditors, 182 ; in command at Darien, 183, 185, 187 ; and Enciso, 185, 187, 189 ; explores isthmus, 186 ; hears of Peru, 187, 189, and Pedrarias, 191 ; prepares expedition for Peru, 192–194 ; character, 192, 198 ; false charges and conspiracy against, 194–196 ; horoscope, 196 ; executed, 197.

Bancroft, H. H., American historian, on Herrera as a historian, ii. 286 ; on location of Vespucius's Bermudas, 314 n.; on Vespucius's account of his voyages, 320 n. ; on prehistoric Mexico, iii. 5.

Bandelier, F. A., American archæologist, on veracity of Spanish explorers, i. 107 ; on population of Cholula, 108 ; researches on Mexican society, 117, 118 n., 120, 130, 131 n., iii. 45 n. ; on the Chichimecs, 8 n. ; on strategic strength of Mexico City, 12 n. ; on Quetzalcoatl, 20 n., 21 n. ; on gardens of Mexico City, 57 n. ; on military colonies in Mexico, 136 n. ; on policy of abolishing Indian slavery, 302 n.

Bannocks, Indian group, culture status, i. 47.

Barbarism, and savagery, i. 29–31 ; three periods and the Indians, 32–37, 136 ; and civilization, 38 ; value of the term, 42 ; exemplification in America, 43–45 ; importance of middle period, 149 ; history of the word, 376 n.

Barbaro, Marco, on Zeno, i. 269 n.

INDEX

450

INDEX

birth, ii. 24 ; left at Huelva, 77, 90,
93 ; page at court, 94 n., 191 ;
claims, 266 ; marriage, 266 ; liti-
gation over claims, 267–270 ;
governor of the Indies, iii. 29,
177 ; relation to the Crown,
177–179 ; conquers Cuba, 274.

Columbus, Ferdinand, natural son
of Christopher, on the sloping
ocean, i. 357 n. ; biography of his
father, ii. 1 ; library, 2 ; authority, 4 ; ignorant of father's early
life, 6 ; authenticity of biography,
7 n. ; birth, 80 ; on the visit to
La Rábida, 93 n. ; witnesses his
father's departure for second voyage, 153 ; page to the queen,
191 ; in father's fourth expedition,
200 ; motto, 210 ; makes no
objection to name America, 374 ;
filial defence, 375 n.

Columbus, Giovanni, brother of
Christopher, ii. 10, 16, 20 n.

Communism, Indian, i. 77–81, 93 ;
Mexican, 122.

Compass, necessary to systematic
ocean navigation, i. 297 ; introduction, 360–362 ; deflection
during voyage of Columbus, ii.
106.

Congo River, discovered, i. 375.

Constantinople, importance in twelfth
century, i. 311 ; captured in
Fourth Crusade, 315 ; effect of
capture by Turks, 336.

Copan, ruined city in Central America, i. 158 n.

Copper, use in middle period of barbarism, i. 36.

Corbaria, bishop of Monte-Peloso,
epigram on Columbus' discovery,
ii. 136 n.

Cordeiro, Luciano, Portuguese historian, disparages Columbus, ii.
74 n.

Córdova, Francisco Hernandez de,
(first), expedition to Yucatan, iii.
30–33.

Córdova, Francisco Hernandez de,

(second), in Central America, iii.
205 ; executed, 205.

Coronado, Francisco de, Spanish explorer, compares Zuñi to Granada,
i. 106, 109 ; expedition, iii. 338.

Cortereal brothers, Gaspar and Miguel, Portuguese navigators, voyages, ii. 234.

Cortes, Hernando, compares Tlascala
to Granada, i. 106–109 ; character, iii. 36 ; expedition to Mexico,
37 ; actions due to knowledge of
Mexican conditions, 37, 41–43,
71 ; founds Vera Cruz, 38 ; cuts
loose from Velasquez, 38 ; scuttles
his ships, 38 ; force, 40 ; aided
by circumstances, 41 ; at Cempoala, 41–43 ; reception at Xo-
cotlan, 43 ; line of march, 43,
49, 52 ; conflict with the Tlascalans, 43–47 ; alliance with
Tlascalans, 47 ; treachery and
massacre of Cholulans, 49–52 ;
first sight of Mexico City, 52–54 ;
situation in Mexico City, 69–71 ;
seizure of Montezuma, 71–76 ;
seizure of Cuitlahuatzin, 77 ; de-
stroys idols, 77 ; marches against
Narvaez, 78 ; wins over Narvaez's
troops, 79 ; returns to Mexico
City, 81 ; result of releasing
Cuitlahuatzin, 81–83 ; retreat,
83 ; victory at Otumba, 84 ;
alliance with Tezcuco, 85 ; siege
of Mexico City, 85–87 ; later
life, 87 ; and Pizarro, 217 ; exploration on the Pacific coast,
332.

Cosmas Indicopleustes, monk, geographical theories, i. 306–308 ;
on Sinai inscriptions, 306 n. ; on
India and China, 309.

Cosmographie Introductio, contents, ii. 364, 365 ; editions,
365 ; first suggestion of name
America, 366–368.

Coulanges, N. D. Fustel de, French
archæologist, on functions of early
kings, i. 128.

451

INDEX

Counties, English, origin, i. 112 n.

Cousin, Jean, of Dieppe, voyage, i. 173, 174 n.

Covilham, Pedro de, Portuguese adventurer, in Abyssinia, 380, 381.

Creeks, culture status, i. 35 ; Maskoki Indians, 50.

Crees, Algonquin Indians, i. 51.

Cresson, H. T., American geologist, palæolithic discoveries, i. 9, 11.

Croll, James, English physicist, on glacial period, i. 8.

Crusades, origin, 312, 313 ; effect, 314 ; disastrous Fourth, 315.

Cuba, Columbus discovers and coasts, ii. 117, 159, 161 ; supposed to be Asian mainland, 118, 162–168 ; discovery of insularity, 264, 291, 293, 295, 298 ; confused on maps with Florida, 303–305 ; conquered, iii. 29, 274.

Cuitlahuatzin, Montezuma's brother, seized by Cortes, iii. 77 ; released and supersedes Montezuma, 82 ; death, 86.

Culture, and race, i. 28, 28 n. ; grades, 29–38 ; caution on classification, 39, 41. *See also* Barbarism, Indians, Savagery, and Indian groups by name.

Cumaná, Pearl Coast, Las Casas's attempted colony, iii. 285–288.

Cumberland Islands, discovery, iii. 378.

Cushing, F. H., American ethnologist, at Zuñi, i. 100, 102 n., and the Zuñi priests, iii. 337 n.

Cuvier, G. C. L., French naturalist, on origin of the potato, iii. 114 n.

Cuzco, Peru, founded, iii. 124 ; Pizarro at, 223 ; besieged by Manco, 228 ; seized by Almagro, 229.

Dakotas, Indian group, culture status, i. 35, 47, 57.

Dante Alighieri, Italian poet, cosmical theory, ii. 45 ; on Donation of Constantine, 144 n., 147 n.

Darien, founding of colony, iii. 178–181 ; abandoned and reëstablished, 183 ; Balboa in command, 183, 185 ; arrival of Pedrarias, 189–191.

Darwin, C. R., English naturalist, on the Patagonians, ii. 436 n. ; on Peruvian maize, iii. 114 n. ; on Peruvian methods of improving breed of animals, 171 n.

Dasent, Sir George, English scholar, on Iceland, i. 179 n.

Dati, Giuliano, Italian poet, paraphrase of Columbus's letter, ii. 136, 137 n.

Dávila. *See* Gonzalez, Pedrarias.

Davis, John, British navigator, search for northwest passage, iii. 378.

Dawkins, W. B., English geologist, on antiquity of man, i. 13 n.–15 n. ; on origin of Eskimos, 21.

De Costa, B. F., American historian, on Thorfinn's voyage, i. 209 n. ; on Skrælings, 218 n.

Deane, Charles, American historian, on theory of roundness of earth, ii. 214 n.

Dee, John, English mathematician, map, iii. 357, 358.

Delawares, Algonquin Indians, i. 51 ; mound builders, 168.

Demarcation, bull of, ii. 142–148 ; influence on service of explorers, 407 n.

Deza, Diego, Spanish royal confessor, interest in Columbus, ii. 95.

Dias, Bartholomew, Portuguese navigator, rounds southern end of Africa, i. 381 ; effect of his voyage, 383 ; death, ii. 324.

Diaz de Castillo, Bernal, Spanish historian, on Mexican human sacrifice, iii. 33 ; on first sight of Mexico City, 52 ; on Mexican cannibalism, 62 n.

Dighton rock inscription, Washington's opinion, i. 247 n. ; Mallery's

452

INDEX

i. 19–23 ; relation of American and Siberian, 21 n. ; not Indians, 25 ; not natives of Vinland, 217, 218 n. ; destroy Norse settlements in Greenland, 260.

Espinosa, Gaspar de, chief judge of Darien, iii. 191 ; voyage on the Pacific, 202.

Espinosa, Gonzalo Gomez de, constable of Magellan's fleet, commands the Trinidad, ii. 447 ; disasters, 447 ; pensioned and ennobled, 450.

Estevánico, negro, adventures with Cabeza de Vaca, iii. 331 ; with Fray Marcos, 334 ; reception in Zuñi, 335–337.

Estotiland, Zeno's description, i. 281 ; identity, 282, 285.

Estufa of pueblo Indians, i. 103.

Eudoxus of Cyzicus, Greek navigator, voyages on coast of Africa, i. 347, 348.

Eugenius IV., pope, grants heathen countries to Portugal, i. 373.

Europe, condition in 1000, i. 297–300 ; outlook toward Asia only, 300–303 ; effect of Saracen empire, 310 ; effect of Crusades, 312, 314–316 ; condition in 1300, 318 ; origin of name, ii. 367 n.–369 n.

Eyrbyggja Saga mentions Vinland, i. 234.

Færoe Islands, Zenos at, i. 264–267 ; on Zeno map, 271.

Family, Maine's basis of primitive society, i. 63 ; patriarchal, not primitive, 64, 67 ; primitive kinship through female, 65–68 ; origin of indissoluble marriage, 69, 74 ; earliest forms, 71 ; exogamy, 72 ; change to male kinship, 72, 73, 76 ; development of phratry and tribe, 72 ; Aztec, 140–142 ; growth of patriarchal, iii. 118–120 ; in Peru, 161. *See also* Clan.

Faria y Sousa, Manoel de, Portuguese historian, on Magellan, ii. 427.

Ferdinand, king of Aragon, absorbed in war with Moors, ii. 79, 88 ; no share in first expedition of Columbus, 102 ; reception of Columbus after first voyage, 127 ; gets credit for the discovery, 139 n. ; edicts of 1495 and 1497, 178, 308–311 ; dissatisfaction with Columbus, 190, 192, 307 ; responsibility for Bobadilla, 196 ; and Indian slavery, iii. 255, 264, 271 ; death, 276.

Fernandez, Dinis, Portuguese navigator, passes Cape Verde, i. 374.

Fernandez, Garcia, and Columbus at La Rábida, ii. 92.

Feudalism, and gentilism, i. 112–114, 116 ; kingship under, 129.

Finæus, Orontius (Oronce Fine), French geographer, globe, ii. 352–354.

Finnbogi, murdered in Vinland, i. 195.

Finns, Tacitus on, i. 378 n.

Fire as criterion in savagery, i. 31.

Five Nations. *See* Iroquois.

Florida, Vespucius coasts, ii. 277 ; date of discovery, 297–303 ; confused on maps with Cuba, 303–305 ; discovery by Ponce de Leon, iii. 316 ; attempted Spanish colonies, 341 ; Huguenot colony, 342–344 ; its destruction by Spanish, 344–350 ; founding of St. Augustine, 346 ; destruction of Huguenot colony avenged, 352–354 ; importance of destruction, 354.

Folk-lore, preservation of Indian, i. 61, 62 n.; mediæval, copied from ancient, 214 n. ; Trojan War, 225 ; Saga of Eric the Red, not, 227 ; of fountain of youth, iii. 315.

Fonseca, Juan Rodriquez de, bishop of Burgos, head of Spanish department of Indian affairs, ii.

INDEX

Hudson, Henry, English navigator, his mermaid, i. 224 ; voyages in Arctic Ocean, iii. 379 ; explores Hudson River, 379 ; in Hudson's Bay, 380 ; death, 380.

Hudson Bay Company, origin, iii. 372 ; French interference, 373.

Hudson River, seen by Gomez, iii. 322 ; named San Antonio, 323 n. Hudson explores, 380.

Huguenots, attempted colony in Brazil, iii. 342 ; colony in Florida, 342–344, 346 ; destroyed, 346–351 ; avenged, 352–354.

Huitzilihuitl, Aztec chief-of-men, iii. 13.

Huitzilopochtli, Aztec god of war, i. 132, iii. 27, 66 ; chief-of-men his representative, 73.

Human sacrifice, and middle period of barbarism, i. 136, 138 n. ; in Mexican tribes, 137, iii. 33, 34, 66–68 ; among the Chibchas, 93 ; suppressed by the Incas, 148–150, 150 n., 157.

Humboldt, Alexander von, German scientist, on the reproductive power of maize, i. 121 ; authority on Columbus, ii. 9 n. ; on date of Toscanelli's letter, 38 n., 40 n. ; on Columbus's knowledge of ancient writings, 46 n. ; on enterprise of the Renaissance, 55 n. ; on La Cosa's map, 229 n. ; refutes charges against Vespucius, 263, 397 ; on origin of the potato, iii. 114 n. ; on literary style, 263 n.

Huron–Iroquois, Indian group, i. 52 ; Iroquois conquer rest of group, 55, 56 n. ; status, 57.

Hurtado. *See* Mendoza.

Hylacomylus. *See* Waldseemüller.

Ibn Batuta of Tangier, travels in Asia, i. 333 n.

Iceland, settled, i. 177 ; and Massachusetts, 177, 178 n. ; growth and literature, 178 ; present condition, 179 n. ; effect of trade monopoly, 260 ; not reached by Black Death, 261 n. ; Columbus in, ii. 59.

Iguana as food, ii. 274, 275 n.

Illinois, Algonquin Indians, i. 51.

Imago Mundi, influence on Columbus, ii. 46, 53 n.–55 n.

Immortality, thought on, i. 71 n.

Incas, Peruvian tribe, iii. 123 ; conquests, 124 ; become ruling caste, 124, 139, 167. *See also* Peruvians.

Incas, Peruvian rulers, list, iii. 100 n. ; origin of title, 124 ; power, 141–144, 155 ; vicedeity, 144, 154 ; and the vestal nuns, 153 ; children, 153, 155 ; wives, 154. *See also* Peru.

Indian corn, ethnic importance, i. 33 ; productive power, 121 n. ; mentioned in Vinland saga, 209–211.

Indians, type, i. 1 ; differentiation, 2, 25, 28 n. ; origin, 2–4, 17, 23, 169 ; no intercourse with Asia, 24 ; not Eskimos, 25 ; only one race, 25–28 ; culture status of different groups, 32, 35, 36, 39–41, iii. 92–94 ; none in upper period of barbarism, i. 37 ; differences in language, 45 ; groups, 46–57, iii. 95, 96 ; perpetual warfare, i. 58 ; cruelty, 58 ; cannibalism, 59, ii. 154, 328, morality, i. 61 ; religion, 61 ; folk-lore, 61, 62 n. ; social basis in exogamous female clans, 67, 76, 91 ; marriage, 76, 81 ; communism, 77–81 ; position of women, 81, 83 ; hospitality, 81 ; structure and rights of clan, 82 ; origin and structure of phratry, 84 ; structure of tribe, 85 ; confederation, 86–91 ; common social structure, 93 ; mound builders, 161–168 ; stage of development at time of discovery, 169 ; fear of unknown animals, 193, 216, iii. 40, 217 n. ;

459

INDEX

Lake Champlain, discovery, iii. 359.

Lake Titicaca, Peru, cradle of Peruvian culture, iii. 102.

Lançarote, Portuguese navigator, on coast of Africa, i. 374.

Landnáma-bók of Iceland, i. 178.

Lang, Andrew, English author, on Morgan's views, i. 147 n. ; on Central American ruins, 157.

Lanigan, John, Irish priest, on papal temporal power, ii. 143 n.

Las Casas, Bartolomé de, Apostle to the Indians, on population of Cholula pueblo, i. 108 n. ; on the sloping ocean, 357 n. ; on objections to Prince Henry's enterprises, 371 n. ; on papal grant to Portugal, 373 n. ; authority on Columbus, ii. 1, 4 ; *History of the Indies*, 2, iii. 309 ; on funds for first voyage, ii. 101 n. ; attacks Vespucius, 390–392 ; on Córdova's voyage, iii. 31 n. ; birth and family, 259 ; bibliography, 259 n. ; early years, 260 ; in Hispaniola, 261 ; takes orders, 261 ; character, 261, 272, 310 ; character of his writings, 262–264 ; as a slaveholder, 273 ; in Cuba, 274 ; becomes an abolitionist, 274–276 ; and Fonseca, 276, 284, 285 ; and Ximenes, 277 ; Protector of the Indians, 277 ; and introduction of negro slavery in America, 278–284 ; and Charles V., 284 ; attempt at colonization, 284–287 ; becomes a Dominican, 288 ; obtains decree against enslavement of Peruvians, 289 ; in Central America, 290 ; monastery in Guatemala, 290 ; idea of Christian conquest, 291 ; peaceful conquest of Tuzulutlan, 292–300 ; in Spain, 301 ; *Destruction of the Indies*, 301 ; and the New Laws, 301 ; result of his labours, 303 ; bishop of Chiapa, 305 ; final return to Spain, 306 ; controversy with Sepulveda, 306–308 ; and Philip II., 308 ; death, 310.

Las Casas, Francisco de, father of Bartolomé, in Columbus's second expedition, ii. 153.

Latini, Brunetto, Italian scholar, on the compass, i. 361.

Latitude and longitude, vague calculations, i. 362.

Laudonnière, René de, Huguenot, leads colony to Florida, iii. 343 ; escape, 348.

Lea, H. C., American writer of Spanish history, iii. 402 n.

Ledesma, Pedro de, Spanish pilot, in Columbus's fourth voyage, ii. 203 n., 318 ; in Vespucius's first voyage, 293.

Leif Ericsson, son of Eric the Red, i. 187 ; converted, 187 ; voyage to Vinland, 188–191 ; and Agamemnon, 225 ; called the Lucky, 239.

Lemos, Gaspar de, carries news of Cabral's discovery to Lisbon, ii. 324.

Lenox globe, ii. 349–351.

Lepe, Diego de, Spanish navigator, voyage to Brazil, ii. 322.

Lescarbot, Marc, French colonist, on Indian eyes, i. 219.

Lester, C. E., American historian, on Vespucius, ii. 242 n., 275 n.

Lewis, Sir G. C., English author, on historical material, i. 231 ; on Phœnician circumnavigation of Africa, 344 n.

Lewis, Meriwether, American explorer, expedition to Oregon, iii. 376.

Libya, origin of name, ii. 369 n.

Lima, Peru, founded, iii. 226.

Lisbon, Portugal, founded, i. 345 ; Columbus at, ii. 19, 22 ; centre of nautical science, 21.

Llamas of Peru, iii. 113, 121.

Llorente, J. A., Spanish historian, on Ojeda (second), iii. 286 n.

INDEX

Lloyd, Thomas, English navigator, search for island of Brazil, ii. 215.

Loadstone, superstition concerning mountain of, i. 356 n.

Loaysa, Garcia de, Spanish navigator, at Cape Horn, iii. 317.

Local self-government in Iroquois confederacy, i. 89.

Lok, Michael, English geographer, map, iii. 356.

Longfellow, H. W., basis of *Hiawatha*, i. 54 n.

Loritz, Heinrich (Glaseanus), Swiss humanist, uses name America, ii. 389 n.

Louisiana named by La Salle, iii. 368.

Lowe, Robert, Viscount Sherbrooke, verses on Iceland, i. 177 n.

Lubbock, Sir John, English archæologist on race evolution, i. 28 n., 169.

Lud, Walter, René's secretary, at Saint Dié, ii. 361; plan for edition of Ptolemy, 363.

Ludewig, H. E., on Indian languages, i. 46.

Luque, Fernando de, Spanish priest, share in Peruvian expeditions, iii. 206, 207.

MacCauley, Clay, American ethnologist, on Indian marriage, i. 76 n.

McClure, Sir Robert, British navigator, finds northwest passage, iii. 320.

McLennan, J. F., Scottish sociologist, on Bachofen, i. 65; *Primitive Marriage*, 66; and Bachofen, 66.

Machin, Robert, visits the Madeiras, i. 370.

Macrobius, Roman grammarian, on the torrid zone, i. 355.

Madeira Islands, known to Phœnicians, i. 348; visited by Portuguese, 369; visited by Machin, 370; colonized, 370.

Madoc, Welsh prince, voyage, i. 49.

Magellan, Ferdinand, birth and character, ii. 419–421, 443; sources of information, 419 n.; early years in East Indies, 421; and the Malay plot, 422; friendship with Serrano, 423; interest in the Moluccas, 424; service in Morocco, 424; plan to circumnavigate the earth, 425; plan rejected by Portugal, 426; enters service of Spain, 427; expedition fitted out by Spain, 428; fleet and crew, 428; Portuguese machinations, 429; source of information on his voyage, 430; crossing of the Atlantic, 430; winter quarters in Patagonia, 432; mutiny, 432–436; voyage through the strait, 437; desertion of one ship, 438; on the Pacific, 438–442; at the Ladrones, 442; at the Philippines, 442; death, 443–445; massacre of leading men of the crew, 445; voyage continued to the Moluccas, 445; fate of the Trinidad, 446; return of the Victoria, 447–449; greatness of the voyage, 449; honors for survivors, 450.

Magellan Straits, seen by Jaques, ii. 402; on Schöner's globe, 425; Magellan's passage, 437.

Magnusson, Finn, Icelandic archæologist, on Columbus and Vinland, ii. 60.

Mahaffy, J. P., Irish historian, on contrast in former and present Asia Minor, i. 313 n.

Maine, Sir Henry, English jurist, *Ancient Law*, i. 63, 68; views criticised, 64.

Maine, aboriginal shell mounds, i. 5.

Major, R. H., English historian, on St. Olaus monastery, i. 185 n.; on Zeno narrative, 262, 267 n., 272 n.; authority on Portuguese voyages, 369; misstatement on

INDEX

INDEX

INDEX

of the Chibchas, 94. *See also* Barter.

Mongol empire, power, i. 319; character, 319; friars visit, 320; Polos in, 323–327; why not Christianized, 324; overthrow, 334.

Montejo, Francisco de, Spanish officer, in Grijalva's expedition, iii. 34.

Montesino, Antonio, Dominican monk, crusade against Indian slavery, iii. 270–272; in Virginia, 321; death, 321.

Montezuma I., Aztec chief-of-men, iii. 14.

Montezuma II., Aztec chief-of-men, mistaken for a king by Spanish, i. 111, 127; elected, iii. 18; and the Great Khan, 36; seized by Cortes, 71, 74–76; priest - commander, 72–74; deposed, 82; killed, 83.

Montreal, Canada, Cartier at, iii. 325.

Moors, character, i. 312. *See also* Moriscoes, Spain.

Moquis, pueblo Indian group, i. 96; pueblos, 105.

Morales, Gaspar de, Spanish explorer, in Gulf of San Miguel, iii. 200.

Morgan, Lewis, American archæ-ologist, his criteria of culture, i. 29–38; caution on his classification, 37 n., 39; on Iroquois "long houses," 78–80; on Iroquois confederacy, 84; adopted by Senecas, 86 n.; on status of pueblo Indians, 97; on change from clan to township, 113 n.; views on Mexican society, 116, 132 n.; on population of Mexico, 121 n.; rules on narratives of Spanish explorers, 143, 144; inconsistencies, 145–150; on mound-builders, 164; on Aztlan, iii. 8 n.; on population of Mexico City, 59 n.

Moriscoes, converted Moors in Spain,

condition, iii. 391; rebellion, 396; expulsion, 397; effect on Spain of expulsion, 397.

Morley, John, English author, on moral obligation to lower races, iii. 281 n.

Mormon, Book of, on origin of Indians, i. 3 n.; pure fiction, 4 n., 206 n.

Morse, Edward, American naturalist, on ancient shell-mounds, i. 6.

Morton, Thomas, of Merrymount, on relation of Asia and America, iii. 357 n.

Moscoso, Luis de, Soto's lieutenant, iii. 340.

Mound-Builders, vague speculations, i. 161–163; antiquity of mounds, 163; compared with Mexicans and Zuñis, 164; culture status, 165; mounds by different tribes, 166–168; and Indians, 168.

Mundus Novus, Vespucius's letter published under title of, ii. 339–341; success, 342; Ringmann's edition, 343. *See also* New World.

Munsees, Algonquin Indians, i. 51.

Münster, Sebastian, German geographer, use of term America, ii. 381, 389 n., iii. 327.

Muscovy Company, ii. 221.

Music, ancient Nahuatl, iii. 295, 296 n.

Muyscas. *See* Chibchas.

Mycenæ, Greece, excavations, ii. 37 n.

Nahuas, pueblo Indian group in Mexico, i. 96; invasion of Mexican tableland, iii. 5, 8; music, 295, 296 n. *See also* Aztecs, Mexicans.

Nakuk Pech, Maya chief, chronicle of Spanish conquest, i. 158.

Names, queer transformations, i. 270; ii. 329 n.

Narragansetts, Algonquin Indians, i. 52.

466

469

INDEX

and Mayas, 172–176 ; humaneness, 173 ; intellectual culture, 174 ; fear of horses, 217 n. ; paralyzed by presence of Spaniards, 219, 220. *See also* Peru.

Peschel, Oscar, German geographer, error on Dighton rock inscription, i. 249 n.

Philesius Vosgesigena. *See* Ringmann.

Philip II. of Spain, and Las Casas, iii. 308 ; and the Huguenots, 351.

Philippine Islands, Magellan discovers, ii. 442 ; Magellan's death, 443–445 ; retained by Spain, iii. 319.

Phœnicians, voyages on African coast, i. 342–348.

Phratry, growth from clan, i. 72 ; origin and structure of Indian, 84 ; analogy to Teutonic hundred, 85 ; of Mexico City, 121, 123, iii. 59.

Pietro d' Abano, astrologer, and the mountain of loadstone, i. 356 n.

Pigafetta, Chevalier Antonio, journal on Magellan's voyage, ii. 430, 437, 438, 440, 448 n. ; on Magellan's death, 445.

Pilot major of Spain, duties, ii. 250.

Pineda, Alvarez de, Spanish explorer, discovers the Mississippi, iii. 316.

Pinkerton, John, Scottish historian, on the Zeno narrative, i. 262.

Pinotl, Aztec tribute gatherer, first sees the Spaniards, iii. 18, 34.

Pinta, caravel in Columbus's first expedition, ii. 104.

Pinzon, Martin Alonzo, and Columbus at La Rábida, ii. 92 ; in Columbus's first expedition, 104 ; deserts, 119 ; overtaken, 122 ; treacherous attempt to get credit of the discovery, 126 ; death, 127.

Pinzon, Vicente Yañez, Spanish navigator, in Columbus's first expedition, ii. 104 ; date of voyage to Mexican coast, 283–291, 310, 321 n. ; identity of voyage with Vespucius's first, 291–293 ; probable origin of voyage, 307–311 ; voyages to South America, 321, 412 ; proposed voyage to the La Plata, 409.

Pirua, traditional Peruvian dynasty, iii. 103, 112.

Pizarro, Fernando, brother of Francisco, accompanies his brother, iii. 211 ; character, 211 ; in Spain, 221 ; return to Peru, 226 ; besieged in Cuzco, 228 ; captured by Almagro, 230 ; released, 230 ; executes Almagro, 230 ; reception in Spain, 231.

Pizarro, Francisco, in Darien, iii. 181 ; early years, 199 ; partnership for expedition to Peru, 206 ; first attempts, 207–209 ; at Gallo Island, 209 ; on coast of Peru, 210 ; in Spain, 211 ; captain-general, 211 ; brothers, 211 ; in Peru, 212, 214 ; considered a god, 215, 220 n., 224 ; meeting with Atahualpa, 215–217 ; and Cortes, 217 ; seizes Atahualpa, 218 ; receives ransom, 219 ; executes Atahualpa, 221–223 ; march to Cuzco, 223 ; proclaims Manco Inca, 224 ; founds Lima, 226 ; created a marquis, 226 ; extent of his government, 226 ; assassinated, 235.

Pizarro, Gonzalo, accompanies his brother Francisco to Peru, iii. 212 ; besieged in Cuzco, 228 ; captured by Almagro, and escapes, 230 ; expedition over the Andes, 233–235 ; successful rebellion, 237 ; defeat and execution, 238–240 ; aims at independence, 302 n.

Pizarro, Juan, goes to Peru with his brother, iii. 212 ; death, 229.

Pizarro y Orellana, descendant of

470

INDEX

474

INDEX

INDEX

on the inhabitable world, 356 n.; ignorant of savagery, 378 n.; prophecy on America, ii. 44; on the loneliness of the sea, 48 n.

Sumptuary laws, prevalence in time of Columbus, ii. 13 n.

Sun worship in Peru, iii. 145–154.

Susquehannocks, Huron-Iroquois Indians, i. 53.

Switzerland, culture status of lake-dwellers, i. 36.

Szkolny, John, Polish pilot, voyage in northern seas, i. 292 n.

Tacitus, Roman historian, on the Finns, i. 378 n.

Talavera, Fernando de, confessor to Isabella, interest in Columbus, ii. 79, 95.

Tallegwi, identified with the Cherokee Indians, i. 167.

Tasso, Torquato, Italian poet, on the Canaries, i. 349 n.

Taxes, tribute to Aztec confederacy, i. 119, 133; Peruvian, iii. 164.

Taylor, Isaac, English philologist, on Maya hieroglyphics, i. 152 n.

Tecpanecas, Mexican tribe, alliance with Aztecs, iii. 13; alliance against Aztecs, 13; defeated and destroyed, 14.

Tenochtitlan (Mexico City), significance of name, iii. 11. *See also* Mexico City.

Terrarossa, Italy, claim as birthplace of Columbus, ii. 17.

Tezcatlipoca, Aztec god of darkness, rival of Quetzalcoatl, iii. 24; human sacrifice to, 27, 66.

Tezcucans, Mexican tribe, in Aztec confederacy, i. 118, iii. 14; attack on Aztec, 13; alliance with Cortes, 85.

Tezozomoc, H de A., Mexican historian, on Tollan, iii. 9.

Thomas, Cyrus, American ethnologist, on mound-builders, i. 166; on Maya hieroglyphics, 151 n.

Thomson, Sir William (Lord Kel-

vin), English physicist, on age of earth, i. 7.

Thorbrand Snorrason, killed by Indians in Vinland, i. 219; mentioned in Eyrbyggja Saga, 235.

Thorfinn Karlsefni, marries Gudrid, i. 192; unsuccessful colony in Vinland, 192–194; descendants, 193 n.

Thorhall Gamlason, called the Vinlander, i. 190 n., 235 n; accompanies Thorfinn to Vinland, 192 n.

Thorir, Northman, Arctic voyage, i. 244 n.

Thorkell Gellison, uncle of Ari, authority on Greenland and Vinland, i. 237.

Thorne, Robert, Bristol merchant, on Cabot's landfall, ii. 225; interest in Rut's voyage, 232.

Thorstein Ericsson, brother of Leif, unsuccessful voyage to Vinland, i. 191.

Thorvald Ericsson, brother of Leif, in Vinland, i. 191; killed by Indians, 191.

Thorvard, evil deeds in Vinland, i. 194–196.

Thule, use of term by ancient writers, i. 351; Columbus on, ii. 57, 59.

Titu Cusi Yupanqui, Inca, iii. 246.

Tizoc, Aztec chief-of-men, iii. 16.

Tlacatecuhtli, Aztec military executive, i. 126. *See also* Chief-of-men.

Tlacopans, Mexican tribe, in Aztec confederacy, i. 118, iii. 14.

Tlaloc, Mexican elemental deity, iii. 21, 22.

Tlascala, Mexican independent pueblo, compared to Granada, i. 106; population, 108; hostile to Aztecs, iii. 17; fight with Cortes, 43–46; night attack frustrated, 46; alliance with Cortes, 47, 84.

Tlatelulco, part of Mexico City, iii. 59 n.

477

INDEX

THE END

The Riverside Press

Electrotyped and printed by H. O. Houghton & Co.

Cambridge, Mass., U. S. A.